Boatbuilding with Baltek DuraKore

BOATBUILDING WITH BALTEK DURAKORE

DAVID G. BROWN

International Marine
Camden, Maine

International Marine/
Ragged Mountain Press

A Division of The **McGraw·Hill** *Companies*

10 9 8 7 6 5 4 3 2

Copyright © 1995 International Marine, a division of The McGraw-Hill Companies.

Library of Congress Cataloging-in-Publication Data
     Boatbuilding with Baltek DuraKore / David G. Brown.
       p. cm.
     Includes index.
     ISBN 0-07-008212-X
     1. Boatbuilding. 2. Fiberglass boats—Design and construction.
    3. Baltek Corporation. I. Title.
    VM321.B85   1995
    623.8'207—dc20   94-39680
                                      CIP

Questions regarding the content of this book should be addressed to:

International Marine
P.O. Box 220
Camden, ME 04843

Questions regarding the ordering of this book should be addressed to:

The McGraw-Hill Companies
Customer Service Department
P.O. Box 547
Blacklick, OH 43004
Retail customers: 1-800-822-8158
Bookstores: 1-800-722-4726

Boatbuilding with Baltek DuraKore is printed on acid-free paper.

Printed by *Quebecor Printing*, Fairfield, PA
Design by *Chris McLarty*, Silverline Studio
Production and page layout by *Janet Robbins*
Edited by *James R. Babb, Hilary Swinson, Tom McCarthy*
Photographs by *Carol Brown* unless otherwise noted

To Arnie Duckworth and the many others who helped

develop strip composite construction. And to

Adam Pendleton, who wanted his boat.

DuraKore Scantling Booklet

As a companion to *Boatbuilding With Baltek DuraKore*, noted naval architect Dave Gerr has prepared a booklet titled "Baltek DuraKore Scantling Handbook." Written in clear, easy-to-understand language, it is a guide to determining suitable DuraKore/FRP laminate and core specifications for power and sail boat construction. For a free copy, more information on DuraKore and other Baltek boatbuilding products, and the address of your nearest DuraKore distributor, write Marine Department, Baltek Corporation, P.O. Box 195, Northvale, NJ 07647-0195; FAX 201-387-6631.

CONTENTS

ACKNOWLEDGMENTS

Naval architects, professional boatbuilders, chemists, computer programmers, and—most important—amateur boatbuilders around the world have contributed ideas and suggestions to this book. Writing a definitive volume on composite strip construction would not have been possible without their willingness to share their hard-won expertise. Those who deserve particular mention include:

John Allin—an amateur builder in Ohio, who is winning races in a monohull sailboat he built to plans by Tim Jackett.

Bret Blanchard and Dean Pike of the Washington County (Maine) Marine Trades Center, who opened their facility and shared their experiences building in DuraKore.

Christopher Copeland—designer of the Kit Cat S-28, who provided information on the engineering of catamaran bridge decks.

Ian Farrier—naval architect and boatbuilder, who designed the F-9A and F-25 sailing trimarans for amateur construction.

Abbot Geer—Baltek Corporation's public relations consultant, who spent hours tracking down people, information, and photographs.

Meade Gougeon—one of the famed Gougeon brothers, who developed West System epoxies. He was most helpful in discussing all aspects of amateur boat construction—particularly the problems amateurs create for themselves.

Colin Haigh—builder of an Ian Farrier X9A catamaran in Surrey, British Columbia, who shared his experiences with outgassing and ripping strips from DuraKore planks.

Steve Hollister—of Nautilus Systems software, who explained computerized lofting, specifically how to output lines drawings as full-size frame mold patterns.

Helge von der Linden—of Hamburg, Germany, who gave valuable

insights into preventing movement of strips during the planking stage of hull construction.

Wilbur "Spike" Meredith—designer of the balsa-cored, patented V-Cat hull, who provided details on constructing high-speed powerboats and installing high-performance engines.

John Shaw—president of Shaw Boats, Inc., and one of the most experienced DuraKore builders in the United States.

Gary and Bonnie VanTassel—owners of Ocean Systems in Solomons, Maryland, who opened their shop and their minds to share critical information about working with DuraKore.

Keith Walton—director of marine products for Baltek Corporation, who supervised the development of DuraKore and DecoLite.

James R. Watson—technical advisor for Gougeon Brothers, Inc., who provided key insights into the relationship of epoxy resins and DuraKore strips. His research into the outgassing problem provided the keys to its solution.

PREFACE

Today you can build a high-tech cored laminate boat in less time than it once took just to loft the design for conventional construction. Computers have all but eliminated the onerous lofting stage. A new manmade wood composite and special marine epoxy glues allow you to build virtually any hull shape in just days instead of weeks or years. By taking full advantage of modern technology, you can go from dreaming about a boat to sailing your dreamboat in a fraction of the time needed to build a boat using conventional methods.

Building your own boat is still no small undertaking. The long hours of hard work involved require true dedication to what is essentially a dream. Traditional boatbuilding methods have often intimidated amateurs to the point that they fear beginning a boat project. This is particularly true of old-fashioned lofting, which Meade Gougeon says has stopped more would-be boatbuilders than any other part of the process. Old-fashioned construction techniques, particularly spiling planks, also have caused many amateur boatbuilders to throw down their tools in disgust. Those days are gone.

Strip composite construction utilizing Baltek Corporation's new DuraKore strips and DecoLite panels eliminates the drudgery of painstakingly spiling each plank into the hull. Quick shaping of pre-cut strips with a hand tool is all that's needed. Epoxy resin glues hold everything together better than the polyester resins used in most boat factories. Once sheathed in special fiberglass or aramid reinforcing, the strip composite hull gets its strength in the same way as a steel I-beam does, at a fraction of the weight of other boat construction methods.

Strip composite construction is in its infancy. Building methods are in a state of flux as builders experiment with this new concept. One thing is certain, this is the high-tech method of the future for home builders who want to spend their time on the water and not in the boatyard.

Boatbuilding involves multiple processes occurring at the same time. This is in conflict with writing a book, which is a linear process requiring words to be organized in straight lines called sentences. There is no way in a book to present the simultaneous operations typical of building a boat. Each process must be considered separately in words and placed in the linear organization of paragraphs and chapters.

As a boatbuilder, I urge you to read the entire book to gain an understanding of all of the work involved before starting any construction. Then study your building plans and read all instructions from the naval architect. Spend a few days mentally digesting all of this information before you prepare your personal "game plan" for building your boat.

Disclaimer

This book explains only the general methods and procedures for using DuraKore strips and planks, DecoLite panels, epoxy resins and hardeners, and various reinforcement fabrics in the construction of pleasure boats. It is not an engineering manual, and there is no intention to provide specific suggestions or specifications on scantlings, strengths of materials, or other engineering concerns regarding a specific boat or boats. Readers must seek assistance from qualified marine engineers for this information. For details regarding the design of vessels appropriate for this form of construction, readers should seek assistance from qualified naval architects. Readers without specific knowledge of marine engineering or naval architecture should not attempt to convert existing vessel plans to this form of construction without consulting the original naval architect or engineer. This book provides general information about the use of various materials, but is not meant to replace specific data provided by the manufacturers of those materials. Readers should follow specific instructions from manufacturers in cases of conflict with information presented in this book.

TRADEMARK INFORMATION

AutoCAD is a registered trademark of AutoDesk, Inc.

DecoLite, AL-600, and ContourKore are registered trademarks of Baltek, Corp.

DuraKore is a trademark of Baltek Corp.

IBM and IBM-PC are registered trademarks of International Business Machines Corp.

MS-DOS is a registered trademark of Microsoft Corp.

SYSTEM THREE is a registered trademark of SYSTEM THREE Resins, Inc.

West System is a registered trademark of Gougeon Brothers, Inc.

Chapter I
INTRODUCTION

nventive Australian Arnie Duckworth gets the credit for bringing one-off boatbuilding into the high-tech age. A leading designer-builder of fast sailboats, he's always searching for the perfect boatbuilding material. And, like other builders engaged in that quest, he knows wood offers an ideal combination of light weight, flexibility, and strength. Unfortunately, none of the woods supplied by Mother Nature satisfies Duckworth. So, in the early 1980s he created his own by combining end-grain balsa with hardwood veneer. The resulting composite material is perfect for strip planking boat hulls using epoxy glue and fiberglass reinforcement cloth. It is now sold under the *DuraKore* trade name.

Duckworth's high-tech method, known as "DuraKore strip composite construction," produces cored composite hulls that are amazingly lightweight for their strength. More important, strip composite construction allows graceful hulls with fully rounded sections. The slab-sided look of amateur-built sheet plywood boats is gone. Today's home builder using DuraKore can reproduce the rule-beating bumps and hollows of an I.O.R. sailboat or the sweeping lines of a classic Herreshoff design.

Admittedly, DuraKore sounds too good to be true. Haven't other building methods made the same promises to amateur boatbuilders? In a word, yes. Since World War II at least two major building techniques have seized the public fancy. Both created waves of home boatbuilding that washed across the country like pet rocks, hulahoops, and other passing fads.

The most recent boatbuilding fad was ferrocement. It too promised easy construction of complex hull shapes. However, most amateur builders found that concrete is an industrial product with little affinity for the world of yachting. Many people, ranging from big-name naval architects to individual home builders, got burned when the concrete fad fizzled. Half-finished hulls started in the 1960s still litter backyards from Maine to California.

Prior to the concrete fad, plywood home building was promoted by major boat companies. Chris-Craft once produced kit versions of its most popular boats. Plywood is excellent for home building because it is readily available and familiar to woodworkers. Unfortunately, plywood bends in only one direction at a time. Sharp chines are needed to join flat panels into the three-dimensional shape of a boat. The result is a flat-sided hull with little of the grace of its more rounded sisters.

Plywood hulls built before the advent of epoxy marine glues proved sensitive to the wracking forces of movement in a seaway. Additional complications arose when builders substituted cheaper household caulking for marine-grade material or steel hardware store screws for bronze fasteners. Some plywood boats built in backyards during the 1950s had lifespans measured in months rather than years.

Plywood boats are still being built by amateurs, and for a lot of good reasons. They are simple to construct and the materials are readily available. Hard chines, which come naturally to plywood boats, lend themselves to planing hull powerboats. Thanks to modern epoxy glues and coatings, plywood boats can have lifespans competitive with conventional fiberglass hulls. The big drawback of plywood is its inability to bend in two directions at once. Boats built of plywood continue to have a somewhat boxy appearance.

Now comes DuraKore strip composite construction. What makes this new method so different from its predecessors? The answer is engineering. Neither plywood nor concrete was originally created specifically for building boats. Instead, those materials have been adapted to the purpose. Like most adaptations, the results are not always acceptable. On the other hand, the factory-made wood and the epoxy materials of DuraKore strip composite construction were engineered specifically for building boats. There's no adaptation involved.

DURAKORE AND DECOLITE

DURAKORE COMPOSITE STRIPS

Arnie Duckworth's "wood" is an evolutionary rather than revolutionary material that combines the best characteristics of wood with lightweight, high-tech cored composite construction. DuraKore is end-grain balsa bonded under heat and pressure between hardwood veneers. It comes either as 12-inch wide planks or as strips ranging

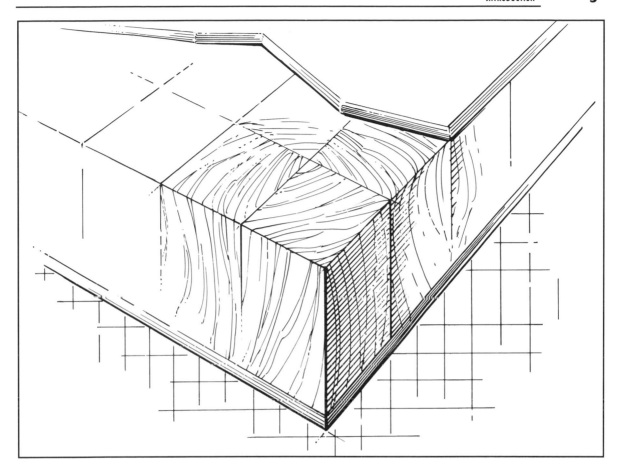

from ¾ inch to 1¼ inch in width and from ¾₆ inch to 1 inch in thickness. Planks and strips are both 8 feet long. Strips are finger jointed at both ends to eliminate tedious scarfing when gluing up battens the full length of the hull.

The concept for this manufactured wood product goes back to the early 1970s, when Arnie Duckworth was looking for a better way to build light, strong sailboat hulls. Duckworth turned to the favorite wood of model airplane builders: balsa. This gave him a lightweight hull, but durability was a serious problem. There was no practical way to orient the balsa fibers across the thickness of the skin instead of in the weaker fore-and-aft direction. Fore-and-aft orientation exposed the long grain of the planks to the Achilles heel of balsa-core construction, rot.

Duckworth knew that the proper orientation for the balsa is with the end grain at right angles to the outside and inside skins of the

Many production boats use composite construction in which blocks of end-grain balsa are sandwiched between conventional fiberglass skins. DuraKore allows custom builders to accomplish the same sandwich construction without the need for expensive fiberglass boat tooling. (Courtesy Baltek Corp.)

hull. The Australian boatbuilder needed a way to create long end-grain balsa strips to plank his boats. Gluing thin blocks of balsa together wasn't the answer. He reasoned, "What if I bond the end-grain blocks to a very thin substrate?" That solution would combine the durability of hardwood veneer with balsa's light weight.

The quest to outdo natural wood led Duckworth to Northvale, New Jersey, in the United States, headquarters of the world's largest supplier of balsa wood products, the Baltek Corporation. The Australian spent hours in long-distance telephone consultation with Keith R. Walton, head of Baltek's marine products. Those globe-spanning conversations led to hand-laminating a hardwood veneer to both sides of end-grain balsa. In this way Duckworth laboriously created the first few planks of what would become DuraKore.

Wood has long been a favorite of high-performance sailboats in the Land Down Under. The late Ben Lexcen, who won fame by designing Australia's winning America's Cup yacht, was always a fan of wood. "Wood, weight-for-weight, has better engineering proper-ties than most steels or composites," Lexcen said. In 1985 he backed that opinion by building his personal 30-foot racing sailboat in the still-experimental strip composite system. From the day Lexcen's *Eclipse*, with its revolutionary balsa core, hit the water, it set records for speed and performance in both light and heavy air.

Not being in the business of manufacturing wood products, Duckworth assigned the rights to his manmade wood to Baltek. The company was already producing a variety of balsa products engi-neered for boat construction. Its end-grain balsa-core materials are accepted for hull and deck construction in fiberglass boats by certifi-cation agencies such as the American Bureau of Shipping in the United States, Lloyd's Register of Shipping in Great Britain, and Det Norske Veritas in Norway. Baltek quickly went to work testing proto-type samples of Arnie Duckworth's wood to develop methods of putting it into production.

"We named it DuraKore and created precise gluing, machining, and production specifications to very tight tolerances," said Baltek's Walton. "Quality assurance tests were developed and are applied to every batch of DuraKore the company makes, including the uniform perfect match to the finger joints."

DuraKore consists of Baltek's presealed AL-600 end-grain balsa wood laminated between two $\frac{1}{16}$-inch hardwood veneers. Sandwich construction gives DuraKore excellent physical properties at very

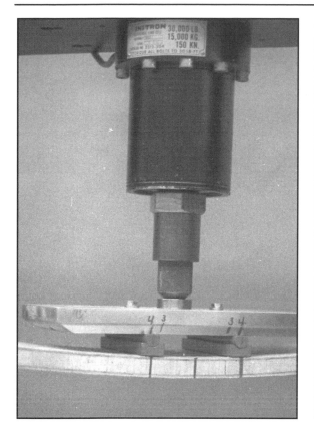 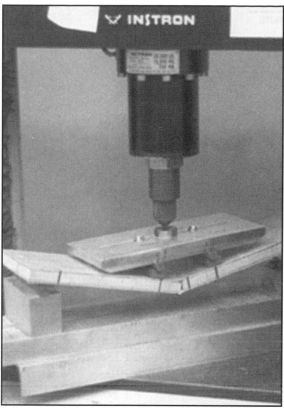

light weight. More than six months of experimentation went into the development of the waterproof glue used in this manmade wood. The ratio of the width of the strips to their thickness was carefully established to assure bending properties that allow the smooth compound curves required in boats.

As it turns out, the ¹⁄₁₆-inch-thick wood veneers on both surfaces of DuraKore give the material some pretty sophisticated characteristics. This product has a stiffness matched only by carbon fibers on a weight-for-weight basis. The veneer grain runs parallel to the strip on what engineers call the strip's "zero axis." Because of its low density, veneer increases the panel thickness more than a comparable weight of fiberglass and resin laminate. This enhances the stiffness of DuraKore and provides fore-and-aft strength to the completed boat.

According to Baltek's Walton, manufacturing of DuraKore starts by milling end-grain balsa to precise thickness. "The end grain is coated with our AL-600 polymer to prevent excess absorption of the glue," he says. Precision milled hardwood veneers are then bonded

Extensive testing ensures that DuraKore planks and strips and DecoLite panels meet quality standards. Here, a hydraulic ram deforms a DecoLite test sample until it fails. Electronic instruments record the pressure and the amount of deflection.

This sample panel was built of DuraKore strips to show how their narrow width conforms to a rounded shape. Note the finger joint showing in the middle of the front edge of the panel.

to the balsa using heat and pressure. Walton explains, "We use resorcinol glue because it's better than epoxy when you are using presses to get a very thin glue line."

Resorcinol glues were the original waterproof boatbuilding glues. The special version used by Baltek meets the highest marine testing standards. "You can even boil DuraKore and it won't come apart," claims Walton. The AL-600 polymer coating controls penetration of the glue into the balsa. Without the coating, too much glue would get into the grain, increasing the weight of the finished composite and reducing its flotation qualities. Pressure applied during the manufacturing process forces some resorcinol upward through the hardwood veneers, sealing them against most water penetration.

The first boat built with Baltek's brand-name DuraKore was *Ocean Surfer* designed by Dick Newick in 1987. This 40-foot racing trimaran was laid up on temporary wooden female jigs. Each half-hull was completed by four people in just six hours. After sailing to England, *Ocean Surfer* competed in the Transatlantic C-Star singlehanded race, where she placed second in class and 16th overall.

More than half of the boats built with DuraKore have been multihull sailboats, which particularly benefit from the material's light weight, conformability, and high strength.

DuraKore construction is key to the performance of White Wings, *a cruising trimaran designed by Dick Newick. The owner made a 2,000 mile solo circumnavigation of Lake Superior and is now sailing in Florida waters. (Courtesy Baltek Corp.)*

Despite the fact that about one-third of all the DuraKore hulls launched to date have been constructed by home builders, DuraKore was not developed for amateurs. Professional boatbuilders were the intended customers and they remain the biggest users of this engineered wood. The prototype for Carl Schumacher's new 28-foot *Alerion-Express* sailboat was built using DuraKore. It was the first monohull sailboat in the Western Hemisphere to be built of strip composite construction. In an interview Schumacher said, "The new DuraKore technique provides a simple, great way to build one-off balsa-cored fiberglass boats."

Baltek deliberately avoided the amateur DuraKore market for half a decade. The company was concerned that its new product get only good reports in the public press during those first years. Baltek wanted to avoid the possibility of negative publicity from failures by inexperienced amateur builders. Professional builders using the product were almost hand picked. They had to demonstrate their knowledge of high-tech composites. The plan worked, and DuraKore has gained an enviable record of success.

New England boatbuilders and boat buyers tend to be conservative, favoring traditional boats and methods. Yet designer and builder Malcolm L. Pettegrow of Southwest Harbor, Maine, is constructing 36- to 56-foot sportfish yachts using DuraKore. "The beauty of the DuraKore technique is that it gives us the flexibility to provide the customer whatever design he wants," Pettegrow says. "We're not locked into existing tooling. It's fast, cost efficient, and there are no limitations on the hull designs possible with DuraKore."

The first powerboat built in the Western Hemisphere from DuraKore is the Pettegrow 36, a single-diesel offshore fishing boat. Although traditional looking, the DuraKore construction allows this vessel to achieve speeds above 30 knots. (Courtesy Baltek Corp.)

DecoLite Composite Panels

Baltek offers a companion line of products sold under the trade name, *DecoLite*. These are hot-pressed composite panels based on an end-grain balsa core bonded within fiberglass laminates with a variety of facings. Sold in 4 × 8-foot sheets, DecoLite panels are perfect for decks, cabin sides, interior bulkheads, and permanent furniture. They are available with clear fiberglass, decorative hardwood, or paint-based overlay (PBO) surfaces.

From a boat construction standpoint, DecoLite panels are cut and fitted in the same manner as plywood. However, these panels have significant advantages. They are extremely light without sacrificing strength. High strength-to-weight ratio is critical in building high performance sail- or powerboats. Another advantage comes from the fiberglass laminate skins, which allow direct bonding of panels into the hull. Also, permanent furniture can be glued together, saving the weight and installation time of metal fasteners.

Weight savings achieved by using DecoLite panels instead of plywood are considerable. Conventional fir plywood weighs more than 35 pounds per cubic foot. DecoLite comes in at under 15 pounds per cubic foot. If a boat requires 12 sheets of 4 × 8-foot material 1 inch thick for the interior bulkheads and furniture, the total weight saved would be more than 600 pounds.

Balsa-Core Construction

Using balsa as a core material inside fiberglass skins is not a new idea. Crosby outboard runabouts were the first production boats to feature balsa-core construction back in 1951. It gave those boats improved strength and stiffness over the single-skin laminate construction typical of the era. The boating industry got the idea of using balsa core from World War II aircraft. The U.S. Navy's legendary Catalina PBY flying boat had balsa-cored aluminum skins designed to withstand repeated rough-water landings.

After World War II both Goodyear and Chance Vought Aircraft pioneered in the development of end-grain balsa construction. In recent times, balsa-cored panels have been aboard virtually all U.S. manned spacecraft. Aluminum-faced balsa panels provide strong, lightweight bulkheads in modern passenger aircraft. Balsa core is now an accepted material for lightweight parts on planes as well as boats and trains.

Baltek claims that more than three million fiberglass boats, ranging in size from canoes to 150-foot motor yachts, have been built using end-grain balsa-core materials. Since 1975 Britain's prestigious Lloyd's Register of Shipping has approved end-grain balsa as a marine core material for use both above and below the waterline. The American Bureau of Shipping (ABS) followed suit in 1984.

HOW COMPOSITES WORK

Understanding the advantages of end-grain balsa requires a basic knowledge of composite laminated construction. What Americans call "fiberglass" is actually a composite made of reinforcing fiberglass fabric and plastic resin. Separately, the resin is too brittle to make a good boat and the reinforcing glass fibers are too floppy. It is only when the two are combined in the proper ratio that a tough, resilient laminate results. Most of the world calls this laminate "fiber-reinforced plastic," or "FRP" for short. In the United States, the "P" likely stands for "polyester," the most popular plastic resin used in boat construction.

Weight is the problem with conventional FRP laminates. A standard 30% glass, 70% resin layup weighs just under 100 pounds per cubic foot. That's nearly triple the weight of equivalent fir plywood and almost seven times as heavy as DuraKore strips. The greater weight of FRP might be acceptable if it brought additional benefits. But that's not the case. A balsa-cored FRP laminate is considerably stronger than a conventional glass and resin layup of the same thickness. In modern engineering, it's axiomatic that weight does *not* equal strength.

WEIGHT COMPARISONS
(APPROXIMATE POUNDS PER CUBIC FOOT)

MATERIAL	WEIGHT
DuraKore	15
FRP Layup	96
Teak	55
Fir Plywood	36
Honduras Mahogany	35
Douglas Fir	33
White Cedar	23

Balsa as it comes from the tree is actually a composite material produced by nature. Cellulose fibers are bonded together by lignin, a natural resin. Much of balsa's strength comes from the complex orientation of the cellulose in the various layers that make up the cell walls. Pound for pound, wood fibers are stronger than steel. Balsa has also been shown to have better shear and compressive strength than structural polyvinyl chloride (PVC) foams or plastic honeycomb materials.

A quick aside on environmental considerations. Balsa is a farm crop. The Baltek Corporation owns balsa tree plantations in South America, where timber is grown to exacting specifications. Trees growing on these plantations could supply the company's needs for at least twenty more years. However, Baltek plants new ones as older trees are harvested, ensuring a continuing supply. More important to boatbuilders, since the trees are tended as a crop, they grow straight and tall for best grain structure. Balsa from trees grown in the wild often has a bent or twisted grain structure unsuitable for boats.

CORED LAMINATE STRENGTH

It takes imagination to understand why a cored laminate outperforms just glass and resin. Cored construction is strong for the same engineering reason that steel I-beams are strong. The two outer skins of the laminate function in the same way as the flanges of an I-beam— they take the tension and compression loads. The balsa core acts as the "web" of the I-beam, carrying shear and compression loads between the skins. Careful engineering is required to design a composite material with the right relationship between the thickness of the core and the outer laminates. This was done for boatbuilders in the development of DuraKore strips.

The cellular nature of balsa provides additional benefits. Balsa is a natural honeycomb made of microscopic hexagonal closed cells. Because they're closed, they provide the natural buoyancy associated with wood. Their hexagonal shape also allows epoxy resin to penetrate the structure of the wood and bond to exposed cell walls. This produces a strong mechanical as well as chemical bond. Surprisingly, end-grain balsa is actually more crush resistant than the closed-cell plastic foams also used as cores in boat construction. Balsa is a better choice than plastic foam for boats expected to withstand severe impact loads.

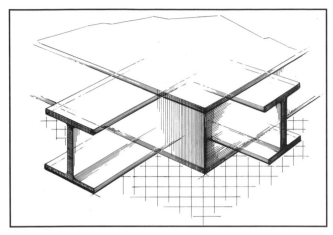

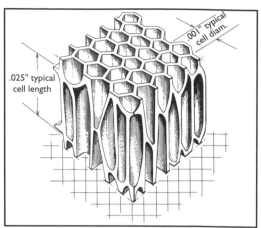

.025" typical cell length

.001" typical cell diam.

(left) A DuraKore composite covered by fiberglass set in epoxy resin functions much like a continuous I-beam. The skins or "flanges" take the tension and compression while the core acts as the "web" to carry shear and compressive loads between the skins. (Courtesy Baltek Corp.)

(right) Its cellular structure makes Balsa a natural "composite" material. The complex orientation of the cellulose in the cell walls makes wood fibers stronger than steel on a pound-for-pound basis. (Courtesy Baltek Corp.)

With all of its benefits, any natural material is subject to normal deterioration if not properly protected. In other words, it can rot. Every boatyard has horror stories about balsa core that became saturated with water and rotted. While these stories are true, they are seldom the *whole* story. What's left out of the telling is the reason for the deterioration. Invariably, rot problems result from either improper initial construction or improper installation of fasteners through the balsa core.

Balsa can't rot if it doesn't get wet. Factory-made DuraKore strips go a long way toward preventing water intrusion and migration. The end grain of the balsa is sealed by the hardwood veneer surfaces and resorcinol glue. Strip composite construction automatically seals the side grain with thickened epoxy resin as the strips are glued together. Then the entire hull is encased inside and out within epoxy FRP laminates. Water is effectively blocked from the core by the nature of the construction process. No water, no rot.

Installation of hardware, particularly hardware that will be under water, still creates problems. Care must be taken to seal with epoxy any core exposed when holes are drilled for fasteners or fittings. In some cases it is necessary to prevent crushing of the core when fasteners are tightened. These preventive measures aren't particularly difficult or time consuming. Techniques for accomplishing them are detailed throughout this book.

MARINE EPOXIES

Marine epoxy is the glue that holds a DuraKore strip composite boat together. Mixed with thixotropic agents (better known as thickeners), epoxy simultaneously bonds strips to each other and fills gaps in the seams between them. The gap-filling characteristic of thickened epoxy is a key factor in creating strong hulls that can be sanded fair. Epoxy resin also can be combined with various fiberglass, Dynel, Kevlar, or carbon-fiber reinforcement materials to create smooth, virtually impervious outer skins for hull or deck.

Ordinary FRP boats are built with polyester resins. While these resins combine well with fiberglass cloth, they do not bond well to wood. Nor do they form good secondary bonds, a critical factor when installing bulkheads and decks. That's why *only* epoxy resins should be used in strip composite construction. Admittedly, epoxy resins are several times the cost of polyester materials. But attempting to save a few bucks is almost certain to lead to disaster. Don't be tempted to use less expensive polyester resins.

The biggest reason for not using polyester is hydrolysis. Believe it or not, polyester resin is not completely waterproof. This point has been driven home by osmotic blistering of FRP boat bottoms. A contributing factor to this blistering is the migration of water through polyester laminates. The longevity of wood composite construction depends upon its ability to keep moisture out of the laminate. Moisture allows rot to develop in any wood, whether balsa, mahogany, spruce, or oak. Unlike polyester, epoxy resins are excellent at blocking water. As few as two coats of epoxy form the required moisture barrier to prevent rot. Properly coated surfaces will not become saturated with water unless that coating is damaged or broken.

Better paint adhesion is another benefit of epoxy coatings. The smooth, mechanically stable surface of epoxy provides a perfect substrate for paint or varnish. Epoxy surfaces should never be left unprotected against sunlight because they break down under direct ultraviolet exposure. Linear polyurethane paints are particularly good at protecting epoxy coatings. Not only do they block ultraviolet light, but they also provide a glossy surface that can be superior to gelcoat on an FRP boat.

Special coating resins are available for use where it is desirable to show off the underlying wood grain. Like all epoxies, however, those intended for clear coating are subject to ultraviolet degradation. Topcoating the epoxy with several coats of ultraviolet-resistant varnish is the answer. Conventional marine spar varnish works well, but polyurethane clear coats give an even longer-lasting finish.

NOT A WOODEN BOAT

Although DuraKore composite strip construction involves the use of balsa and other hardwoods, it does not produce a wooden boat. The completed hull is correctly described as a balsa-cored, fiberglass reinforced plastic composite. This type of boat has more in common with conventional fiberglass boats than it does with traditional planked wood hulls. Building a DuraKore strip composite boat demands nearly as much chemistry knowledge as it does woodworking skill.

Interior and exterior skins of reinforcing cloth set in epoxy resin are required to provide strength across the long seams between the battens. Engineers call this the "90-degree axis." Reinforcing material can be either directional or knitted fiberglass, Kevlar, or carbon fibers. Depending on the construction of the reinforcing material, additional strength is gained along the "plus or minus 45-degree axis." These strength gains are engineered to complement the natural strength of the wood veneer along the zero axis.

Wooden boat lovers will not find the process of composite strip construction satisfying. While the strips have a hardwood veneer, this wood is not intended to show in the finished hull.

Layers of resin and cloth in the outer skins obscure the veneer of the

The first U.S.-built monohull DuraKore sailboat was the prototype for Carl Shumacher's 28-foot Alerion-Express. Above the waterline it is a slightly modified version of Nathanael Herreshoff's personal boat built in 1916. (Courtesy Baltek Corp.)

Twin diesels driving surface-piercing propellers push the Ocean Tech 34 to more than 50 miles per hour. Stiff, lightweight construction afforded by DuraKore is a key factor in the boat's performance.
(Courtesy Baltek Corp.)

strips. As a result, DuraKore boats receive a final exterior finish of linear polyurethane paint. To the uninitiated, the high gloss luster of these paints appears to be fiberglass gelcoat. The wood is hidden beneath layers of reinforcing fabric, epoxy resins, and linear polyurethane paints.

The general rule is, "If you want a wooden boat, build a wooden boat." That said, a strip composite hull can be dressed out with as much (or little) wood as desired. For instance, the fiberglass reinforcement on the outside of the hull might be replaced with wood veneer. Two layers of veneer strips can be cold molded over the hull at 45-degree angles to the joints in the DuraKore strips. This would provide the necessary strength on the 90-degree axis across the glue joints of the strips. A third layer added in the fore-and-aft direction would give the appearance of conventional planking. Topped off with epoxy and polyurethane clear coat . . . ahhhh!

Even if the hull is not bright wood, the boat doesn't have to look like a bleach bottle. Teak toe rails, hatches, coaming boards, and even planked decks can be added on the outside. The interior can also display enough wood to warm a lumberman's heart. Of course, adding too much wood negates much of the weight savings involved in DuraKore construction. It's all a matter of taste.

TECHNOLOGY VERSUS COST

Whether in computers, airplanes, or boats, high tech is often associated with high cost (and justifiably so). DuraKore strip composite construction is definitely not the cheapest way to build a boat. In fact, when only cost of materials is considered, it may be the most expensive method of amateur construction. However, strip composite construction makes excellent economic sense if you value your time. For instance, if you earn $35,000 per year on your full-time job, your time is worth $16.83 per hour. There is no doubt that using DuraKore speeds up construction of the basic hull and deck. If you save just 200 hours, the value of that time is more than $3,200— enough to pay the extra cost of materials.

Rather than saving money, however, the primary reason for using strip composite construction is to build the best possible boat. If cost is your concern, then a hard chine plywood boat should be your choice. But if the high-tech combination of light weight and strength is your goal, unpack a box of DuraKore and mix up some epoxy.

Chapter 2
SETTING UP SHOP

Spend as much time planning your workshop as you do every other aspect of the boat. After all, you'll be spending a large part of your life there. From lofting to launching, a cruising sailboat or liveaboard powerboat is a multi-year project. Small daysailers or outboard runabouts can take months to build. Working in a cramped shop or one with bad lighting turns what should be pleasurable hours into pure torture. Even small things like the placement of electrical outlets become major frustrations. So take time planning your shop. Like everything else in boatbuilding, careful preparation pays dividends.

Even in the sunny tropics, a DuraKore boat must be built under shelter. The moisture content of DuraKore is carefully controlled at the factory, and the strips should be kept dry until they are fully encapsulated in epoxy. From a practical standpoint, the only way to avoid moisture problems is to build the boat inside a conventional building with a roof, side walls, and a solid floor.

PLANNING THE SHOP

Everyone's familiar with the old joke about the fellow who built a boat in his basement only to discover there was no way to get it out of the house. Unfortunately, it's not always a joke, and when it happens it's never funny. Even professionals have built boats too big to go through the only doorway to the outside world. That's why the first consideration in choosing an indoor workshop should be, "How am I going to get the boat out of here?"

The answer is not always obvious. For instance, the doorway may only be too narrow for the boat at the sheerline. This is often the case at professional boatshops, where they simply cut a small "flap" into one side of the doorway and trundle the boats out. Other builders plan construction so that the hull will fit through a doorway only when tilted on its side. They take advantage of the diagonal of the door, which is longer than its height or width. Removing a large set of windows from the side of the building may also provide the necessary exit.

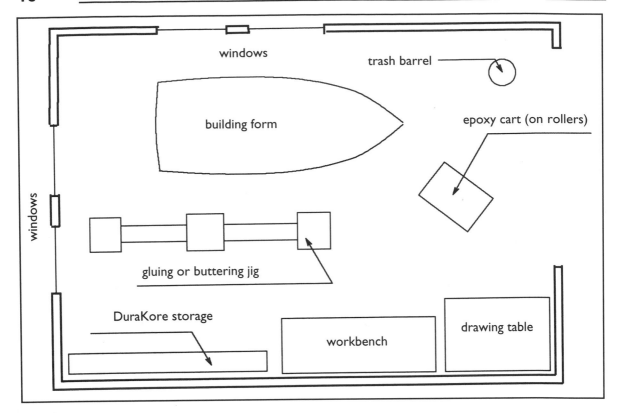

windows

trash barrel

building form

epoxy cart (on rollers)

gluing or buttering jig

DuraKore storage

workbench

drawing table

windows

Convenient layout of building form, workbench and gluing jig is critical to efficient boat building. Pay as much attention to shop layout as to the actual construction of the hull.

Build your boat so that either the bow or stern is pointed straight at the opening to the outside world. This makes things a lot easier on moving day. Outside, there must be enough driveway space for the boat hauler's truck to pick up the completed vessel. Narrow suburban driveways can block the departure of a boat as effectively as a basement stairway can. Extra outdoor space will be necessary if cranes are needed to turn the boat over or to hoist it onto the truck trailer.

Working space inside the shop is the next major consideration. The room should be at least 8 feet longer than the sheerline length of the hull. This gives a minimum 4-foot working space at bow and stern for handling long battens of DuraKore. Keep in mind that the straight planking batten is much longer than the finished boat because of the curve of the hull. Extra work space at the bow or stern is never wasted.

DuraKore strips must be assembled into long planking battens off the hull on a special set of gluing jigs. If possible, these jigs should be located at the stern end of the boat. This allows the planking battens to be carried a short distance in a straight line to where they are needed. Moving long DuraKore battens always raises the possibility of breakage. The less movement—and the fewer corners to go around—the fewer broken pieces.

A number of factors come into play when calculating the minimum width necessary for your shop. Start with the maximum beam of the boat and add 10 feet to provide working space along either side. Then add the space necessary for a workbench, a batten gluing jig, bench power tools, and raw materials. For maximum comfort, this equipment will need another 15 feet of space along the entire length of the shop. A little less may do, but extra space won't remain empty for long.

The typical attached two-car garage is big enough for building shallow boats up to perhaps 20 feet LOA. A dinghy can even be built in the basement, provided that the maximum depth of the hull does not exceed the width of the stairwell to the outside. George Buehler in his most entertaining book, *Buehler's Backyard Boatbuilding* (International Marine, 1991), talks at length about building a temporary shelter out of roll plastic and 2 × 4 framing. This type of structure allows working in your backyard, but it represents one more thing to do before you start actual boat construction. Local zoning laws may prohibit or severely limit building a boat in your backyard. Always check first!

Backyard boatshops usually have dirt floors (the grass dies quickly inside the enclosure). Working on dirt is advantageous for building a conventional plank-on-frame boat because erecting stocks becomes a simple matter of driving timbers into the ground. On the negative side, it is extremely difficult to maintain a constant humidity level in a dirt floor shop covered with a plastic building. This can cause problems of movement of DuraKore strips on the building form.

Basements, garages, and old warehouses have concrete floors. Unless "dished" for water drainage, concrete floors are generally flat and level. That's their biggest advantage. Sore feet and legs are the disadvantage. Anyone who has spent hours walking a concrete floor knows the pain of shin splints. Also, although it may appear dry, concrete passes considerable moisture up from the ground underneath. Once again, this can change the moisture content of the DuraKore, leading to movement of the strips during construction. It is also difficult to attach anything to concrete, so erecting stocks or temporary hull supports may be impossible.

A wood floor over a dry basement or crawlspace probably provides the best working surface. The only real negative of wood floors is that they can never be considered absolutely flat or level. Otherwise, wood is comfortable to walk on and tends to absorb some of the sound of power tools. Building forms and other supports can be nailed right to the floor. And wood floors don't "sweat" the way concrete can. Wood floors have one potentially dangerous disadvantage: inadequate support. You must be certain that the floor is strong enough to support the weight of your boat and all of your shop equipment.

Don't forget to look overhead when inspecting a potential shop location. You'll need enough clearance not just for the boat, but also for your head. A minimum of 4 feet clearance is needed above the highest point on the hull when it's upside down. There should be this much clearance between the top of the cabin if the deck and superstructure will be installed inside the shop. Any less clearance will result in a lot of bumped heads against the ceiling or overhead beams.

Searching out a vacant warehouse or factory to rent for a shop is the most realistic solution for the majority of home builders. If you're forced to look for rental space, there are several considerations:

SHOP CONSIDERATIONS

➤ Driving distance—The farther the boat is from your house, the less work will get done. If possible, find space within a ten-minute drive of home.

➤ Security—Your entire collection of hand and power tools will eventually migrate to the boat shop. Is the building secure against break-ins and theft? Also, you will be leaving the shop late many nights. Is the neighborhood safe?

➤ Utilities—Electric power and water service have often been shut off to vacant commercial buildings. Getting service turned on can be difficult and expensive, especially if the previous occupant left an unpaid balance.

A rent payment of a hundred bucks a month might not sound like much, but many amateurs take three to five years to complete a complex cruising boat during their spare time. If that's the case, you'll have spent $6,000 on rent with nothing but an empty room to show for it. This reality may force you to move the vessel to lower-cost space during construction.

The relative speed with which a DuraKore boat can be built helps limit the cost of renting shop space. A dedicated amateur builder may not need more than a year to build the hull, install interior bulkheads, and deck over a typical 30-footer. Once the boat is waterproof, it can go outside for final finishing of both the exterior and interior. Outdoor space suitable for completing a boat generally rents for a fraction of the cost of an indoor shop.

Back to building in the basement: This may be completely acceptable for a dinghy or a catamaran with narrow hulls. Epoxies do not give off the nose-numbing chemical odors associated with polyester resins. A boat being built in the basement won't announce itself to visitors or neighbors. However, keep in mind that most basements are rather damp. Controlling the relative humidity is usually an exercise in futility. The planking and coating of a basement-built hull will have to be done quickly to avoid problems caused by the changing moisture content of the DuraKore strips.

POWER, LIGHT, AND HEAT

Human beings built ships for thousands of years before the invention of central heat, running water, or electric power. It's still possible to build a conventional wooden plank-on-frame vessel with only human muscles, but that's not high-tech boatbuilding. Modern materials require modern utility services.

ELECTRIC POWER

If precut strips are used, large power tools are not necessary for strip composite construction. More work is done with battery-powered drill motors and hand tools. If foot-wide planks will be ripped into narrow strips on the job site, you'll need a 10-inch table saw with an accurate fence. Because you don't need a number of big power tools, it's possible to construct a boat without heavy wattage electric service. The number and location of outlets are more important than service amperage. Convenient outlet placement avoids excessive use of extension cords or unplugging one tool to use another.

Don't underestimate the need to have lots of outlets. It's not unusual to have a bench sander, palm sander, battery charger, portable light, corded drill motor, and radio plugged in simultaneously. Of these, only the radio will be in use all the time. The rest will be used sequentially as the work progresses. Circuit overloading is seldom as big a problem as just having enough outlets. Work goes smoothest when each tool is plugged into its own outlet. That avoids the hassle of figuring out which power cord to unplug and which one to plug in.

Using extension cords is unavoidable. For safety, these should be heavy gauge cords intended for industrial use. Buy a "cobra head" 3-plug outlet for use when more than one tool at a time is needed. Be sure the 3-plug outlet is rated equal to the maximum amperage of the cord. Plugging three portable tools into one cord isn't a problem as long as you use only one tool at a time. For instance, a corded drill motor and screwdriver can be plugged into the same cord because you're either drilling or tightening screws, but not both. Tools that are to be used simultaneously by two workers should have separate extension cords from separate outlets.

Larger electric tools require dedicated circuits. A 10-inch table saw is about all a standard 15-amp circuit can handle. A big band saw or bench sander also may tax a 15-amp breaker. Compressed air is exceedingly handy both for operating sanders or grinders and for blowing away the dust, but it takes a lot of power to compress air. That's why air compressors must always be on their own circuits.

Corded power tools today are of the "double-insulated" variety. Because of their special construction, they do not require grounding for safety. Older tools, however, usually require a third wire ground to prevent the possibility of electrocution. Never cut off the ground stud from the plug of one of these tools. Also, be sure to purchase 3-wire extension cords. It's not a bad idea to install Ground Fault Interrupters (GFIs) on all shop circuits. These solid-state electronic devices sense when current is leaking (as in a "short" to your body) and automatically cut off the power.

LIGHT—NATURAL AND ELECTRIC

Electric power is an absolute necessity for lighting. The typical amateur does a lot of boatbuilding in the evening after work. At best, these are the hours of twilight but will be full darkness during the winter months. Overhead fluorescent fixtures provide shadow-less light for working into the wee hours. Low-cost fixtures intended for workshops are available at hardware and home improvement stores.

Portable halogen floodlights are also excellent. Buy the type that can be installed on 6-foot stands as well as set on the floor. Halogen floodlights have 500 or 1,000 watt lamps, which put out enormous amounts of light from very small fixtures. One will flood the interior of an overturned hull with light. These fixtures are excellent for checking the application of paints and varnishes.

A lot has been written about how much light is necessary when doing various tasks. Experts talk in terms of "footcandles" or "lux." Few people have the equipment to measure footcandles, but the human eye is extremely adaptable. It will work in dim light as well as in full daylight. The only problem with human eyes is their inability to handle contrast—the difference between the brightest areas and the darkest. In planning shop lighting it's better to have dim but even (often called "flat") illumination than to have "hot" spots with bright light next to darker areas.

Make the best use of natural daylight possible. North-facing windows (in the Northern Hemisphere) are favored because they give practically shadowless light. However, any window is better than none. Another way to provide daylight is to cover the outside frame of overhead garage doors with polyethylene sheeting, which is naturally translucent. Rig the plastic so the door can be opened to admit daylight without loss of expensive heat from the shop. Since the sheet plastic does not interfere with the operation of the overhead door, the door can be closed at night for security.

HEATING THE SHOP

Epoxy resins and most caulks, primers, and paints work best in temperatures above 55°F (13°C). Cold temperatures effectively prevent working during the winter unless the shop is heated. Hot water radiant heat is the absolute best since it does not raise dust by blowing hot air into the room. If hot water heat isn't available, a forced air furnace is the best alternative. In either case, the boiler or furnace should be located where it draws air for the firebox from outside the shop area. This helps prevent flash fires caused by chemical fumes or sawdust.

Northern dwellers shouldn't be too enthusiastic about providing a "shirtsleeve atmosphere" in the shop. Achieving normal living room comfort during the winter is not desirable. A temperature of 55°F (13°C) makes for pleasant work in a flannel shirt and a pair of coveralls. This temperature is also plenty warm enough for all but the most finicky of chemicals. In fact, the cooler temperature can be a positive benefit when working with epoxies because it extends pot life.

The value of central heat in northern climates cannot be overstated because of the ability to maintain a constant temperature. Composite construction works best when the temperatures of the DuraKore, the epoxy resins, and the shop are all the same. This can only be achieved by keeping the shop heated day and night, whether you are there and working or not.

Portable sources of heat are necessary if the shop does not have a central furnace. Small heaters are also handy in drafty shops with odd corners that never seem to get warm. Portable electric heaters can be moved to a variety of locations, but they use large amounts of electricity to produce minimal amounts of heat. You can have one handy for spot application of heat, but it's not practical to use portable electric heaters for the whole shop.

The least acceptable way of getting heat is from one of those so-called "salamander" heaters favored by construction workers. While a salamander will warm a large area, it puts out fumes that make working conditions less than pleasant. Oil-fired units also tend to put out oily soot, which can cause major problems when bonding or coating with epoxy.

Fire is a danger when working with wood, epoxy resins, and other common boatbuilding chemicals. Contact cements used for installing high-pressure laminates or carpeting are almost explosive. Acetone is another common chemical that burns quickly. A salamander or conventional kerosene stove may provide the source of ignition for fumes. The same possibility exists with a wood stove.

Chemical flash fires are awesome events. One minute everything is normal. Then, in an instant, the entire space is filled with a boiling cloud of flame. There's no "base of the flame" on which to spray a fire extinguisher because everything is on fire. Don't get into this situation. Avoid it by scrupulous fire safety practices.

VENTILATION

Good exchange of fresh air is needed even when working with chemicals as benign as epoxy resins. Most buildings leak enough fresh air that power ventilation using outside air is seldom required even during the winter months. However, portable box fans are traditional items in the boatbuilder's tool kit. While the bulk of the air in the shop stays fresh enough, the same can't be said for the deep recesses of the hull. Pockets of stagnant air make working inside the boat difficult without a fan. This is particularly true when coating the inside of the overturned hull with epoxy.

So-called "box" fans in rugged steel cases stand up to hard knocks. Table fans with plastic shrouds seldom survive a fall to a concrete floor. (Somebody always kicks the fan cord.) Remember that ventilation fan motors are not spark protected and should not be used in explosive atmospheres. It is generally better to blow fresh air into a confined space than to try to exhaust stale air out of the hull.

THE WORKBENCH

Every boat shop needs at least one sturdy workbench of ample proportions. At a minimum, it should be 3 feet wide and 6 feet long. Build it using 4-inch square timbers for legs and 2 × 6-inch planks for framing. Bolt everything together. Using a bit of epoxy in the joints isn't wasteful, considering the extra strength the glue provides. Plans for workbenches abound in woodworking books. Any library should yield two or three acceptable designs.

Make the top of the bench out of dressed 2 × 4- or 2 × 6-inch planks laid flat. Planks allow bending jigs to be nailed directly to the bench. Also, there will be plenty of wood to catch the tip of an errant drill bit. Cut a piece of old carpet to the size of the top. Flop this piece of carpet on top

An advantage to DuraKore construction is that it does not require tools beyond those found in the average home toolbox. This flexible plastic toolbox will not scrape or damage the hull, deck or interior during construction.

of the bench when working on finished surfaces, such as varnished wood, to prevent scratches.

Fine woodworking requires a variety of clever vises coupled with an assortment of bench dogs. Nothing this complex is needed for DuraKore boat construction. A simple woodworker's vise proves handy for the odd shaping or cutting. Put this vise at one corner of the workbench. A 6- or 8-inch metalworking vise at the opposite corner is handy for sharpening tools as well as holding metal. If possible, however, put the metal vise on a separate bench from the woodworking table.

A separate table or cart should be dedicated to the epoxy and filler materials. This confines any mess to a small area of the shop.

Shelves beneath the workbench are an excellent place for storing tools, resins, fasteners, and other odd items. Avoid the temptation to install drawers, which serve more to collect sawdust than to hold supplies. Shelves should also be installed above benches placed against a shop wall.

Build a separate workbench for the epoxy resin pumps and thickening agents. Mixing epoxy is a bit messy, so it pays to separate this operation from the rest of the shop. The resin pumps should be at a comfortable working height and have a drip pan. A wheeled cart similar to those used for microwave ovens allows moving the epoxy to the job. This saves lots of walking and allows full use of the pot life for coating and bonding. Be sure the cart has plenty of storage for plastic mixing bowls and other utensils.

RAW MATERIAL STORAGE

DuraKore strips and planks are shipped from the factory in cardboard cartons. These cartons should be stored horizontally and off the floor to protect them from water damage. A simple wall rack can be made to hold cartons of material. Be sure there is enough room at one end to remove an 8-foot strip without bending it. Strips and planks should be left in their boxes until they are glued into long planking battens.

DecoLite sheets can be conveniently stored on a rolling cart similar to those used for plywood. This type of cart is not sold in stores,
but is easily fabricated from 2 × 4-inch studding available at every
lumberyard. The cart holds sheets lying on their sides. Castors make
it easy for one man to move the stock of panels to the saw or the
boat.

THE DRAWING TABLE

Constant reference to the naval architect's blueprints is a normal
part of boatbuilding. These plans can be rolled up in a corner of the
workbench and unrolled as necessary, but they will soon become
smudged, dog-eared, and torn. Blueprints will last a lot longer if they
can be used on a drawing table reserved for that purpose. A fancy
drafting table isn't necessary, just a flat, smooth surface slightly larger than the biggest blueprint. A satisfactory table can be made out of
a piece of tempered hardboard (e.g., Masonite) screwed to a 1 × 3-
inch pine frame. Tack a piece of polyethylene sheeting along one
edge of the table so that it can be rolled over the top to protect the
drawings from dust. A tension-arm lamp over the table should provide plenty of light.

THE TOOL KIT

Composite strip construction does not require the large array of
extensive and specialized tools needed to build other types of boats.
Other than convenience, there's no reason that a large cruising boat
couldn't be built using only non-electric hand tools. Everyone has
personal tastes in tools, but the basic kit required includes:

GENERAL HAND TOOLS

➤ Screwdrivers—Both straight slot and Phillips in a variety of
  sizes.
➤ Hammers—A 12– to 16-ounce carpenter's claw hammer is
  always handy. Other handy hammers include ones with soft
  plastic or rubber faces and a dead blow mallet.
➤ Pliers—The kit should include a pair of standard 8-inch slip-
  joint pliers as well as a pair of arc-joint "water pump" pliers.
  Diagonal cutters and needlenose pliers will come in handy
  when installing electrical wiring.

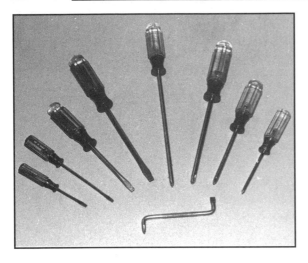

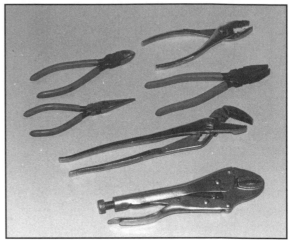

(left) *You'll need an assortment of slotted and Phillips head screwdrivers throughout construction. Most builders prefer Phillips screws, which can be driven with a low-speed drill motor.*

(right) *Pliers have become highly specialized. Here, ordinary slip-joint pliers (upper right) are joined by wire cutters, lineman's pliers, water-pump pliers, and Vise-Grips.*

(below) *Stanley's Surform plane does an excellent job of shaping the end-grain balsa in DuraKore strips. This patented device actually works better than a conventional block plane.*

➤ Wrenches—Full sets of socket and combination wrenches are indispensable when installing an engine and its associated underwater gear.

➤ Knives—A couple of different types of knives will come in handy. The standard shop utility knife with replaceable blades does most of the work, but a pocketknife and a single-edge razor blade scraper are also needed.

SAWS, PLANES, AND CHISELS

DuraKore strips are easily cut and shaped with ordinary woodworking tools. In fact, simple hand saws and shaping devices work better in many situations than the more difficult to use chisels or block planes.

➤ Hand Saws—Smaller saws are more useful than larger carpenter's rip saws. Start with a backsaw and a nest of keyhole saws that fit into a "pistol" handle.

➤ Planes and Surform—A small (6-inch) block plane is handy for trimming the ends of strips or for cutting bevels. A Stanley Surform combines a file-like cutting surface with the body of a plane. Workers who haven't acquired the skill of using a conventional wood plane usually find the Surform easier to use.

➤ Wood Chisels—A good woodworker with a chisel can move the world . . . but chisels in unskilled hands do more damage than honest work. Still, ½- and ¾-inch chisels should be in the tool kit.

➤ Rasps and Wood Files— Useful for taking off small amounts of wood to fit a strip into a tight spot. Fine-cut files and rasps are better on DuraKore than rough-cut tools intended for denser woods.

Sharp-edge tools are the mark of a craftsman. Chisels are useful when fitting timber pieces together. Planes can shape DuraKore strips, although a Stanley Surform is easier for inexperienced workers.

MEASURING TOOLS

Measurements are a critical part of boatbuilding. The nature of boat hulls requires a variety of measuring tools, ranging from a 6-foot folding wood rule to a 100-foot steel tape. Most work is done with either a folding rule or a 25-foot steel tape. Longer tapes are needed only when measuring the overall or gunwale length of larger boats.

➤ Wood Rule—The advantage of a traditional carpenter's rule is that it is self-supporting when measuring beyond the reach of your arms. Buy the best rule because the joints of cheap rules soon get sloppy, as do the measurements.

➤ Steel Tape—A 25-foot self-retracting steel measuring tape is almost indispensable. Small enough to clip to your belt, it's long enough to measure the mid-girth of even large hulls.

PORTABLE POWER TOOLS

Power tools are wonderful devices that allow unskilled hands to make mistakes at a prodigious rate. A benefit of DuraKore composite strip construction is that expensive portable power tools aren't necessary. Still, portable drills and sanders make their purchase worthwhile by saving considerable handwork.

➤ Battery Pack Drill Motor—A ⅜-inch motor powered by a replaceable battery pack (minimum 7.2 volt) is the key power tool for strip composite construction. Buy a spare battery and you'll never run out of power.

➤ Second Battery Pack Drill Motor—Absolutely not a necessity, but a second battery-powered motor greatly speeds up some jobs. One motor can be used to drill pilot holes while the other has the bit for driving the screws. If a second motor is purchased, it should be identical to the primary motor so that the batteries can be interchanged.

➤ Corded Drill Motor—Nothing beats a 120-volt motor for powering through heavy jobs. The motor should have at least a ⅜-inch chuck and variable speed with full reverse.

➤ Corded Power Screwdriver—Not necessary if enough variable speed drill motors are available. An industrial driver that "chatters" screws home is expensive. Avoid less costly units intended for drywall installation, as they operate at too high an r.p.m. for the control needed when driving screws for boatbuilding.

➤ Sabersaw (corded)—If the shop has only one power saw, it should be a full-featured sabersaw. Variable speed and blade orbit improve cutting in a variety of materials. A scrolling feature (allows the blade to rotate) may prove handy, but isn't worth spending extra money on.

➤ Builder's Circular Saw (corded)—Known in the United States as a "Skilsaw" after the brand that made it famous, the 7¼-inch portable circular saw is most useful for rough carpentry

(left) These two corded tools are virtual necessities. Unlike its battery-powered cousins, a corded drill motor never runs out of power. Battery saws don't have the power to match a corded saw. Always buy professional–grade tools.

(right) Breathing protection is necessary when sanding, fairing, or using many two-part paints. The white mask is suitable only for nuisance dust. Wear a true chemical respirator to protect against toxic fumes.

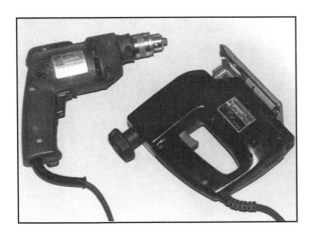

such as building the strongback for the building form.
May have special uses at other
times.

➤ Palm Sander (corded)—
Extremely useful when finishing wood, it will also help during final fairing of the hull.

➤ Router (corded)—A portable
machine with a ¼-inch arbor
should be able to do all of the
necessary work. A router is
needed to make joints in strips
cut from planks. Factory-made
DuraKore strips do not require
routered joints.

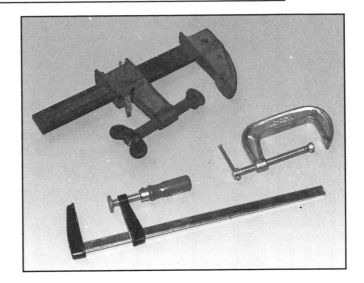

*A variety of clamps will do
the work of two or three
assistants. Lightweight bar
clamps are fine when gluing
DuraKore strips, but you'll
need heavier bar or C-
clamps when bending tim-
ber sheer clamps into the
boat.*

Visit stores catering to professionals when shopping for power tools.
While the brand names may be the same, there is a world of difference between a professional tool and one intended for sale to home-
owners. Electric tools for the pro have stronger motors, better bear-
ings, and stouter cases. In short, they last through the construction
of several boats. Tools for the home shop often die before the work
is done.

BENCH POWER TOOLS

Large bench power tools common for building conventional wood-
en hulls aren't as necessary with DuraKore. Boats have been built
with nothing larger than a portable sabersaw. Still, there are times
nothing works as well as a table saw. This is particularly true if
DuraKore planks are to be ripped into strips for planking.

➤ Table Saw—The larger the diameter of the blade, the
straighter the cut. That's why a 10-inch saw is better than an
8-inch. Look for a cast iron or aluminum top with machined
slots for the miter gauge. Belt-driven saws are preferred by
professionals.

➤ Band Saw—Indispensable for fabricating intricate parts out
of conventional wood. A good sabersaw can do most of the
work of a band saw for less money.

➤ Wood Shaper—Completely unnecessary. Instead, mount a router in one of the commercially available tables and it becomes a serviceable shaper, if you buy the right cutters.

➤ Bench Sander—The most useful machines drive both a disk and a belt simultaneously with the same motor. Purchase one with a minimum 6-inch disk and an adjustable table with a miter gauge slot.

FIBERGLASS TOOLS

Covering the planked hull with fiberglass or other reinforcing material is a major part of strip composite construction. This job involves cutting pieces of fabric taken from rolls or bolts and laying them over the hull. Epoxy resin is then rolled into the fabric, creating the FRP laminate and gluing it to the wood. Special tools are needed.

CLOTH CUTTING

Cutting glass cloth (knitted or woven) requires sharp tools. The cloth tends to be slippery, making it difficult to cut a perfectly straight line.

A dressmaker's wheel cutter used with a special resilient cutting surface works well for cutting and trimming many reinforcement fabrics. Both are available in fabric and craft stores.

➤ Large Shears—Within reason, the longer the better for straight cuts. Eight-inch shears are a practical size.

➤ Small Scissors—These make cutting curves easier. Four and six-inch scissors are equally handy.

➤ Wheel Cutter—Looking like a pizza cutter, a wheel fabric cutter makes both straight and curved cuts. Find these in fabric shops. Buy several extra cutter blades as glass cloth quickly dulls the cutting edge of the wheel.

➤ Cutting Surface—It helps to have a hard, smooth surface on which to cut cloth. The best surface is a piece of plywood faced with high-pressure laminate (e.g., Formica), but a piece of tempered hardboard (Masonite) to lay on top of the workbench should get the job done for a single boat.

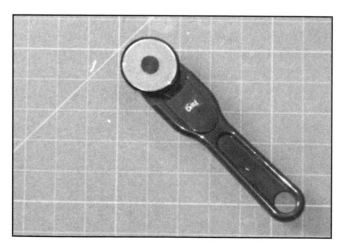

RESIN APPLICATION

Mixed epoxy is poured over the dry cloth, then rolled and squeegeed into the material. Rolling continues until the resin-to-glass ratio is uniform throughout the laminate and all air bubbles have been removed.

- ➤ Paint Roller—A dense polyurethane foam roller cover on a standard paint roller frame is useful for rolling out resin during seal coating.
- ➤ Metal Laminate Roller—Looks like a paint roller, except that it is made out of metal wheels. Used to push resin around in cloth and to reduce wrinkles in cloth. Metal rollers come in various sizes and widths.
- ➤ Squeegee—Made out of flexible plastic. Have several on hand in sizes ranging from 4 to 8 inches wide.
- ➤ Stiff Bristle Brush—This is often useful when breaking up air bubbles or pushing resin into tight corners. Can be made by cutting down a stiff nylon paint brush.
- ➤ Foam Brushes—Used in coating to tip out roller marks, bubbles, and other imperfections.
- ➤ Mixing Containers—Nobody ever has enough plastic bowls and cups for mixing epoxy. Start saving large margarine tubs before you buy the plans for your boat. Cured epoxy doesn't stick to the flexible plastic of these tubs.
- ➤ Mixing Sticks—Wooden tongue depressors work well and are disposable. Find them at full-service drug stores. Cut one end to match the shape of the mixing container.

Chapter 3
WORKING WITH
THE MATERIALS

Although DuraKore strip composite construction produces high-tech boats, the materials involved have decidedly user-friendly, low-tech properties. DuraKore strips are an "engineered composite," but they handle like ordinary wood planks. Epoxy boatbuilding resins are state-of-the-art chemistry, yet they look and act like thick corn syrup. And the weaving and knitting involved in reinforcement material is light years advanced from your cotton flannel shirt, but it cuts and handles much the same as less exotic fabrics.

The high-tech nature of this boatbuilding method is not in the materials, but in the way wood and epoxy and fabric are combined into a final laminate. As mentioned earlier, a DuraKore laminate actually performs in the same manner as a steel I-beam. Strength comes from the physical relationships of the top and bottom reinforcing layers to the inner balsa core. The success of your boat depends on the quality of the bonding of those individual elements. In turn, that bonding depends upon your understanding the nature of the materials involved and the proper ways to use them.

DURAKORE STRIPS AND PLANKS

SHIPPING AND STORAGE

Baltek packs both planks and strips in protective shipping cartons, which should be opened carefully to avoid damaging the contents. This is particularly true of boxes containing DuraKore strips, which have delicate finger joints at each end. The number of strips in a box varies from 63 to 384 depending upon width and thickness of the material. Nine to 18 of the foot-wide planks are contained in a carton. Both planks and strips are 8 feet long.

Unopened boxes of DuraKore material are relatively safe from damage other than dampness. They should be stored off the ground

Machine-cut finger joints permit easy assembly of DuraKore strips into long planking battens. Strips in this photo range in thickness from 3/8 inch to 3/4 inch. (Courtesy Baltek Corp.)

inside weather protection. Once opened, the DuraKore materials should be stored flat on shelves or specially built racks. A series of wall-mounted shelves will hold enough DuraKore for a good-sized

DuraKore Weights & Dimensions

Strip Thickness Inches	Width Inches	Weight Lbs/Sq Ft	Strips Per Box	Coverage Square Ft Per Box
3/8	.75	.65	384	179.52
1/2	.87	.83	252	146.16
5/8	1.09	.92	176	127.89
3/4	1.30	1.01	108	93.60
1	1.75	1.25	63	73.50

DecoLite Weights & Dimensions (FRP)

Thickness Inches	Width Inches	Length Inches	Weight Lbs/Sq Ft
1/2	48	96	0.96
3/4	48	96	1.14
1	48	96	1.35

vessel. Sort the materials by type and size, assigning each shelf a different width strip or plank.

All surfaces of stored DuraKore strips must be protected from chemical contamination. Airborne chemicals (particularly if they are oily or greasy) can make it difficult for the epoxy resin to bond properly. This is a serious concern. Airborne hydrocarbon pollution can come from several sources. Kerosene or propane "salamander" construction heaters are a prime culprit. And expect contamination if you're sharing workspace with someone painting or repairing cars or doing factory work.

ESTIMATING THE AMOUNT OF DURAKORE NEEDED

It's necessary to calculate the square footage of the surface of the hull to know how much DuraKore to order. This calculation requires measurements taken from the lines drawing. While not difficult, the process is time consuming. Start by measuring the distance from sheer to keel along the outer skin as shown on the section view of the lines drawing. Naval architects use an expensive tool to make this measurement. An adequate job can be done with the edge of a blank sheet of paper. Put a pencil mark at one end of the paper and line this mark up at the keel. Rotate the edge of the paper around the outer curve of the hull on the section view. Put a second pencil mark on the paper where it touches the sheerline. Measure the distance between pencil marks to get the section girth.

Convert the measured scale distance to the actual distance on the full-size boat by using the scale of the drawing. For instance, a 6-inch girth measured off a blueprint where $\frac{1}{2}$ inch on the drawing equals 1 foot represents a 12-foot girth in real life. Each section should be measured in this manner and the measurements entered in a table.

The next step is to multiply the girth measurements by the distance between sections. Assume in the above example that the sections are spaced 2 feet apart. Then the 12-foot girth when multiplied by a 2-foot spacing yields 24 square feet. This same process is followed with all sections.

Finally, add the square footages for all of the sections and multiply by two. This gives a very close approximation of the square footage of the entire hull. (Multiplying by two is necessary because the section view shows only half of the hull.) Add about 10 percent to this figure for plank stretch around the curve of the boat. This gives a good approximation of the total square footage in the hull. Here's how our example might work on a 32-foot boat:

SQUARE FOOTAGE EXAMPLE

STATION	MEASURED GIRTH	SECTION DISTANCE		SQUARE FOOTAGE
1	2	2	=	4
2	3	2	=	6
3	4.5	2	=	9
4	5	2	=	10
5	5.5	2	=	11
6	6	2	=	12
7	6.5	2	=	13
8	7	2	=	14
9	7	2	=	14
10	6.5	2	=	13
11	6	2	=	12
12	5.5	2	=	11
13	5	2	=	10
14	4.5	2	=	9
15	3	2	=	6
16	2	2	=	4
	Total Sq. Ft. (Half Hull)	=		$158 \times 2 = 316$ Sq. Ft. (Whole Hull)

Hull Planking Required	=	316 Sq. Ft.
10% Plank Stretch	=	32 " "
15% Scrap Rate	=	48 " "
Total To Order	=	396 Sq. Ft.

Scrap rate is an estimate based on your personal working habits. It's impossible not to waste some material as offcuts, broken pieces, etc. A first-time builder can anticipate a larger scrap rate than a professional. The 15 percent rate illustrated above is not excessive for an amateur builder.

ESTIMATING NUMBER AND LENGTHS OF PLANKING BATTENS

Hulls are planked with long battens fabricated by gluing 8-foot DuraKore strips together. The number and lengths of these battens should be estimated before construction begins, as prefabricating them speeds up the planking process. Also, not all battens need to be the full length of the boat. Near the keel line and the sheerline many

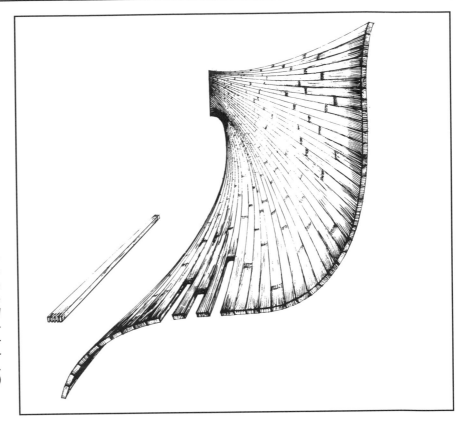

Here's what DuraKore planking would look like without station molds to support it. The ratio of the thickness to the width of the planks allows them to bend in two directions simultaneously to produce a fair surface curved in three dimensions.
(Courtesy Baltek Corp.)

planks will be somewhat shorter, so they do not have to be made full length. Ian Farrier recommends the following method for estimating the number and length of battens that will be needed:

Measure the distance from bow to stern over the outside edges of the section molds at the boat's maximum beam. This gives the length of the longest DuraKore batten needed. Glue up one batten long enough to span this distance. Hold this batten against the mold frames so that it reaches from bow to transom. Move it along the midships mold toward the keel and then back the other direction toward the sheerline. Always keep the batten straight and parallel to the waterlines. This process gives a rough idea of the area of the hull that will require the longest Durakore battens.

All of the other areas of the hull will require shorter battens. By now you should be able to make a rough estimate of the number and lengths of the battens that will be needed. It's better to overestimate the number of various length battens when planking the first side. Extras can be used on the other side of the boat or be cut down into shorter lengths as needed.

This hastily constructed glue-up table made of scrap lumber was sufficient to hold DuraKore strips while they were being glued into planking battens. Note the box of DuraKore strips stored beneath the table on blocks to keep it off the potentially damp concrete.

JOINING DURAKORE STRIPS

Finger joints on DuraKore strips are machined so that when assembled correctly, both edges of each strip fit flush. If one strip is upside down, the joints will slide together but the edges will not be flush. To aid alignment, each finger joint is marked with a black line on one edge of the exposed balsa. The other side is not marked. Match a marked side to an unmarked side to ensure correct alignment.

The gluing jig consists of wooden guide strips screwed to the table. A piece of scrap DuraKore wrapped in poly film serves as a spacer to ensure the guides are the right distance apart and are correctly aligned. The table was covered with poly film before the strips were screwed down.

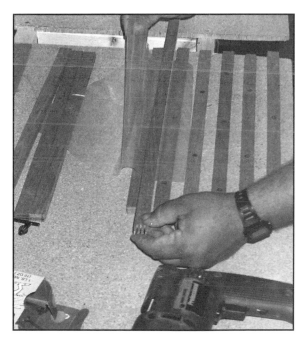

Long DuraKore battens used to plank the hull are assembled off the boat in a gluing jig. In its simplest form, this jig is really just a flat surface as long as the longest batten needed. Different builders have used a variety of methods to ensure the joints remain straight and true while the epoxy cures. Most involve clamping the strips between a long, straight batten and a guide rail along one edge of the jig. Remember to cover the jig with polyethylene sheeting to prevent strips from bonding to it.

In use, Ocean Tech jigs are clamped to sawhorses or other supports spaced 8 feet apart. After the finger joints are glued and pressed together, the strips are pushed into the slots to ensure that the joints remain aligned until the glue kicks. Scraps of polyethylene sheeting keep the DuraKore from bonding to the wooden jigs. The thickness of the plastic helps wedge the strips tightly in the slots.

Finger joints are glued with moderately thickened epoxy. Most builders use a low-density filler mixed to a stiff molasses consistency. Apply the glue with a small paintbrush (disposable metal-handled acid brushes work well). Fully coat the fingers on both strips, then press the joint together in the jig. Wipe off excess glue that squeezes out of the joint. Repeat the process to complete enough battens to plank one side of the hull.

Long DuraKore planking battens are extremely floppy and difficult for one person to handle without breaking. A short, straight approach from the gluing jig to the building form limits the possibility of dam-

OCEAN TECH COMB JIGS

At Ocean Tech in Solomons, Maryland, Gary and Bonnie Van-Tassel build high-speed offshore sportfish boats using DuraKore. They solved the problem of gluing strips into battens by creating sets of "comb" jigs. These jigs are little more than squares of plywood on which ⅜-inch strips of wood have been affixed. The strips run parallel to each other from one side of the board to the other and are set just the width of the DuraKore strips apart. The slots thus formed hold DuraKore finger joints in alignment while the glue cures.

Epoxy glue is brushed into the finger joints of the DuraKore strips before they are pushed together. All surfaces of the joint must be coated to prevent weak joints.

age. Avoid carrying the long battens around corners. If the building shed is not long enough to locate the jig at one end of the mold, an alternative is to make the jig portable. Set it on the side of the hull currently being planked.

After the epoxy cures, sand the glue joints on each batten to remove excess epoxy that has cured on the surface. A power sander with 80-grit paper works well, but caution is advised. Do *not* sand into the DuraKore itself, as this creates an hourglass shape that weakens the joint and causes a gap between battens when fitted to the mold frames.

BATTEN BUTTERING JIG

DuraKore battens are seamed together on the building form using thickened epoxy. Applying this thickened glue is known as "buttering" the battens. It's a messy procedure at best. Trying to butter on the building form can be wasteful of materials and can slow down the planking process. A much cleaner, faster method is to butter the long battens on another special jig designed for this purpose.

A simple jig for "buttering" the edges of planking battens can be constructed from scrap lumber. The secret lies in making the guide rails slightly taller than the DuraKore strips. A disadvantage is that glue may begin to cure before the batten can be installed on the building mold.

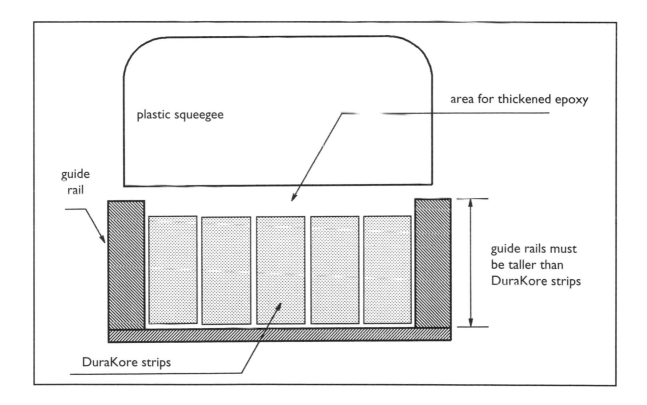

plastic squeegee

area for thickened epoxy

guide rail

guide rails must be taller than DuraKore strips

DuraKore strips

The buttering jig is a U-shaped trough just wide enough to hold four to six battens on edge. The sides of the trough extend above the DuraKore strips by the thickness of the desired layer of thickened glue. Buttering the strips in the jig is a matter of pushing a gob of thick glue ahead of a flexible plastic trowel held against the sides of the trough. The exact thickness of epoxy bog putty is left behind the trowel.

As with any other gluing jig, the buttering jig must be protected against epoxy buildup with clear package sealing tape or scraps of polyethylene sheeting. The buttering jig becomes quite messy with use. Replacing the protective tape or plastic several times during construction of the boat is normal.

The capacity of the buttering jig is deliberately limited to the number of battens that can be installed on the building form during the pot life of one mixing of epoxy glue. This number varies with the ambient temperature, the skill of the workers, and the complexity of the hull shape.

Sometimes it's advantageous to attach the planking batten to the building mold dry and apply the glue later. Troweling or brushing thickened epoxy onto the edge of a strip is time consuming. It's much faster to fill a plastic bag with thickened epoxy. Snip a corner off the bag and squeegee the glue out of this opening onto the strip. This is known as the "pastry bag" technique because of its similarity to the method used by cake decorators for applying frosting.

USING DURAKORE PLANKS

Cost saving is the primary advantage of the 12-inch wide DuraKore planks. Money can be saved by cutting planks to size and creating your own joints. However, these savings come at the expense of the biggest advantage of DuraKore strip composite construction: speed. Prefabricated strips with their machined finger joints allow rapid hull construction. Ripping planks into strips and then cutting joints slows the boatbuilding process. It's well known that the longer an amateur takes to build a hull, the less likely that the boat will be completed.

There are times, however, when ripping DuraKore planks to size may be the best way to build a boat. This is particularly true of hulls with large, flat sections. A single 4-inch wide plank takes a lot less time to install than five ¾-inch battens. Knowing when to use planks in place of battens is a matter of judgment based on boatbuilding experience. If you're not sure, stay with the precut DuraKore strips.

RIPPING DURAKORE PLANKS

Planks are seldom used in their full 12-inch width. They must be ripped lengthwise to an appropriate size. This can be done with a band saw, table saw, or portable builder's saw (Skilsaw). Stacking several planks together during the cutting operation speeds up the process. The low-density balsa wood cuts easily without slowing down the saw motor. A narrow kerf, fine-tooth blade usually makes the cleanest cut with the least waste of materials.

Jim Gentry of Clarkston, Washington, ripped all of the planking battens for his F-32 from DuraKore planks using a 10-inch table saw. He did this partially to save money and partially to custom tailor the width of the battens to various areas of the boat. "You have to be careful when you push the planks through the blade to keep the cut accurate," he says. Gentry needed coffee breaks every ten minutes or so to interrupt the tedium. He used a carbide-tipped, 60-tooth general-purpose blade.

CUTTING PLANK JOINTS

The ends of DuraKore planks are square cutoffs without finger joints. It is necessary to create your own method of joining planks into long battens. A traditional 8:1 or 12:1 scarf joint could be made, but takes time without necessarily improving the strength of the completed boat. A cored hull gets its strength from the *continuous* nature of the outer skins and inner core material. It's more important that joints ensure the core is continuous than that they make the long planking batten as strong as possible. Two methods produce this type of joint quickly:

➤ Finger Joint Cutter—Special cutters are available to convert an ordinary router into a finger joint machine. These require the use of a router table. As the "fingers" should go through the hardwood veneer, the width of plank that can be finger jointed is limited by the length of the cutter.

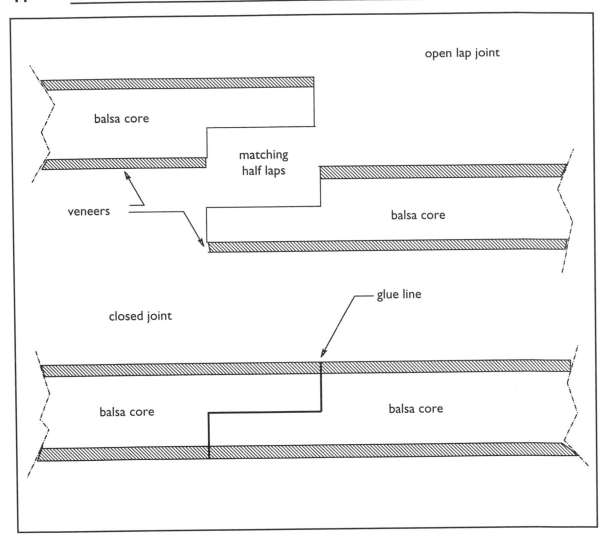

DuraKore planks and DecoLite panels can be joined with simple open "ship lap" joints, an easy cut on a table saw using either a dado blade or a horizontal cutter/shaper. Extra strength can be achieved by applying a strip of reinforcement fabric set in epoxy over both external glue lines.

➤ Overlapping Butt—This method requires no special cutters. The outer layer of veneer is removed for the full length of the joint from one side of both planks. The balsa core is cut to half its depth for the length of the joint, also from both planks. This produces mirror-image stair steps, which can be glued together.

As with the factory-made DuraKore strips, planks should be assembled into long battens and buttered with thickened glue before being installed in the hull.

EPOXY RESINS AND HARDENERS

The term "epoxy" does not refer to a single product but to a wide range of chemicals. Epoxies for boat construction are carefully blended to produce a tenacious bond on wood and to be virtually waterproof. In addition, they exhibit good working properties such as flow and pot life. A single epoxy "blend" seldom does everything. Chemists have found that different jobs require different chemical composition. That's why an epoxy mixture that's good for bonding is usually not the best to use for clear coating wood.

Fortunately, you don't have to have a Ph.D. in chemistry to decide which epoxy to use. Boatbuilding epoxies are sold as "systems" that combine a basic epoxy resin with a variety of hardeners to suit the job at hand. Additional materials known as fillers (thixotropic agents) can be added to the mixed resin to create troweling putties for fairing the hull or thick bog putty for filleting and bonding bulkheads.

Jan and Meade Gougeon of Bay City, Michigan, pioneered the use of epoxies in boatbuilding. Their company, Gougeon Brothers, produces West System epoxy products that have become the industry standards. However, "West" is part of the Gougeons' trademark and not a generic term for epoxy or for a boatbuilding technique. Many other companies worldwide produce excellent marine epoxy glues and filler materials.

Epoxy consists of a base resin and a hardener. Neither has any glue properties by itself. They must be mixed together in specific amounts to start a one way chemical reaction known as "curing." The speed of this reaction is determined by the formulation of the hardener and the ambient temperature of the material. As molecules in the mixture begin to cross-link, the epoxy hardens and gives off heat. Curing resin goes through several distinct stages ranging from rubbery to glasslike. Final strength and flexibility are not reached until the epoxy is fully cured, about 24 hours after it was mixed.

Epoxy has two drawbacks for marine use, both involving sunlight. The first is the susceptibility of cured epoxy to ultraviolet degradation. Even the relatively mild sun of New England or the upper Great Lakes is sufficient to break down unprotected epoxy solids. The other drawback is heat deformation. Some cured epoxy formulations will soften at temperatures that may be reached in the tropics when bright sun beats down on dark surfaces. (That's why decks should be painted white or light colors.)

Both sun-related drawbacks can be overcome through the use of proper coating materials. Light-colored linear urethane paint blocks ultraviolet light and keeps the surface cool by reflecting much of the sun's energy. Bright finished wood that has been coated with epoxy can be topcoated with ultraviolet-resistant varnish or urethane clearcoat. If uncoated epoxy is to be exposed to sunlight for an extended period of time (such as during construction outdoors), it should be protected from sun degradation by adding special aluminum powder or white pigment.

MIXING EPOXY

According to Meade Gougeon, the biggest reason for epoxy failure is improper mixing of the resin and hardener.

Anyone who has worked with polyester resins is familiar with the trick of adding extra catalyst to speed up the chemical reaction. *Never* promote a fast cure of epoxy by adding extra hardener. Always mix epoxy resin and hardener in the exact ratio specified by the manufacturer. Adding extra hardener does not speed up the cure of epoxy, it only reduces its cured strength. Even worse, if too much hardener is added, all of it may not cross-link. Excess hardener can remain a bubble of liquid surrounded by cured resin.

Not stirring thoroughly is the other big mistake made with epoxies. It takes a lot of mixing to get the hardener evenly dispersed through the resin. A couple of quick swishes with a mixing stick doesn't get the job done. Professional boatbuilders worry enough about this problem that they color resins with yellow dye and hardeners with blue. They know a pot of glue isn't mixed until both colors disappear into a uniform green. Home builders don't need to get that colorful as long as they stir the mixture for at least two full minutes.

DISPENSING RESIN AND HARDENER

Don't even think about trying to use epoxy glues without purchasing the correct mixing pumps. These pumps come in matched sets, one for the resin and the other for the hardener. They are calibrated to dispense exactly the right resin-to-hardener ratio on the basis of

Epoxy manufacturers supply special metering pumps that ensure a proper resin-to-hardener mixture. Pumps should be replaced when they become worn or clogged with chemical residue. Using two or three sets of pumps to build one boat is not unusual nor unwise. (Courtesy Gougeon)

one pump of each. This is accomplished by having the resin pump deliver more material than the hardener pump. Dispensing pumps do more than just assure the correct ratio. They also prevent waste that's inevitable when using measuring cups.

There's a trick to using mixing pumps when larger quantities of glue are required. The wrong way is to put five or six pumps of resin into the mixing bowl and then add the same number of pumps of hardener. Don't do this! It's far too easy to lose count, which results in an improper ratio. Instead, always pump once on the resin and then once on the hardener before going back to the resin. In addition to avoiding the problem of losing count, alternate strokes allow both pumps to fully recover for the next stroke. Continuous strokes on one pump can result in less than a full measure being dispensed.

Do not attempt to pump cold materials. Both the resin and the hardener become extremely thick at low temperatures. This can lead to inaccurate dispensing by the pumps, which may not produce enough vacuum to suck up a full stroke of material. Even if the pump does work, the strain will cause its premature death. Pumps used to handle cold resin do not last long.

STIRRING THE POT

The Gougeon manual recommends stirring resin and hardener for up to two minutes to ensure full dispersal. A disposable wooden paddle shaped to fit the contours of the mixing container is recommended. Scrape the sides and bottom of the container as you mix. Although this is boring work, it may be the single most important task in building a strip composite boat. Your hull will only be as good as the epoxy holding it together. Stir at least two full minutes (longer for larger batches).

Soft plastic mixing containers are suggested. Have a supply of several sizes on hand. Small margarine tubs are good for one or two pump jobs. Larger margarine tubs can hold four or five pumps. Really large jobs require the plastic buckets that come from the store filled with peanut butter. All ex-food containers must be thoroughly scrubbed clean to remove all traces of contamination.

Wide, flat mixing containers are better than tall, narrow cans. This is because the chemical reaction that causes epoxies to cure is what chemists call "exothermic." It gives off heat, which is retained better in a tall, thin container than in a wide, flat bowl. Warm epoxies cure faster. That's why a soup can of mixed epoxy turns into a steaming froth in a few minutes while glue mixed in a flat dish remains workable for its full pot life.

Disposable wooden tongue depressors can be purchased in bulk through full-service drug stores. They make excellent epoxy mixing sticks. Their round ends fit into the contours of most small plastic margarine tubs. If you're using a mixing container with a square bottom, cut off one end of the depressor to match the container.

THICKENING AGENTS

Mixed epoxy glue has a consistency about like corn syrup. This consistency is fine for most gluing and coating jobs but is much too thin for bonding strip seams, installing bulkheads, or creating fillets. For these jobs it is necessary to add a filler. Various materials are used as fillers, ranging from cotton fibers to microballoons and powdered garbage bag plastic. The selection of the proper filler depends upon the strength needed and the sanding or fairing requirements.

High-density fillers make the strongest bonds but are the most difficult to sand. They are excellent for bonding hardware or for filleting and gap filling where maximum strength is the overriding consideration. Low-density fillers give minimal strength but are easier to sand. They are most often used in fairing putties ("bog" to Australians) that sand easily to a smooth finish. Some low-density fillers are subject to heat deformation, so should not be used on flat deck surfaces.

Always mix the resin and hardener fully before adding fillers. Don't be fooled by first appearances. The mixture will seem to thicken almost immediately, but will become considerably thinner with more stirring. Continue adding small amounts of filler until the proper consistency is reached. If mixing to a fairing compound recipe, measure the full amount of thickener but add only small portions at a time. Continue stirring for a full minute after the last thickener is added to ensure there are no pockets of dry powder in the mixture.

There is no easy way to unthicken a batch of putty. You can't just add another pump of resin and hardener because it will be impossible to properly mix them together and blend them into the batch. The only solution is to mix extra epoxy in a separate container and then add it to the putty, a tedious process that uses up valuable pot life. So add filler slowly to avoid over-thickening in the first place.

SURFACE PREPARATION

Surface contamination is a key factor in bond failures. Epoxies won't stick to waxy, oily, or greasy surfaces. All bonding surfaces must be properly cleaned and prepared for coating or bonding.

NEW DURAKORE AND NEW WOOD

New DuraKore straight from the box needs no surface preparation before use. The same is true of most other wood straight from the mill. Teak, with its high natural oil content, is the major exception. Wipe down teak with acetone to remove the natural oil from the bonding surface. Use a clean white rag and turn the rag often as it picks up oil from the teak wood. Let the acetone "flash off" for about 30 minutes to be sure all traces of solvent have evaporated. Observe fire safety precautions. Using flammable solvents such as acetone around open flames invites a disastrous flash fire.

Solid hardwoods and all non-porous surfaces should be thoroughly sanded with 80-grit aluminum oxide paper to provide a good texture for the epoxy to "key" into. This sanding is often referred to as "giving the surface a tooth." Remove sanding dust before applying any epoxy glue.

Beware of wood that has been thickness planed. An old woodworker's trick is to lubricate the bed of a thickness planer with beeswax or paraffin. Some of this wax rubs off the planer and onto the surface of the wood, where it becomes a chemical contaminant. Epoxy glue does not stick to wax.

EXISTING MATERIALS

On occasion it may be desirable to incorporate recycled materials into a new boat. (The usual motivation is saving money.) The surfaces of these materials are often contaminated with everything from kids' handprints to old engine oil. All contaminants must be removed before application of epoxy glue. DuPont's Prep-Sol 3919S is an excellent silicone and wax remover available from professional paint stores. Acetone and lacquer thinner work well on some contaminants. Beware of fire when using flammable solvents. Also, test the solvent on an inconspicuous spot before wiping it over the entire object to be sure it won't damage the surface. Finally, don't forget the cleaning power of hot soapy water.

No matter which solvent is used for cleaning the surface, it must be allowed to dry thoroughly. Minute traces of solvent (even water) are themselves contaminants that can cause bonding problems. An electric fan can speed up the drying process. Bonding surfaces should be cleaned thoroughly *before* sanding. If contaminants aren't removed before sanding, the grit of the sandpaper forces them deep into the surface, where they become all but impossible to remove. Sand with 80-grit aluminum oxide paper and remove the sanding dust.

REMOVING AMINE BLUSH

Many steps in building a DuraKore strip composite boat require bonding to a hardened epoxy laminate or coating. A typical case is bonding interior bulkheads or furniture to the inside of the hull. Newly cured epoxy often has a thin wax-like film known as *amine blush*. It is a natural result of the curing process that clogs sandpaper and inhibits secondary bonding of additional layers of epoxy.

Fortunately, amine blush is water soluble, so it is easily removed with clean water and an abrasive pad, such as 3-M's Scotch-Brite 7447 General Purpose Hand Pads. Wipe the surface clean with plain white paper towels to remove the dissolved amine blush before it is redeposited by the evaporating water. Once the surface is completely dry, sand with 80-grit aluminum oxide sandpaper.

According to James R. Watson, a technical advisor for Gougeon's West System, an unthickened coat of epoxy used to seal open grain wood like DuraKore soaks deeply enough into the base wood that amine blush is seldom a problem. He advises against washing an unfinished DuraKore hull due to the possibility of water soaking into exposed wood. This could result in unwanted strip movement. On later coats, when the cured epoxy takes on a glassy appearance, Watson strongly advises a washdown with water and a scrubbing pad.

Some coating and bonding procedures, particularly vacuum bagging, involve the use of a release fabric (e.g., Peel Ply) over the wet epoxy film. This fabric remains on the glue as it cures. Pulling the release fabric off the cured epoxy also removes the amine blush, so the clean water wash is not necessary.

Epoxy coatings must be allowed to fully cure if they are to be topcoated with paint or varnish. Wash off the amine blush and sand before topcoating.

PRIMARY VERSUS SECONDARY BONDS

Epoxy glue joints fall into two distinct categories: primary bonds and secondary bonds. A primary bond occurs when wet epoxy is applied to both surfaces to be joined. The surfaces are then clamped together until the glue cures. In a primary bond the glue keys equally into both surfaces and is chemically the same throughout the joint. Primary bonds normally occur when new materials are glued together, such as during planking of the hull.

A secondary bond occurs when something new is attached to an existing structure that has previously been coated with epoxy. In this case, the wet glue must bond to already cured epoxy. Although this type of joint can be extremely strong, it is never as strong as a primary bond.

Always attempt to make primary bonds unless there is no alternative to a secondary bond. If a secondary bond is necessary, the cured epoxy must be properly prepared. Use water to wash off any amine blush. Let the cured epoxy dry before sanding it with 220-grit sand-paper to give a "tooth" into which the new epoxy can bond.

Epoxy surfaces that have not cured to the "hard rubber" stage may be bonded to or coated with epoxy without washing or sanding because the amine blush has not yet formed. To test whether a primary bond is still possible, press a gloved finger into the curing epoxy. Primary bonding is possible if this results in the impression of a fingerprint. If there is no impression, the surface should be allowed to fully cure and then be prepared for a secondary bond.

ONE-STEP BONDING TECHNIQUE

The majority of bonds in a strip composite boat are made using the one-step procedure. Thickened epoxy is simply troweled onto one surface of the joint and the pieces mated together. This is the technique involved in buttering planking battens. To make a good one-step bond, the epoxy glue should be as thin as possible. Thicken it only enough to bridge gaps in the joint or to keep it from sagging out of the joint before it cures. Thinner glue penetrates deeper into the wood fibers to give a stronger bond.

The one-step procedure is simple but is not recommended for highly stressed joints. The reason is that thickened epoxy does not penetrate the wood fibers as well as glue without fillers. The two-step bonding technique is always recommended for highly loaded joints.

TWO-STEP BONDING TECHNIQUE

Two-step bonds are stronger, because unthickened glue is used to saturate both mating surfaces before the joint is made with thickened epoxy. The first step in this procedure is using an unthickened resin/hardener mixture to wet out the wood fibers. Unthickened glue penetrates much deeper into both surfaces than a thick putty.

The second step involves applying thickened glue to one piece and bringing the mating surfaces together. This is exactly the same procedure as a one-step bond. The thickened glue should be just viscous enough to bridge the gaps in the joint and not sag out before it cures. Making two-step bonds is not as difficult as it sounds. Mix up enough resin and hardener for both steps. Apply the straight glue in step one before adding filler to the mixture for step two.

CLAMPING PRESSURE

Epoxy joints do not need the hard clamping pressure required by conventional woodworking adhesives. Apply only enough clamping pressure to cause some thickened glue to squeeze out of the joint. Too much pressure causes a weak, "dry" joint. Several strips of masking tape may give enough pressure when bonding light structures. Rubber bands, spring clamps, and conventional C-clamps also can be used. Use small squares of polyethylene sheeting to keep clamps from bonding to the work. Remove excess glue that squeezes out of the joint while it is still soft.

"With hardwoods like oak, the glue doesn't soak in very far," says Gougeon's Watson. "If you clamp it too hard, you'll squeeze all of the glue out of the joint. Also, clamping pre-stresses the joint. When you remove the clamps, that stress comes out of the wood and the joint can fail."

CONTROLLING CURE TIME

It is not possible to change the cure time of epoxies by altering the ratio of resin to hardener. Alteration of the ratio only reduces the strength of the cured epoxy and not the time it takes to cure. There are only two practical ways to control cure time. One is to change hardeners, and the other is to change the temperature of the mixed glue. Adding heat causes the chemical cross-linking to speed up and the glue cures faster. Conversely, cooling the glue slows down the chemical reaction and gives longer pot life.

CHANGING HARDENERS

Hardeners are manufactured to provide different working times when mixed with epoxy resin. You can also custom blend your own hardener. Mix different hardeners produced by the same manufacturer to achieve a specific cure time. See the technical data sheets packed with the hardeners to determine which is best for a specific purpose.

ADDING HEAT

Speeding up the chemical reaction can be tricky business. It is seldom a good idea to heat the glue in the pot, as this can result in a runaway fast cure. The glue is already warming itself through heat generated by the cross-linking chemical reaction. When a runaway cure starts, the pot first gives off the characteristic "popcorn" smell of cooking epoxy. Then it begins to steam and froth. The pot quickly becomes too hot to hold. Plastic mixing containers distort in the heat and may rupture.

Don't panic when this happens. Everyone has a container or two of epoxy run away, particularly during the hot summer months. Just put the pot on the floor well away from anything flammable and let it cook off. In a few minutes the glue will have turned itself into a solid glob of frothy plastic, which can be safely tossed in the trash.

Rather than heat the pot, it's usually best to heat the epoxy after it has been applied to the joint. Heat lamps or hot air can be directed on a joint to cause the glue to kick faster. A great deal of heat is not required. Raising the temperature of the curing epoxy to 85° or 90°F (29° to 32°C) should be sufficient. Never raise the temperature to more than 120°F (49°C). Heating epoxy causes it to become much thinner. This results in distorted fillets and sagging coatings on vertical surfaces. It may also result in a problem called "outgassing," which will be discussed in Chapter 7.

CHILL OUT

More often than not, the need is to stretch the pot life of mixed epoxy. Planking on a hot August day is an example. Under those conditions, cooling the resin slows down the chemical reaction. A small electric fan may provide enough air circulation to keep the epoxy from kicking too quickly, but old-fashioned ice is about the easiest way to really chill out epoxy. Put the mixing container in a slightly larger pan of ice water, and the chemicals get very lethargic. Cooling causes the glue to become extremely stiff. If it gets too cold, uncured epoxy can't even be spread with a putty knife. Put the mixed epoxy on ice for only a minute or so out of every five minutes to achieve the combination of pot life and working consistency required.

Some workers chill their resin in a refrigerator overnight, especially in the tropics or during the months of deep summer. Cold resin obviously reacts much more slowly with the hardener (which does not have to be chilled). The problem with this method is that cold resin is extremely difficult to move through a mixing pump. Each stroke of the pump may not produce exactly the same amount of resin, so the ratio to the hardener may be inaccurate. Also, pumping extremely thick resin can cause premature failure of the mixing pump.

CLEANUP

Beginners find working with epoxy to be extraordinarily messy. Later, as skill is developed, the process becomes cleaner and less wasteful. As with any job, the smaller the mess, the easier the cleanup. Spilled resin or gobs of dropped putty should be cleaned up immediately, before they have a chance to bond themselves in place. Tools should be cleaned as soon as the glue begins to thicken noticeably. At this stage, epoxy can still be removed with cleaning agents. After it cures, removal from tools is difficult to impossible.

WATERLESS HAND CLEANER

Auto mechanics have long depended on waterless hand cleaner to remove black dirt and grease from their hands. The same gloppy stuff removes uncured epoxy resin from hands, tools, and even clothing. Experience has shown that the GoJo brand works best. Get the largest can available—it is cheap and does not go bad on the shelf.

Disposable brushes can be saved for another day by rubbing GoJo into their bristles. Mush the cleaner into the head of the brush to emulsify as much epoxy as possible. Use a paper towel to wipe out most of the cleaner. Then thoroughly rinse the brush with water. Shake out the bristles and hang the brush to dry overnight. A similar technique works to clean uncured epoxy from rollers, putty knives, and other tools. The final rinse is usually not necessary after wiping steel tools clean with a paper towel.

DON'T CLEAN YOUR BOWL

Don't attempt to wipe uncured epoxy from soft plastic mixing containers with a rag and solvent. Instead, let dirty containers collect so that any residue epoxy kicks to full hardness overnight. The next day, flex the sides and bottoms of the containers to crack the cured epoxy away from the soft bowls. In a few minutes you'll have a full set of absolutely clean mixing containers with no messy cleanup. Wear work gloves and eye protection to crack cured epoxy, as chips fly and sharp edges may cut the skin.

ACETONE AND OTHER SOLVENTS

Acetone, lacquer thinner, and several other industrial solvents can be used to clean up uncured epoxy. The use of these solvents should be discouraged because of their toxic nature and flammability. Many less dangerous cleaners can be substituted. Vinegar works well to wipe up spilled resin, and hot water is effective in cleaning up spilled hardener.

Warning: Do not use solvents directly on your skin. Read directions and precautions on solvent containers before using.

SAFETY TIPS

Epoxies are relatively benign chemicals. The basic resin rarely causes problems. Hardeners are more likely to cause skin irritation, but their toxicity is greatly reduced when they are properly mixed with resin. The following safety recommendations are quoted from the WEST System manual:

1. Avoid all direct skin contact with resin, hardener and mixed epoxy by wearing protective clothing. Wear plastic gloves whenever you handle WEST System [*or other brand*] epoxy materials. Barrier skin creams provide additional protection. Use a waterless skin cleanser to clean uncured epoxy from skin. **Never** use solvents to remove epoxy from your skin. Always wash thoroughly with soap and water immediately after skin contact with resin, hardeners or solvents.

2. Protect your eyes from contact with resin, hardeners, mixed epoxy and solvents by wearing safety glasses or goggles. If contact should occur, immediately flush the eyes with liberal quantities of water under low pressure for 15 minutes. If discomfort persists, seek medical attention immediately.

3. Avoid inhalation of vapors. Use epoxy only in areas with good ventilation. In close quarters, such as boat interiors, be especially careful to exhaust the space and provide a supply of fresh air. Wear a dust mask when you sand epoxy, taking extra care if it has cured for less than a week.

4. Stop using the product if you develop a skin rash while working with epoxy. Resume work after the rash disappears, usually three or four days later. When you go back to

work, improve your safety precautions and prevent any skin contact whatsoever with resin, hardeners and mixed epoxy, as well as their vapors. If problems persist, consult a physician.

5. Do not operate power machinery or climb ladders if you have been working with solvents in a confined area. If you feel tired, nauseated, high or irritable while using solvents, move immediately to fresh air.

6. Clean up spills with a squeegee and paper towels. Scrape up as much material as possible with a squeegee before using paper towels. Sand or clay-type absorbent material may be used to contain or soak up large spills. Clean residue with acetone, lacquer thinner, 855 Cleaning Solution, or waterless hand cleaner. Scraped up resin or hardener that is uncontaminated may be strained for use.

7. Dispose of empty resin and hardener containers safely. Before disposing of resin and hardener containers, puncture corners of can and drain residue into clean containers for re-use. Do not dispose of resin and hardener in a liquid state. Waste resin and hardener should be mixed and reacted to a non-hazardous solid before disposal. Place pots of mixed resin and hardener outside on the ground to avoid danger of excessive heat, fumes and possible fire. Dispose after reaction is complete and mixture has cooled. Follow federal, state, or local disposal regulations.

8. Keep resins, hardeners, fillers and solvents out of the reach of children.

For additional safety information on epoxies, write to SAFETY, Gougeon Brothers, Inc., P.O. Box 908, Bay City, MI 48707 USA.

Some workers develop a sensitivity to epoxy materials, especially the hardeners. Those most susceptible are people with fair skin who sunburn easily or who are particularly vulnerable to poison ivy. Skin contact with epoxy materials is usually on the hands, but this is not where sensitization usually shows up. It most often appears as a mild rash on soft skin around the eyelids or the insides of the arms. At the first sign of sensitization, the worker should stop handling uncured materials and breathing the fumes of curing epoxies. In other words, take a vacation from boatbuilding.

During the layoff period the worker should attempt to build up his immune system. A healthy diet and adequate sleep are strongly recommended. Some workers have reported benefits from taking vitamin supplements. After four to six weeks the rash should have subsided and the person can resume work as long as on-the-job hygiene is improved. "Work neat, like a surgeon," Jim Watson advises.

Hardeners are the primary culprits in sensitization. In some cases, just changing from one formula hardener to another has solved the problem. Workers should always wear protective clothing, and there should be adequate air exchange in the shop. As with any health problem, consulting a doctor in cases of epoxy sensitization is prudent.

WEST SYSTEM

The following is a brief description of West System products of particular interest to strip composite construction boatbuilding. It is not a complete listing of all of the boatbuilding adhesives, fabrics, and thickening agents offered by the Gougeon Brothers. For a full listing, write the company for product literature: Gougeon Brothers, Inc., P.O. Box 908, Bay City, MI 48707 USA; (517) 684-7286.

105 RESIN

The key to the popularity of Gougeon Brothers' epoxy products is that they are part of a complete system based around a nearly crystal-clear epoxy resin. West System 105 Resin was formulated specifically to wet out wood fiber. 105 Resin is not considered flammable and has little odor.

205 FAST HARDENER

This is the most popular hardener in the West System. It is a medium-viscosity curing agent used in the majority of situations to produce a rapid cure that quickly develops its physical properties. The cured resin/hardener mixture yields a rigid, high-strength, moisture-resistant solid with excellent bonding and coating properties. The amber color of 205 Hardener slowly darkens when an open can is stored in the shop, but this color change is harmless.

Pot Life (at 72°F [22°C]) . . . . .9 to 12 minutes
Solid Cure . . . . .6 to 8 hours
Maximum Strength . . . . .1 to 4 days
Minimum Recommended Temperature . . . . . . .40°F (4°C)
Hardener-to-Resin Ratio 1:5

206 SLOW HARDENER

This low-viscosity epoxy curing agent allows extended cure time for extended working time, especially at higher ambient temperatures. When properly mixed with 105 Resin, it produces a rigid, high-strength, moisture-resistant solid with excellent bonding and coating properties. Not recommended for clear coating.

Pot Life (at 72°F [22°C]) . . . . .20 to 25 minutes
Solid Cure . . . . .9 to 12 hours
Maximum Strength . . . . .1 to 4 days
Hardener-to-Resin Ratio 1:5

207 SPECIAL COATING HARDENER

This hardener was specially developed for use with 105 Resin in coating applications where a clear, moisture-resistant natural wood finish is desired. An ultraviolet inhibitor improves the resistance of the cured solid to ultraviolet light, although further protection with a quality ultraviolet-filtered varnish is recommended. 207 Hardener also works well in humid conditions without clouding. It is more difficult to thicken, so is less cost effective for this purpose than 205 or 206 Resin.

Pot Life (at 72°F [22°C]) . . . . .20 to 25 minutes
Solid Cure . . . . .20 to 24 hours
Maximum Strength . . . . .4 to 9 days
Hardener-to-Resin Ratio 1:3

403 MICROFIBERS

This blend of fine fibers is used as a thickener to create a multipurpose adhesive especially for bonding wood. Epoxy thickened with microfibers provides good gap-filling qualities while retaining excellent wetting and penetrating capabilities. Color: off-white.

404 HIGH-DENSITY FILLER

This additive provides maximum physical properties for bonding hardware where high cyclic loads are anticipated. It can also be used for filleting and gap-filling where maximum strength is necessary. Color: off-white.

405 FILLETING BLEND

This wood-toned filler is good for use in glue joints and fillets on natural-finished wood interiors. It creates smooth fillets that require little sanding. Color: consistent brown.

406 COLLOIDAL SILICA

Used most often to control the viscosity of the epoxy, it is the most versatile filler. Colloidal silica can be used in conjunction with other WEST System fillers to control working characteristics. Excellent for preventing epoxy runoff on vertical and overhead surfaces. Improves abrasion resistance. Color: off-white.

407 LOW-DENSITY FILLER

This microballoon-based filler produces an excellent fairing putty that is easily sanded. Reasonably strong on a strength-to-weight ratio. Color: dark red to brown.

410 MICROLIGHT

A specially blended low-density filler for creating an easily worked fairing compound especially suited for fairing large areas. Mixes easier and feathers to a finer edge than other low-density fillers. Not recommended under dark paint or surfaces that will be subject to high temperatures. Color: tan.

GOUGEON LAMINATING SYSTEM

Although produced by the same company as the WEST System, these special materials are quite separate. They use their own resins and hardeners at different ratios from WEST System epoxies. Known as "GL" epoxies, they are not recommended for general bonding applications unless the bonds are required to be post-cured at elevated temperatures. Standard West System epoxy should be used for secondary bonding of GL components after they have been post-cured. Post-curing is the controlled heating of an epoxy laminate to shorten the overall cure time and to improve the strength and thermal properties of the cured epoxy.

GL formulations are designed to give maximum strength along with good moisture resistance. When properly cured, these resins have an outstanding ability to withstand vibration, fatigue, and the harsh marine environment. Their primary use in DuraKore strip composite construction is to laminate reinforcement fabrics to the planked hull. GL resins work well with fiberglass, aramid, carbon fiber, or hybrids by wet lay-up procedures.

GLR-125 RESIN

When used with one of the two matching hardeners, this product ensures fast and thorough wetting of the reinforcing fabric because of its low viscosity and air-displacing properties. Lower viscosity results in a higher fiber-to-epoxy ratio in the cured laminate. This resin is especially good when working with thick fiber weaves or bundles of fibers. It maintains excellent working properties until a rapid gel occurs in five to seven hours at room temperature. A complete cure is reached after two weeks at 72°F (22°C). Elevated post-curing is not necessary for many applications, but will speed the mixture through the cure and increase both mechanical properties and high-temperature performance.

```
Pot Life
    GLH226 Hardener (72°F [22°C]) . . . . . . . . . .37 minutes
    GLH229 Hardener (72°F [22°C]) . . . . . . . . . .77 minutes
Solid Cure . . . . . . . . . . . . . . . . . . . . . . . . . . . . .5 to 7 hours
Maximum Strength . . . . . . . . . . . . . . . . . . . . . .1 to 4 days
Hardener-to-Resin Ratio . . . . . . . . . . . . . . . . . . .100:35
```

GLR-145 RESIN

This medium-viscosity resin is designed for vertical draping applications, where minimum drainoff is required. The viscosity makes wetting out reinforcement fabrics more difficult. GLR-145 is not recommended as a general laminating resin. It should be reserved for those special problem areas where reducing drainoff is more important than ease of lamination.

Pot Life
      GLH226 Hardener (72°F [22°C])..........32 minutes
      GLH229 Hardener (72°F [22°C])..........67 minutes
Solid Cure................................5 to 7 hours
Maximum Strength............................1 to 4 days
Hardener-to-Resin Ratio.........................100:35

SYSTEM THREE RESINS

The other major supplier of epoxy materials to amateur boatbuilders is SYSTEM THREE Resins, Inc. This company's products include special resins for composite cored construction as well as for more traditional wooden boat building. For a full listing of all products offered, see the company's literature: SYSTEM THREE Resins, Inc.; P.O. Box 70436; Seattle, WA 98107; (206) 782-7976.

SYSTEM THREE EPOXY RESIN

This resin is the original offering by this company. It is intended primarily for new wood construction and repair, as well as for fiberglass boat repair. Use at a 2:1 volume ratio with any of the company's three hardeners. Can be used at temperatures as low as 35°F (2°C) with no limitations on humidity. Cures to a tough, resilient, clear film.

PHASE TWO EPOXY RESIN

Use Phase Two epoxy for building balsa-cored boat hulls and high-tech composites. This resin should be used only for the skin laminates and cored structural frames and/or bulkheads. Use SYSTEM THREE Epoxy Resin filled with microballoons and silica thickener for fairing. Phase Two's long pot life makes it ideal for vacuum bagging.

CLEAR COAT EPOXY RESIN

This resin is designed for dry rot repair, clear-coating wood, and wetting out cloth for bright-finished boats. Use as a primer for clear linear polyurethane coatings.

SYSTEM THREE HARDENERS

Three hardeners are offered, each with a different cure time. These hardeners may be custom blended to achieve a specific cure time.

Hardener #1 (Low Temperature) has a 15-minute pot life at 77°F (25°C). Thin films set tack free in about two hours. Uses include coating and glassing at all temperatures and general purpose use below 70°F (21°C).

Hardener #2 (Intermediate Temperature) has a 30-minute pot life at 77°F (25°C). Thin films are tack free in about four hours. This is a general-purpose hardener for use from 60° to 85°F (16° to 29°C).

Hardener #3 (High Temperature) has a pot life of 70 minutes at 77°F (25°C). Thin films are tack free in about nine hours. Works well for gluing jobs where long open assembly times at elevated temperatures are necessary.

F-9 EPOXY FAIRING COMPOUND

This is a premixed fairing compound that avoids the fuss of mixing dusty powders. A 1:1 ratio non-sag epoxy paste dries to a purple-brown color.

Chapter 4
CHOOSING THE RIGHT DESIGN

A WORD OF WARNING

Building a boat carves out large slices of your family life, social life, and work life. Why go through the effort of building your own boat if somebody already has what you want on the market? As you study boat designs, it may become apparent that one particular factory-built boat offers just about everything you want. Buy it and go sailing. There's no point in delaying your fun on the water by building a duplicate of an existing boat.

There's one and only one valid reason for the average person to build a boat: overwhelming desire. In this case, the word "desire" means a burning passion to build a boat. This passion must be so strong that the would-be builder doodles boats during important business meetings. If you have that kind of overwhelming desire, you'll probably get through a small project, say a saucy whitehall rowing dinghy.

But to undertake construction of a larger craft with a cabin and interior accommodations, having a burning passion isn't enough. You need one more factor: lack of choice. No existing boat on the market should answer your needs and desires. If the boat you want already exists, it makes no sense to spend a year or three working with wood strips, epoxy resins, and polyurethane paints. You could better spend the time enjoying the water. The frustration of being stuck in your shop while everyone else is sailing soon overcomes enthusiasm for building your own boat.

The final price of the vessel should not be important in the decision to build a boat. The dollar cost of building your own boat in DuraKore may not be much less than buying a factory-built model. More important than the ultimate cost is your ability to borrow money—your credit. Many people can't qualify for a bank loan on their dream boat even though they have enough spare cash to sustain a boatbuilding project. Building a boat allows you to pay as you go. You may not save much money building your boat, but when it's built... it's paid for.

CHOOSING A DESIGN

The opening paragraphs of this chapter were meant to be discouraging. If you're still enthusiastic, you're a qualified candidate to build a boat. But which boat? Picking the right design should be more a matter of self-analysis than of searching through plan catalogs. Know yourself and you'll automatically choose the right boat: How will you really use this boat? . . . racing? . . . cruising? Will you be keeping it in a shoal harbor or in a deepwater anchorage? If you're going to race, what handicap rule will it be under? If you're going to cruise, will it be coastal or offshore passagemaking? How many people will be in your regular crew?

Begin the search for your "perfect boat" by collecting drawings, advertisements, and literature about every boat you discover that's vaguely related to your dreams. Your goal is to collect ideas for better galley arrangements or improved deck layouts. Everything's fair game. As the old saying about the need to borrow ideas goes, "good people copy, the great steal." Boat designers expect clients to arrive with a box full of clippings showing the ideas they want in their dream boats.

Interior accommodations are a key factor influencing the purchase of factory-built boats. However, don't be overly concerned about the interior layout of the particular design you intend to build. As long as structural members remain in place, the interior furniture can be rearranged to meet your needs. In fact, amateur builders traditionally eschew the original designer's interior plans in favor of a "design as you build" approach. There are obvious dangers to this method, but it does have the significant advantage of putting a personal stamp on the finished yacht. Once again, that box of clippings is a good source of building ideas.

DuraKore strip composite construction lends itself to high-performance racing sailboats. If that's your goal, become an expert on the rating system or class rules under which the boat will sail before choosing a specific boat design. There are lots of really fast designs available, but how do they rate under the IOR, IMHS, JAM, or PHRF rule? A fast boat with a killer rating can be a real frustration when time comes to collect trophies. You may be the first skipper back to the yacht club bar every Wednesday night, but the guys with slug boats, blown-out sails, and sweetheart ratings will collect the trophies.

One-design class rules can be equally troublesome. At this writing there are no classes of one-design sailboats designed around composite strip construction. As a result, most class rules envision a hull built of much denser materials. Getting a DuraKore hull to meet the required weight may be a significant problem, especially if the amount and location of ballast are tightly controlled.

Consider resale even before starting construction. During the planning stages few amateur builders anticipate selling their masterpieces. That sad day comes eventually. Home-built boats admittedly have a narrow market compared to cookie-cutter yachts churned out by boat factories. One way to overcome this is to build to a plan by a name architect. Following that plan *very* carefully increases the value of your boat. Also, a boat that is more "middle of the road" has a wider acceptance than some radical design intended for one specific purpose.

CHOOSING A DESIGNER

Although DuraKore strip composite construction is relatively new, it has attracted the attention of naval architects worldwide. As might be expected, multihull sailboat designers were the first to take advantage of the high strength, extreme light weight, and stiffness of this new method. In addition to the late Ben Lexcen, fellow Australians Tony Grainger and Lock Crowther have also drawn up plans for DuraKore. In the United States, multihull sailboats have been designed by Dick Newick, Ian Farrier, Kurt Hughes, Gino Morrelli, and Hans Geissler.

While the majority of boats built in strip composite construction have been multihull sailboats, there is nothing that limits this technique to one type of boat, power or sail. Any design that benefits from lightweight yet strong construction is a candidate. So far, the largest boat built in DuraKore is a 65-foot monohull sport fisherman built by Ocean Tech Marine in Solomons, Maryland, U.S.A. Designed by Gary VanTassel, president of Ocean Tech, this "war wagon" has three diesel engines and will reach speeds in excess of 50 knots.

Honors for the first powerboat built using DuraKore in North America go to *Varns Infinity* designed by Harry Schoell of Fort Lauderdale, Florida, U.S.A. A futuristic design intended for offshore powerboat racing, it was skinned with knitted biaxial glass vacuum-bagged in epoxy. Designer Schoell says it tops 100 miles an hour with its triple 650-horsepower Merlin diesels.

As with any method, the easiest and best boat to build in strip composite construction is one designed "from the ground up" for it. A small but increasing number of naval architects have stock plans for DuraKore boats. If an original design can't be obtained, the next best choice is a plan modified by the naval architect for strip composite construction. Modification to DuraKore construction is easiest done on hulls originally designed for either conventional strip planking or cold molding. The hardest type of boat to convert is one drawn for traditional wood construction.

"While we have many designs for cold-molded strip plank wood construction, we don't specifically mention DuraKore even though no doubt that product could be substituted in most cases," says California naval architect Ken Hankinson. His company, Ken Hankinson Associates, sells plans for boats ranging from dinghies to world cruisers. None of the plans has been adapted to strip composite construction. According to Hankinson, "We have yet to include specific details for DuraKore, choosing to take a wait-and-see posture."

Converting some designs is possible, but not practical. A boat designed for sheet plywood is an example. The hard chines and flat surfaces of this type of boat do not make the best use of DuraKore's ability to create smooth compound curves. Reuel Parker, who is widely known for his traditional cold-molded boats, describes the comparison he did between DuraKore and plywood for building one of Bruce Kirby's Norwalk Island Sharpies. "After the DuraKore core was glassed, in and out, it weighed every bit as much as my marine plywood hull did," Parker says. His plywood boat was covered with a Xynole-polyester skin.

Much the same is true of steel or ferrocement boat designs intended for amateur construction. A design for either of these materials would not prove a problem on the basis of shape, but the lightness of strip composite construction compared with steel or concrete would seriously change the boat's displacement.

Every boat is an individual. There is no simple conversion factor or table that allows quick translation of design from one medium to another. The process is one of making a series of educated guesses. Even the best boat designer is treading unfamiliar water when he attempts the process. Baltek's Keith Walton suggests this rule of thumb: The thickness of DuraKore should be approximately equal to the plank or skin thickness of the original design.

A boat built of DuraKore strip composite construction is significantly lighter than one built of other materials. Changing a boat design involves more than just adjusting the table of materials. It may be necessary to increase the ballast or to revise the underwater shape to reflect the reduced displacement of the strip composite vessel. These changes are not jobs for the untrained amateur. The work should be done by a professional naval architect who understands the complicated interrelationships of weight, ballast, and hull shape.

Adapting a design for a carvel planked wooden vessel is also fraught with complications. A conventional wooden boat is somewhat analogous to a woven basket. Keel, stem, frames, transom, planks, stringers, and longitudinals all work together to give the boat both shape and strength. A strip composite construction boat relies on its monocoque construction for those qualities. The framing required for carvel construction isn't needed. Converting a conventional design involves eliminating keels and stem pieces without eliminating the strength they provide. This takes knowledge of engineering, so is also best left to a professional.

WORKING WITH THE DESIGNER

Dealing with a naval architect is a lot less intimidating than might be expected. Virtually all of them are in love with boats. They enjoy nothing more than discussing the details of bringing a new boat to life. Good architects realize that your opinions as the customer are as important to the success of the boat as is their design skill. But don't just rush off to your favorite boat designer's office. Instead, seek out someone who has experience working with lightweight composite laminates. Designers tend to choose the materials they know when drafting plans for new boats. A designer who loves wood draws wooden boats. Likewise for steel, conventional fiberglass, or DuraKore.

As with other professionals, the stock in trade of a naval architect is knowledge, which is dispensed for a fee. Your first visit may be gratis, but after that expect to pay an hourly consultation rate to partake of the expert's knowledge. This is only fair. You may be dreaming, but the designer is trying to earn a living. Do your homework before calling on the naval architect. Have a good idea of the kind of boat you intend to build and how you will use it.

A meeting or two is all that should be needed for you and the designer to firm up the basic concept of the project. At this point it's customary for the naval architect to ask for a retainer to cover the early phases of the work. The amount of the retainer is normally a percentage of the anticipated total cost of the design. Once it is paid, the real work of creating the necessary drawings begins. Additional payments are scheduled at specific points in the project until the entire cost of the architect's professional services is paid.

Included in the fees are the rights to build only one boat from the plans supplied. It's normal for the designer to retain ownership of the building rights to the design. This allows selling the same plans to other builders. Constructing a boat to a set of copyright plans without a royalty payment is thievery punishable under federal copyright laws.

Most naval architects want to participate in building the boats they design. In fact, they usually include several consultation hours in their fees for this purpose. They encourage the builder to talk over any problems that arise or changes to be made. Most designers make it a practice to visit the boat a time or two during construction if the building site is anywhere near their offices.

CUSTOM VERSUS STOCK PLANS

Without doubt, purchasing a custom design from a "name" naval architect is one of life's great pleasures. It's also the most expensive method of obtaining plans for your dream boat. Far less expensive is having that same designer modify an existing stock plan to meet your needs. Even less expensive is purchasing unmodified stock plans from the architect. Stock plans are entirely workable, but few designers offer more than a couple of consultation hours as part of their stock plan service. If you want to do alterations, you're pretty much on your own unless you're willing to pay for having the plan customized.

Custom plans represent 10 percent or more of the final cost of an amateur-built boat. A lot of home builders balk at this level of spending. The objection is probably more imaginary than substantial. Money for custom plans is spent before the first step of construction begins. It's psychologically more satisfying to buy a box of DuraKore strips or a couple gallons of epoxy resin than it is to pay for a dozen hours of telephone consultation. Everyone who has built a custom boat will agree, however, that the cost of custom plans is always offset by the value of having the designer as an active member of the building team.

Buying a stock plan and paying for minor modifications is the most cost-effective approach. In fact, if only minor modifications are needed, the final cost can be little more than a stock plan. The usual price of a modified plan is less than five percent of the total cost of building the boat. Another benefit of this approach is speed. It takes the designer a lot less time to modify an existing plan from his file than it does to create a completely new boat.

Stock plans are available both from conventional naval architects and from companies that specialize in selling boat designs to the public. Of the two, it's always better to deal with a real live designer than with a stock plan house. That said, if the stock plan company has the boat you want, buy it. Stock house plans sometimes come with extensive instructions for lofting and building the hull. Other times they are little more than a set of lines drawings and a bill of

The majority of multihull floats are not symmetrical. An asymmetrical float allows the designer to achieve better performance. Since the halves of an asymmetrical hull are not mirror images, both must be fully lofted before construction can begin.

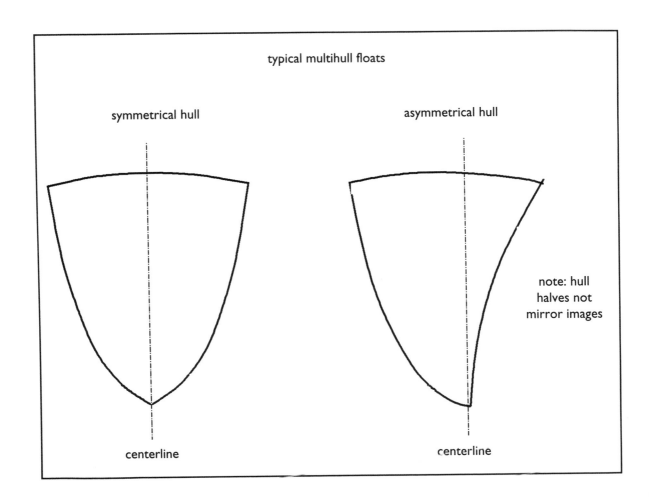

typical multihull floats

symmetrical hull

asymmetrical hull

note: hull halves not mirror images

centerline

centerline

materials. The cost for stock plans usually runs less than two percent of the cost of the completed boat.

DECIPHERING THE PLANS

Step one in boatbuilding is learning to read the drawings supplied by your naval architect. The key blueprint is known as the *lines drawing*. To the uninitiated, this sheet appears to be a jumble of information because it presents the hull in three views: plan, profile, and section (or half-breadth). To complicate matters, it's common for the profile

---

A WORD ABOUT "FAIR"

Naval architects and boatbuilders use the word "fair" to describe several related but separate concepts. Although this word is one of the most-used terms in boatbuilding, it has no firm definition.

The broadest use of the term refers to overall shapes such as hull sides or sheerlines. In this use, "fair" means that the shape or curve is both smooth and pleasing to the eye. A smooth curve is obviously one with no sharp breaks or changes in direction. Which lines are "eye sweet" and which are not is a discussion that has spawned legendary arguments. Beauty is in the eye of the beholder, so there is no way to concretely define "fair" in this sense of the word.

The second definition involves the boat designer huddled over a drafting table. "Fair" to the naval architect means that all of the lines in the three views of the lines drawing cross at the same point. In other words, if a buttocks crosses a waterline at 3-6-2 (3 feet, 6¼ inches) on the section view, it makes the same crossing on the plan view. The worker on the loft floor uses exactly the same definition of "fair."

While we now seem to have a concrete definition, the people writing boat design software for computers have discovered there is no mathematical definition of "fair." Mathematically correct solutions can occur with crossing points skewed slightly. For this reason, if two people or two computers loft two boats from the same set of blueprints, the resulting hulls are not always identical. Once again, a precise definition of "fair" eludes us.

Finally, the third concept of "fair" applies to the actual three-dimensional hull. Here again, the word refers to the larger aspect of the curves of the hull and the sheerline. "Fairing" is the process of reducing the inevitable roughness of the raw hull to the smooth, flowing shape of the completed boat. While a number of methods are used to achieve "fairness," there is no exact definition.

Don't confuse "fairness" in a completed hull with "smoothness." A highly unfair hull could be polished so smooth that it will reflect your face. In fact, a fun house mirror is a good example of a smooth but unfair surface. On the other hand, the surface of a very fair hull still could be quite rough.

and section drawings to be superimposed. This superimposition seems confusing, but there is a purpose. It allows you to determine where various lines are tangent to each other in the two views. This becomes important in lofting.

The plan view is often presented as a separate drawing. Only half of the hull is shown, mostly to save paper. There's no need to reproduce the lines for both sides of a conventional monohull boat because they are mirror images. The section view normally shows the bow view on the right and the stern view on the left.

Special note for multihull builders: It is often necessary to draw and loft both sides of multihull floats that may not be symmetrical. The center hull is almost always symmetrical, so may be drawn conventionally.

A lines drawing is far more complicated than a simple 3-view mechanical drawing you might have done in high school drafting class. A boat is an object with a continuously varying shape, so it

The plan view is a fish's perspective. Horizontal slices, known as waterlines, are parallel to the actual waterline when the hull is floating. On this drawing they are graceful, sweeping curves. (Courtesy Jay R. Benford)

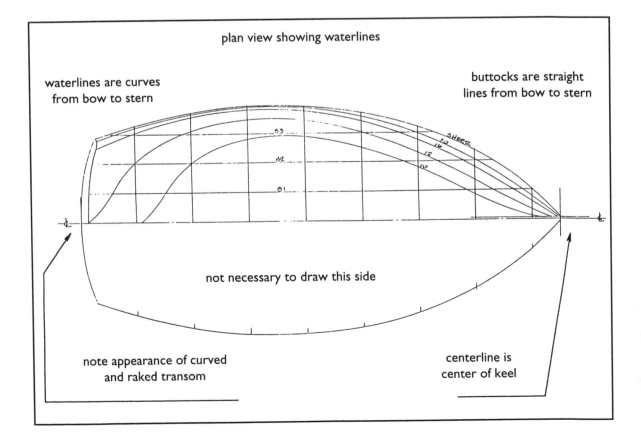

plan view showing waterlines

waterlines are curves
from bow to stern

buttocks are straight
lines from bow to stern

not necessary to draw this side

note appearance of curved
and raked transom

centerline is
center of keel

does no good to draw just the outline of one plane on the boat. For instance, the shape of the deck at the sheerline may have little relationship to the boat's shape at the waterline. Likewise, the profile of the hull along the centerline is quite different from the profile inboard from the gunwale.

A lines drawing shows only the outside shape of the hull. It does not include any of the interior, which is shown on the *accommodations plan*. Nor does it indicate the scantlings of the hull or any details of the mechanical equipment.

WATERLINES

The lines drawing effectively cuts the boat into "slices." Horizontal slices are known as "waterlines" because they lie parallel to the boat's actual waterline. In fact, one of the waterlines normally is the designed waterline of the boat. Waterlines are drawn equidistant at specific heights from the baseline.

The section view shows the stern on the left and the bow on the right side of the centerline. Waterlines have become flat horizontal lines, while the stations are now curves representing the outside shape of the hull. (Courtesy Jay R. Benford)

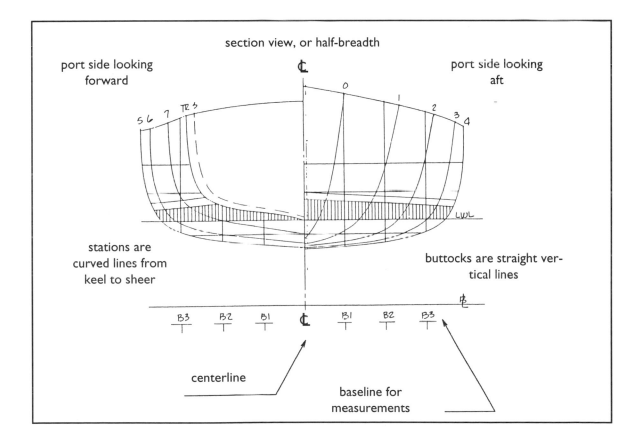

SECTIONS

Slices across the hull at right angles to the keel are known as "sections." Most drawings show the forward (bow) end of the boat to the right of the centerline and the aft (stern) end on the left side. Sections appear as straight vertical lines on the profile drawing. On the section drawing they display the transverse (across the keel) shape of the boat.

BUTTOCKS

The lines that give beginners the most problems are the vertical slices made in a fore-and-aft direction parallel to the keel, known as "buttocks," or "buttocks lines." They show on the plan view as straight lines equidistant from the keel. Buttocks are curved lines on the profile drawing. One way to understand them is to think of buttocks as vertical slices of boat stacked one upon another from the centerline outward toward the viewer.

THE LINES DRAWING

In the profile view the waterlines and stations are straight lines but the buttocks are curves. (Courtesy Jay R. Benford)

Since all three views are drawn on one sheet of paper, it's proper to use the plural "lines" when describing this drawing. The concept of "slicing" the boat with sections, buttocks, and waterlines is no acci-

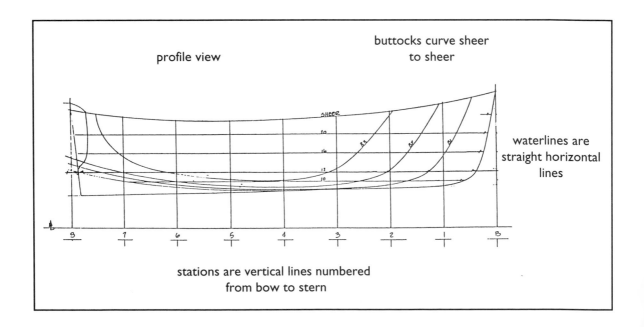

dent. That's exactly what builders did two hundred years ago before paper drawings were common. They would carve out a model of the hull, then mark the stations on it. This model would then be cut (sliced) into what were called "lifts." Since the port and starboard halves of the boat are mirror images, time was saved by carving only half of the hull. This was the origin of those half models that now decorate yacht club bars and other gathering places of sailors.

The first line drawn by a naval architect is always the horizontal baseline along the bottom of the paper. The waterlines are drawn horizontally parallel to this line. Next, vertical lines known as "stations" are erected at right angles to the baseline. The distance forward to the bow and aft to the stern is divided into an equal number of "stations." They are given numbers starting from "0" in the bow and going up toward the stern. Most designers use 10 to 12 stations for a yacht.

Station lines usually double as the location of the transverse sections discussed earlier. However, there is no law requiring that the sections be placed on the stations. If the sections are not on the stations, it is customary to letter the sections separately from the numbered stations, starting with "A" in the bow. Knowing the difference between "sections" and "stations" becomes critical in placing the mold frames on the building jig.

TABLE OF OFFSETS

The lines drawing is always accompanied by a grid of numbers known as the "table of offsets." These numbers, called "offsets," are measurements that describe the hull shape. All U.S. and many British and Australian naval architects use feet and inches. Three numbers are used for each measurement. The first indicates feet, the second inches, and the third eighths. These numbers are separated by dashes. Reading a measurement is simple:

$$2 - 3 - 5$$

translates into "two feet, three and five-eighths inches." A plus (+) or minus (-) sign following the last number indicates that $\frac{1}{16}$ inch should be added or subtracted from the dimension. Drawings from European designers are normally in meters expressed to three decimal places.

Two types of offsets are presented. They are normally labeled as "Height Above Baseline" and "Half-Breadths." As might be expected,

	STATIONS	0	1	2	3	4	
height above baseline	Top of deck	6-1-3	5-10-3	5-7-4	5-5-3	5-3-3	**height above baseline**
	Butt 3	—	—	5-7-4	2-10-1	1-10-1	
	Butt 2	—	4-5-6	4-10-1	4-9-1	1-1-0	
	Butt 1	4-9-7	2-11-0	1-0-4	0-5-3	0-5-0	
half-breadth from CL	Top of deck	1-4-6	2-7-1	5-5-7+	4-1-2	4-8-2	**half-breadth from CL**
	WL2	0-3-2	2-2-1	3-2-6	4-0-1	4-8-0	
	WL1	—	1-5-7	2-9-7+	3-10-4	4-5-7	
	LWL	—	0-7-3	1-1-0	2-1-1	3-4-0	

This hypothetical table of offsets illustrates the general layout. Dimensions are given in feet, inches, and eighths. A plus sign (+) indicates that $1/16$ inch should be added to the dimension shown. Dashes indicate the lines do not cross at that point. For instance, buttock lines 2 and 3 do not cross station 0.

a height above baseline is measured on the profile or plan view vertically at right angles to the baseline. The half-breadths are measured on the sections at right angles to the centerline. These two measurements become a system of coordinates allowing naval architects to specify any point on the surface of the hull.

DIAGONALS

An additional set of slanting lines appears on the section view of most large boat plans. These are known as "diagonals." Naval architects use diagonals to increase the number of measuring points on the hull. Additional points allow a closer check on the fairness of the lines, both on the drawing and in the full-size lofting. Diagonals do not represent structural elements in the completed vessel. They are only a convenience for the designer and builder to make fairing the hull easier during the lofting process.

Diagonals are always drawn on the section view at as close to right angles to the outer skin of the hull as possible. At their inner end, they land on the centerline of the view at an angle the designer supplies. This information is used to plot diagonals in the full-size lofting. While large hulls always have diagonals, simple hulls may not require them.

STANDARD ABBREVIATIONS

Boat designers use a system of abbreviations to identify various items on the lines drawing. The most common are:

B.L.	Baseline
C.B.	Center of Buoyancy
C.L.	Centerline
C.G.	Center of Gravity
Diag.	Diagonal
L.O.A.	Length Overall
L.W.L.	Load Waterline
Sect.	Section
Sta.	Station
W.L.	Waterline

Knowing how to read the lines drawings is necessary before the next step, lofting, can be undertaken. High-tech designers today produce their final drawings on a computer. Their boats go straight into production without being printed as a standard blueprint on paper. This skips the time-consuming and expensive step of traditional lofting. It's becoming increasingly possible for amateur builders to do the same. However, even if you plan to use computerized lofting, a knowledge of old-fashioned lofting is still necessary.

OLD-FASHIONED MANUAL LOFTING

The best naval drafter cannot draw a perfect set of lines using paper and pencil. A small variation in the width of a pencil line not visible in the drawing may translate into a noticeable unfairness on the full-size hull. Builders have always recognized that they cannot construct a boat directly from the architect's small-scale plans. So their first task on a new boat is to make a full-size version of the lines drawing. This process is known as "lofting" because it was normally done on the floor of a loft above the building shed.

In the good ol' days the loftsman would start by painting the floor with flat white paint. The floor then became a large sheet of "drawing paper" on which all the lofting would be done. Working from the table of offsets, he would laboriously recreate the lines drawing full size. As he worked, the loftsman would discover the inevitable small errors in the table of offsets. Using lofting battens, he would fair the lines and correct the table as he went. Once the full-size plan was completed, he would transfer the shapes to patterns for constructing the building mold.

The corrected table of offsets would be sent back to the naval architect for inclusion in later editions of the plans. This step made it easier for another builder to build the same boat sometime in the future. Unfortunately, it's not always possible to determine by studying a set of plans whether or not the table of offsets has been corrected through lofting. A call to the original designer may settle the issue, but only if that person is still alive or the company is still in business. Assume the table of offsets is uncorrected unless proved otherwise.

Lofting a boat intended for assembly line production can be an arduous procedure. However, the amateur does not need to go into the detail required by professional builders. In fact, the home builder working with DuraKore need only loft the hull sections, the stem shape, the sheerline, and the transom full size. These shapes are then traced onto plywood or particle board and cut out. Fairing previously done on the loft floor is now being done in three dimensions on the building mold using battens.

Books have been written about lofting. This is not one of them. Perhaps the most entertaining discussion of the process is found in *Buehler's Backyard Boatbuilding* by George Buehler. Another author, Robert M. Steward, gives a more in-depth study of the process in his *Boatbuilding Manual*, 4th Edition (International Marine, 1994).

PREPARING YOUR "LOFT"

To loft a boat the old-fashioned way, start by preparing a space at least 10 feet longer than the overall length of the boat. (Allow extra room if the transom must be expanded.) The lofting space should also be at least 10 feet wider than the height of the hull from the bottom of the keel to the top of the sheerline. Lofting can be done directly on a wood floor; however, it's much preferable to join sheets of ¼-inch plywood as the lofting surface. (Concrete floors require preparing a plywood lofting surface.) The surface should receive two coats of semi-gloss white paint. It is very difficult to erase pencil lines from the flat white paint often suggested for lofting. Gloss white erases easily, but does not take ballpoint pen ink, which will smudge as you crawl around on the drawing.

Some builders (notably Buehler in his *Backyard Boatbuilding*) recommend lofting on heavy paper. This does not eliminate the need for building a lofting floor out of plywood. It does, however, allow the final lofted drawing to be picked up and tacked to a shop wall for future reference. This is necessary if your mold loft is the same floor where the boat will be built.

LOFTING TOOLS

Some tools used in lofting must be purchased, but others are best manufactured on the spot. Here's the typical list:

➤ Pencils and Pens—Professionals do their final lines in ballpoint pen after first working in erasable pencil. Different colored inks are used to denote the sections from the buttocks or waterlines.

➤ Large T-square—A carpenter's L-shaped framing square is big enough for dinghies and small craft. For larger boats, construct a large T-square out of ¼-inch plywood or straight, clear 1 × 3 pine. The vertical arm should extend beyond the boat's sheerline. The horizontal arm should be about one-third the length of the vertical arm. Use the straight mill edge of the wood for drawing lines.

➤ Measuring Tape or Folding Rule—Because they are longer, tapes are usually easier to use. The tape should be longer than the overall length of the boat.

➤ Lofting Battens—Battens used for lofting are long, thin pieces of wood (or plastic), which are bent as guides for drawing smooth curves. The thickness of the lofting batten determines its flexibility, and it is customary to have several of different thicknesses. Lofting battens can be ripped from a 1 × 4-inch by 12-foot length of *clear* white pine.

➤ Hammer and Nails—Small finishing nails are driven into the plywood to provide points around which the lofting battens are sprung.

> ➤ "Ducks"—Also called "lofting weights," these are used for the same purpose as the hammer and nails. Commercial ducks are shaped like mini-whales with brass pins to hold the battens. Make low-tech ducks out of bricks wrapped in burlap.

A large bar compass, an adjustable T-bevel, and "pickup sticks" also come in handy. All of these items can be purchased, but it's a lot cheaper to spend an afternoon making them. Descriptions of do-it-yourself tools are given in *The Gougeon Brothers on Boat Construction*, 4th edition (Gougeon Bothers, Inc., 1985).

DRAWING THE GRIDS

Lofting starts by laying down the baseline and erecting the vertical station lines, just as the architect did on the scale drawing. The large T-square can be used; however, it's more accurate to erect the station lines geometrically using a compass. Once the stations are erected, the horizontal waterlines are drawn parallel to the baseline. At this point it pays to measure all dimensions and every angle to make sure that the stations really are square and the waterlines are absolutely parallel to the baseline. Errors in lofting are cumulative, so avoid making any this early in the game. Once everything is perfect, ink all these lines.

Now it gets confusing. It's easiest to fair the lines if all three views—plan, profile, and section—are superimposed, on top of each other. So the next step is drawing in the buttocks lines for the plan view, using the baseline as a reference. Remember, buttocks lines are straight and parallel to the baseline in the plan view. Use a second color ink to avoid confusion. All lines should be given a written label in addition to their color code. If a buttocks line and a waterline happen to coincide, draw a single line but label it as both.

At this point there are two sets of straight lines drawn on the lofting board in different color inks. One is for the plan view, the other for the profile. A third set, for the section plan, must now be added. It is drawn right amidships on top of the two existing grids. Naturally, a third color ink is called for and more labels are necessary.

A section plan is actually two views of the boat, sharing the same vertical centerline. Typically, the righthand side shows the bow and the left shows the stern. Again, the symmetrical nature of boats allows this because both the port and starboard sides should be identical. In this drawing, the buttocks are vertical lines at the same distance apart as they are on the plan view. It is not necessary to draw waterlines, as they are the same lines you drew for the profile view.

Once the straight line grids have been inked in various colors, the lofting is ready for drawing the curved shapes of the boat.

CURVED LINES

Curved lines, such as the sheer or the stem, are created by using measurements from the table of offsets. These points are marked on the appropriate station lines, waterlines, or buttocks. Small finishing nails are driven into the plywood at these points and a lofting batten is sprung around the nails. Alternatively, ducks (special weights) can be used to hold the lofting batten at the control points. Using ducks avoids creating pesky nail holes in the plywood but creates the possibility of unexpected batten movement.

Unfairness is adjusted out by moving the reference points slightly. (Remember, the table of offsets was prepared from a small drawing, so expect it to be in error.) Once the line is fair, it is drawn on the lofting surface.

Here's the rub. Changing an offset on one view affects that same point on all three views: plan, profile, and body plan. The process of bringing all three views into agreement is known as "fairing" the drawing. This takes time and patience. Dick Minier, the head loftsman for Matthews Boats in its heyday, recalls spending a full eight-hour day getting just one point to come into agreement. Of course, he was lofting a 56-foot boat that had never before been built. The table of offsets on most stock plans will have been corrected enough to avoid the agony he experienced.

"Sometimes I would spend all day trying to get something to fit," Dick has said. "The problem would go home with me at night and I'd wake up at two in the morning with the solution." Eventually, he began keeping a "little black book" of solutions to common problems.

Most people loft the profile view first, then the plan view, and finally the body plan. There is no magic to the sequence. Some prefer to work on all three views simultaneously, fairing a single point on all three views before going on to the next. One thing is certain, no line should be inked until it is completely fair on all three views.

SKIN THICKNESS SUBTRACTION

Naval architects always draw hulls to the *outside* of the skin. This is no problem if you plan to use a female form, since you will be building inward from the outside. Difficulty arises on a male form, which requires building outward from the section molds to the skin. Section molds for a male form must be reduced by the thickness of the skin, or the finished boat will not have the designed shape, especially in the bow. "Skin thickness" in discussions of lofting refers to the full thickness of the DuraKore planking plus the inner and outer reinforcement laminates.

Right amidships there is no problem subtracting the thickness of the skin from the mold. Just draw a new line inside the original outside shape. This new line is exactly parallel to the outside shape line and separated from it by the exact thickness of the skin. Easy.

The process isn't nearly as simple in the bow where the boat rapidly changes shape. Here, skin thickness cannot be measured perpendicular to the station mold. Rather, it must be measured at right angles to the outside skin of the boat. Because of the angle at which the skin crosses the section mold, the effective skin thickness is considerably more than the actual measured thickness of the materials. Mold stations forward must be reduced more than molds amidships.

The process of reducing the station molds is more complicated to discuss than it is to accomplish. The process starts on the waterlines. Use a pair of dividers or a compass to tick off the actual thickness of the skin on each section line where it crosses a waterline. This tick mark should be *parallel* to the waterline so that the section line crosses both it and the waterline at the same angle.

Next, set your dividers to measure the distance between the tick mark and the waterline *along* the station line. Amidships this new setting should be very close to the actual thickness of the skin. Close to the bow (and stern of a sailboat), the distance along the station line should be noticeably greater than the true skin thickness. Subtract this new distance from the outside of the section by making a tick mark on the appropriate waterline where it crosses the station line. Note that the amount of reduction changes from sheerline to garboard, so a specific deduction must be made at each waterline.

Join the reduction ticks with a fairing batten to create the shape of the reduced station.

Is it really necessary to account for skin thickness? Every first-time boatbuilder has asked the question. The answer is, maybe. Boats have been built—and quite successfully—without adjusting for skin thickness. As one naval architect says, "If you don't reduce for skin thickness, you'll get a boat all right. But it won't be the boat the designer intended. That may be OK for a rough workboat, but it could be disastrous on a racing sailboat designed to a specific rating rule."

EXPANDING THE TRANSOM

Unless the transom is absolutely perpendicular to the waterline, its true shape will not appear on the lines drawing. The outline of a raked transom is foreshortened whether the transom slopes outward, as on a traditional powerboat, or inward, as on a reverse transom sailboat. Expanding the transom is one of the final steps in lofting a hull. It is always done *after* the plan, profile, and section views have been drawn and faired. As with other sections, only half of the transom is expanded, the other half being a mirror image.

FLAT TRANSOM

Tradition places the stern at the left side of the lofted boat. Start by establishing a new centerline specifically for the transom just to the left of the lofted hull. Draw this line *parallel* to the transom shown on the profile and not at right angles to the original baseline.

Pick up the distances between waterlines from where they cross the profile transom and transfer them to the new expanded transom centerline. Note that these distances on the sloping transom are greater than the distances between the waterlines on the profile grid. Transferring measurements can be done with either a large pair of dividers or a batten marked with appropriate pencil lines. In a similar manner, transfer the location of the top and bottom of the expanded transom.

Waterlines for the expanded transom are then drawn at right angles to the new centerline at the required locations. Erect these using a large T-square, or do it geometrically with a compass. Buttocks lines can then be drawn parallel to the new centerline at their appropriate distances apart. The grid for the expanded transom is now complete and can be inked.

Creating the curved line representing the outer edge requires picking up points from the profile drawing and transferring them to the new grid. Marking a stick of scrap lumber (called a "pickup stick") is the easiest way. Lay the stick on the profile transom and mark where each buttock lands. Move the stick to the centerline of the expanded transom and tick off the appropriate locations. Draw a line from each point outward at right angles to the expanded centerline. The points where these lines cross the buttocks establish the outer edge of the expanded transom. Use pencil and label everything to avoid confusion.

Next, on the profile drawing measure upward from the baseline to where each waterline crosses the angled transom. Move to the expanded transom and transfer these measurements to the new waterlines. Once again, your tick marks on the expanded waterlines represent the outer edge of the transom. Join all of the points marking the shape of the expanded transom with a lofting batten and draw the curved line. Check everything twice, then ink it.

CURVED TRANSOM

A sloped, curved transom is a delight to see but confusing to loft. It involves steps similar to those described above, with the additional complication of "unrolling" the curved shape of the transom. Examination shows that nearly all curved transoms are a small portion of the circumference of a cylinder and that the buttocks are straight line elements of that cylinder. Lofting involves "unrolling" the cylinder and drawing the correct expanded shape.

Before sharpening a pencil, consult the plan set for the radius of the transom. If this information is not given, contact the designer. Someone skilled in lofting can recreate the radius, but the task is nobody's favorite way of spending a Sunday afternoon.

A flat transom requires only one auxiliary drawing, but a curved transom requires two additional loftings. One is an accurate plan view of the stern, and the other is the expanded shape of the transom. The special plan view provides the dimensions required to make the expanded drawing. Allow space for these additional drawings when laying out the lofting surface. They must be drawn adjacent to the stern of the existing views. The expanded stern is drawn to the left of the profile, while the auxiliary plan view is placed above the profile.

The centerline of the new plan view is drawn at right angles to the face of the transom at the centerline of the profile view. With a conventional raked transom, the new centerline will go up and away from the profile sheerline. However, a reverse rake causes the new centerline to plunge downward into the profile view. A bit of position juggling may be necessary to keep one set of lines clear of the other. Buttocks lines are added to the auxiliary plan view parallel to its centerline and at the same distance apart as on the lines drawing. The last three or four section lines are erected at the appropriate locations. These sections are used to draw the auxiliary plan view of the stern, especially the sheerline.

Locate the center of the transom radius on the auxiliary plan view centerline. Drive a small nail into the loft floor at that point and tie a string to it. Measure an exact length of string equal to the transom radius and tie a pencil to the string. Keeping the string taught (but not stretched), swing the arc of the transom on the auxiliary plan view.

Until now, buttocks have always been at the same equal distance apart as shown on the lines drawings. In developing the lofting of the expanded transom, this distance increases to accommodate the "flattening" of the cylindrical surface. Expanded distances between buttocks must be found on the auxiliary plan view *along the surface of the arc of the transom.*

The grid for the expanded transom is started by drawing its centerline parallel to the centerline of the face of the transom in the profile drawing as was done for a flat transom. Use the new buttocks distances (found above) to draw buttocks lines for the expanded transom grid. To find them, spring a lofting batten along the arc of the transom in the auxiliary plan view. Mark the spots on the batten where each buttock touches the batten. Similarly mark the edge of the deck.

Allow the lofting batten to spring back straight. Move it to the expanded transom grid. Use the markings on the batten to establish the distances between buttocks lines on the expanded grid. Draw and ink the buttocks parallel to the centerline of the expanded transom grid.

Use a large T-square to hold a straight lofting batten square to the centerline of the expanded transom. This batten crosses the profile view at one end and extends beyond the expanded transom at the other. Move the batten until it touches the locations on the profile view where the buttocks cross the outside edge of the transom. Draw a pencil line from these locations to where the lines cross, matching buttocks on the expanded transom. The outline of the expanded transom's shape is established by the locations where the batten crosses the expanded buttocks. Spring a lofting batten through these points to draw a fair line.

The upper edge of the transom where it meets the deck is also curved to accommodate deck camber. Some architects specify camber in terms of the radius of a circle. Others give it as a percentage of the beam at the particular section. A few designers actually draw the crown of the deck above and roughly parallel to the sheerline on the lines drawing. Use a batten to spring a smooth curve, then draw the upper edge of the transom.

PICKING UP THE LINES

The final step in lofting is transferring the section shapes to patterns so the actual molds can be fabricated. This is known as "picking up the lines." The time-honored method is to use small tacks laid on their sides so that their heads lie along the line to be transferred and the points shoot away from the line. Push the edge of each head into the plywood slightly so the tack stays in place. Then lay a piece of heavy paper over the tacks and rub it down softly with a block of wood. The tack heads indent themselves into the paper. These indentations are linked with a line drawn along a lofting batten to create the final pattern.

This tack trick also works to transfer shapes directly to the particle board, which becomes the section mold. Simply press the tack heads into the board instead of the paper. Use a lofting batten to join the tack marks in a smooth line.

HIGH-TECH LOFTING

Electronic microchips have almost eliminated the onerous job of manual lofting in professional boatshops. A computer armed with the proper program can perform the fairing formerly done on the loft floor. More important, a computer-generated lines drawing can be printed full-size on Mylar drafting film. Since Mylar is dimensionally stable, it's ideal for full-size patterns from which the mold forms can be cut. This type of computer lofting allows professionals to cut weeks off the construction time of a new vessel.

Computer lofting is just beginning to appear in the world of amateur boatbuilding. Several designers now sell sets of full-size Mylar patterns for their boats, created from computerized lofting. The patterns allow going straight to constructing a building form, escaping the tedious work of old-fashioned lofting. A few home boatbuilders are doing their own electronic lofting. While the process has pitfalls, a computer-literate amateur can produce Mylar patterns for any boat using an ordinary personal computer.

Computer programs capable of lofting a boat hull are more complex than traditional CAD (computer-aided design) software. Boat programs must define the hull as a series of interconnected three-dimensional curved surfaces. Suitable software is available for both MS-DOS (IBM and clones) and Apple/Macintosh computers. The cost ranges from well under a thousand dollars to tens of thousands. Naturally, the more costly programs have more options, but even entry-level software will produce faired lines drawings.

The easiest way to obtain a lofting on a computer disk is to ask the designer of your boat for one. Don't expect to get it. There should be no objection to supplying the boat's lines on a disk since you already have them on paper. However, your architect will worry about unauthorized duplication of the lines. Anyone with a copy of the disk could build the boat without paying the required design royalties.

Expect your request for a computer disk to be answered by an offer from the architect to print the lines full size. Don't be upset by this offer. In fact, you might hint that you would rather have Mylar loftings than a disk. That way, the architect goes through the problems of having his work translated to a plotting machine. You have one less problem to solve.

INPUTTING OFFSETS

Difficulties arise if the lines drawing exists only on paper and not as a computer file. (This is the case with a dwindling number of paper-and-pencil naval architects or when a design by a long-deceased architect is being reused.) The table of offsets must be input to the computer and a lines drawing generated before full-size patterns can be printed. Some boat design shops are willing to translate drawings from paper to computer. This avoids the cost of buying a program and learning how to use it. The charge for this service usually runs between $50 and $100 an hour. For a small boat, it may take only one working day to input the offsets into the computer and fair the lines drawings. A more complicated vessel may require several days to a week of computer work.

You can expect the shop to require proof that you own the rights to build a boat from the plans, or that the plans are in the public domain. They don't want to get involved in the theft of another architect's design, which is a federal offense.

BUY YOUR OWN PROGRAM

Purchasing a simple yacht design program costs about double what a design shop will charge to do the work. However, owning the program allows you total control of the lofting procedure, a real advantage if alterations are anticipated. Many programs come broken down into "modules." The basic module is usually sufficient for creating and printing a lines drawings. Some programs may require a second module for proper fairing of lines from a table of offsets.

The basic process of computer lofting involves entering data from the table of offsets. Methods vary depending upon the program, but most take numeric information straight from the table. "Once the data from the table of offsets is typed into the computer, the next step is plotting the sections," says Steve Hollister of New Wave Systems. "It will probably be necessary to adjust the sections slightly, but you have to be careful. In the process you can end up with a fair boat, but not the boat the designer intended."

After the sections are fair, the surface of the hull is fitted to them. In essence, the computer does the work of drawing the waterlines and the buttocks. At this point, the hull will be fair at the intersections of all sections, buttocks, and waterlines, but unfairness may exist between sections. This unfairness must be taken out before the lines are ready for plotting.

An advantage of computerized lofting is being able to "see" the hull in 3-D. The computer electronically combines all three views of the hull into one isometric projection. The hull floats in space somewhere inside the computer screen. By giving the proper commands you can rotate the boat to see either side or just the bow or stern.

You can electronically crawl underneath to get a fish's eye view. Switching into this 3-D view from time to time erases some of the tedium of fairing the hull.

Learning a CAD program is an intimidating task even to computer-literate people. A variety of keystroke commands must be committed to memory before any serious work can be done. The "learning curve" is reported to be up to two years in length with a lot of mistakes being made along the way. You get to be good at computerized lofting the same way a pianist gets to Carnegie Hall: practice, practice, practice.

SKIN THICKNESS SUBTRACTION

Adjusting for skin thickness the old-fashioned way on a full-size lofting takes hours. These days the same work can be done in seconds by a few keystroke instructions to the computer. Good programs are written with the capability of deducting skin thickness for you. No calculations or measurements are required. All you have to do is give the computer the measured skin thickness and it does the work. The ability of the computer to reduce for skin thickness makes it possible to print full-size patterns for internal bulkheads and furniture. These patterns are lofted fair by the computer, so pieces made from them should fit perfectly into the boat.

COMPUTER HARDWARE REQUIREMENTS

Lofting takes megabytes of computing power. Most programs require advanced computers with math coprocessors. High-definition monitors with the latest graphics cards are also required. In the IBM clone world, the computer should have at least an 80386 chip, although an 80486 is preferred. Both chips need their companion math coprocessors. Two megs of random access memory (RAM) is about minimum. The SVGA graphics adapter card should have a high resolution driver option (compatible with AutoCAD). The monitor should be capable of accepting the VGA and SVGA output. A mouse is necessary, while a digitizing tablet and perhaps a scanner are useful peripherals.

It's best not to purchase hardware until a specific boat CAD program has been chosen. Purchase your computer and peripherals based on the recommendations of the software supplier.

PRINTING FULL-SIZE PATTERNS

Computer lofting is still in its infancy. Although standard file formats are supposed to allow easy exchange of data, it doesn't always work out that way. Bugs creep in. For instance, one popular marine design program records its files on the basis of 1 inch on the drawing equals 1 inch in reality (a 1:1 ratio). AutoCAD imports files on the basis of 1 inch on the drawing equals 1 foot in real life (1:12 ratio). This discrepancy is easily corrected, but it can create some unexpected results for the unwary.

Even the people who write these programs admit they have problems transferring data from one computer to another. "You still have to be a bit of a hacker," one programmer admits. Glitches arise most often when a generic CAD program tries to reproduce the drawing created by a boat design program. Curved lines can become bumpy or flatten entirely. If this happens, call the company that produced the boat design software for help.

The typical office printer or desktop plotter isn't capable of printing out full-size boat patterns. For that job you need an industrial plotting machine costing big bucks. These machines are so costly that many engineering firms and naval architects can't afford to make the investment. Instead, they "print" the drawing to a disk, which is then sent to a blueprint service bureau that owns a plotter. For a small fee the service bureau puts the lines on either vellum paper or Mylar.

Look under "Blueprinting" in the yellow pages of the phone book for shops that can plot on Mylar. Major cities will have dozens of companies, but this type of service bureau is common even in smaller urban areas. Look for a bureau with a plotter that can print a strip about 34 inches wide and up to the full length of the roll of paper or Mylar.

Check with your service bureau for its exact requirements on disk size and file format. Most can use 5¼-inch or 3½-inch floppies. By far the most popular file format is DXF, which was created for the AutoCAD program. This format allows the exchange of information between computers and from a computer to a plotting device. DXF files are pure ASCII files, which can be created by popular yacht design programs.

Another popular file format is the Hewlett Packard Graphics Language, or HPGL. This is also an ASCII file, but written in the "move" and "draw" commands used by Hewlett Packard plotters. One advantage of HPGL is that files in this format can be imported by many advanced word processing and graphics programs.

The drafting service bureau will call up your file on its computer using a generic CAD program, not a program written for the complex curves found in boats. The bureau's CAD program then drives the plotter. Interface problems between your disk and the bureau's CAD program probably won't appear until the plotter begins working. It may be advisable to start plotting on cheaper vellum until you are sure everything is working correctly. Then the more expensive Mylar can be loaded into the plotter.

VELLUM OR PAPER PATTERNS?

Full-size section molds can be plotted on vellum paper or Mylar. Either material is fed through the plotter from a large roll. The length of the plot is limited only by the size of the roll. Width is a different story. The typical plotter is limited to a working width of about 34 inches. Full-size patterns wider than the plotting device are printed in several strips. These strips are taped together to make the full pattern. Not all service bureaus have the ability to separate a drawing into strips, so check first.

Plotting services do not come cheap. Rates for plotting on Mylar currently vary from $5.00 to $15.00 per running foot. (The cheaper rates are for a small city, the big rates are from a big city. Get the hint?) Reduce the amount of Mylar needed by stacking items on top of each other. Do this on your computer at home before you go to the service bureau. Sections are normally "stacked" as drawn, but you might rotate the curve of the stem 90 degrees so it will print next to the station molds. Or, if the boat is simple, the stem could be printed over the sections.

To save money, don't bother plotting those portions of the lines that will automatically be recreated when the building form is built. For instance, you absolutely need the lofted shape of the stem and forefoot, but you may not need the shape of the bottom of the boat along the keel. That shape is often created automatically when the station molds are erected and planking battens installed over them.

Ask the service bureau to print grid lines over the station mold shapes. Grid lines help align the patterns, especially if they have been printed in strips. Whether grid lines are printed or not is a decision made at the time of plotting, so be sure to request them.

Vellum or Mylar? There's no doubt that Mylar patterns are more dimensionally stable and longer lasting than paper patterns. They are also far more expensive and may not seem worth the cost to the amateur builder. Paper changes size as humidity goes up or down. The amount of change is small, usually under one percent. That sounds insignificant. Yet a half of one percent (0.005%) change over the length of a 40-foot vessel is 2.4 inches, more than enough to cause major problems. Also, paper may change size more in length than width, skewing the shape of the boat.

That said, many successful boats have been built from paper patterns. The key seems to be working quickly to transfer the lines to the mold station before the paper changes shape. True, the exact size of the patterns may be slightly different from what the plans call for, but all of the patterns will have exactly the same amount of error. This may not affect the fairness of the hull. How fast is fast? That depends upon the weather and the humidity conditions inside the shop. During the winter, paper plans may not change for months at a time in the hot, dry air from a forced air furnace.

The longevity of Mylar is most important to professionals, who may build more than one boat off a set of patterns, than it is to amateurs. If you're planning to build only one boat, the longevity of the patterns shouldn't be a factor since you're only going to need them once. Mylar is the logical choice if the patterns must be printed in strips and taped together. The dimensional stability of this material allows for exact alignment of the grid squares. Perfect alignment is never possible with paper patterns.

CAD-CAM STATION MOLDS

DXF and HPGL files can be used to drive a numerically controlled pin router. This is a computerized robot that routs shapes out of wood or aluminum with extreme accuracy. Material to be cut is flopped down on the table and the machine does the rest. Big boat companies like Hatteras use these machines to create absolutely identical parts for assembly line production. The same technique can be used to cut station molds from a computerized lines drawing.

A good robot router and its accompanying table come with a price tag that includes six zeros, so it's not a practical tool for the home workshop. However, machines are owned by job shops in cities. These shops are always looking for work. The problem is finding a local shop with an appropriate machine and an owner willing to tackle a slightly off-beat project. Start in the yellow pages under "Computer-Aided Design." Don't expect to score a hit with your first call.

INTELLECTUAL PROPERTY RIGHTS

Computerized lofting makes it easy to build any boat if you have a table of offsets. A creative computer hacker may even find a way to digitize a set of lines from a study plan and enter them into the computer. Once the data is entered, it's easy for a boat CAD program to fair the lines and

Industrial pin routers can be driven by the computerized lofting data. This router is cutting two duplicate curved pieces from a DecoLite panel.
(Courtesy Baltek Corp.)

print out a set of full-size patterns. There's an awful temptation to avoid naval architect's fees by this simple means. Bluntly, that's theft.

Boat designs are something lawyers call "intellectual property." As such they fall under federal copyright laws. You may own a set of blueprints, but the original architect owns the copyright to them. It's analogous to this book. You own the book, but the writer, David G. Brown, owns the copyright. You can read this book or use it as a doorstop, but you can't copy it or print your own version without violating the law. In a similar way, you cannot copy a boat design without violating the law.

Most design shops are sole proprietorship businesses. When you copy a design, you're stealing directly from the person who drew the lines. Worse, you may be stealing shoes from the architect's children. The concept of intellectual property is serious business and should be treated with respect.

Chapter 5
ERECTING THE BUILDING FORM

Up to now, all of the work has been done on the loft floor or the computer keyboard. Either way, lofting seems only vaguely connected to the finished boat. Nothing appears to be getting done despite hours of work invested. The situation changes rapidly when sawdust is underfoot and the physical shape of the hull begins to appear. The excitement of setting the first station mold is probably second only to the launching.

A building form is a transitory element that disappears as soon as the hull is planked and coated. But the ghost of the building form remains as long as the boat exists. Mistakes made in erecting and fairing the section molds become a permanent part of the boat to haunt you as long as you own the vessel. Because you're the builder, you will have intimate knowledge of minor imperfections that other people can't see. Avoid these ghosts. Take time when erecting the building form to make sure that everything is true, square, and fair.

MALE VERSUS FEMALE FORMS

Composite strip boats are built either inside a female form or over the outside of a male form. Both methods produce equally good vessels. The choice of male or female form is based on the nature of the boat under construction and is entirely up to the builder. Factors to be considered include the size of the work area, number of assistants, and complexity of hull shape.

If possible, discuss the choice of male or female mold with the designer of your boat. Find out which type of building form was used by other amateur builders who have constructed a similar boat. Then contact one or two of those builders directly for their comments. Most amateurs prefer a male form because they can see the boat's shape in positive space. It's difficult for some beginners to visualize 3-D shapes in the negative space of a female mold. On the other hand, the shapes typical of multihull sailboats can be done only in female molds.

SPACING BETWEEN SECTION MOLDS

Whether in male or female configuration, DuraKore strip composite technique requires fewer mold frames than other methods of one-off construction. They can be spaced up to 42 inches apart, depending upon the hull shape and DuraKore thickness. Closer spacing of mold frames is necessary in areas of greatest curvature. Kit boat instructions or plans from many designers specify the exact spacing of mold frames. If this information is not provided on your plans, attempt to discuss it with your designer.

If information cannot be obtained from the designer, building a mockup can allow mold spacing to be determined by experimentation. Construct a small-scale test building form that approximates the greatest area of three-dimensional hull curvature of the boat. Plank the mockup with several DuraKore strips. If the molds are close enough, the planks will follow the required curve. Otherwise, there will be unfair high spots or flat areas in the planking. Add intermediate section molds to your mockup until the DuraKore strips lie fair around the curve.

This male mold was used to build the prototype of the Freedom 35 sailboat. Plywood stations were set up and ready for planking in less than two months. DuraKore strips butted together end-to-end into 40-foot planking battens are on sawhorses in the foreground. (Photo by Billy Black courtesy of Baltek Corp.)

FEMALE BUILDING FORM

In a female mold, the boat is built rightside up on the inner edge of the section molds. Laminating the inner skin and installing permanent interior stiffeners, stringers, or bulkheads are easy because the hull is upright with the open interior exposed. The hull remains supported by the building form during this work.

There are drawbacks to a female mold for building larger cruising sail or powerboats. Unless your workshop is twice as long as the boat, you must lift each DuraKore strip batten up and over the sheer of the mold frames. This can be messy because the battens are flexible and one edge may be coated with thickened epoxy glue. Also, close quarters near the keel make difficult work of trimming and fitting the planking battens into a female mold.

Another problem of a female building form is that you have to work inside the uncompleted hull. Naturally, you can't walk on the DuraKore strips until the epoxy glue

Colin Haigh of Surrey, British Columbia, built these two float halves for his Farrier trimaran. The float half on the right is still in the building mold. Half bulkheads have been positioned in both pieces, which await covering with reinforcement material. (Courtesy Colin Haigh)

hardens and the inner reinforcing skin has been applied. You can step safely only where the station molds support the strips and straddle the spaces between.

By far the biggest problem with building inside a female mold is that the hull must be rolled over twice. You must first roll it upside down to laminate the outer reinforcing skin and to do the final fairing and painting of the outside. Then the hull has to be turned rightside up again for completion of the interior, decks, and superstructure. Every rollover costs money if cranes must be hired to get the job done. And two rollovers offer twice the opportunity for dropping or otherwise damaging the hull.

Few of these objections to female molds come into play when laminating a long, thin hull typical of a catamaran or trimaran.

These pieces are usually light enough to be handled by a small crew of workers without resorting to industrial machinery. A female mold is also the best way of obtaining the often complex shapes of multihull floats and main hulls.

MALE BUILDING FORM

Male building forms are popular for larger monohull sail- and powerboats. The hull is built upside down by attaching DuraKore battens to the outside edges of the station molds. The outer skin is laminated, faired, and painted before the boat is rolled over for installation of the interior. Male forms are popular because it is much easier to work from the outside of the boat while attaching the DuraKore. From a cost-saving standpoint, a crane is needed just once to turn the hull over.

A major disadvantage of building over a male form is that the hull may have little or no permanent internal bracing before the rollover. Without internal support the hull can be damaged during rollover. Support must be installed inside the hull to prevent warping or distorting the boat's shape. Many builders solve this problem by incorporating permanent bulkheads in the building form in place of station molds. This solution slows the process of attaching the planking battens and laminating the inner skin.

Another problem of using a male mold is that a worker must crawl underneath the overturned hull to scrape excess glue from batten seams. Then that worker has to roll a coat of epoxy onto the DuraKore veneer. At first it's easy to step inside the building form, but it becomes increasingly difficult as planking nears completion.

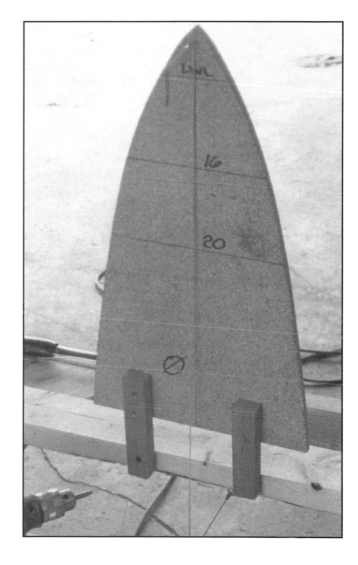

Erecting a station mold requires attention to detail. The plumb line used to make sure the centerline is vertical can be clearly seen. The waterlines are marked on the mold to help in alignment of the molds.

A crawlspace has to be engineered into the mold so this job can be done even when the hull is fully planked.

BUILDING THE STRONGBACK

The hull must be built on a flat, level surface. Since few workshop floors qualify, most boatbuilders construct a foundation known as a *strongback*. This is a ladder-like structure slightly longer than the overall length of the boat. It's made of stout materials so there is no possibility that it will be twisted or distorted during the planking of the hull. The "rungs" of the ladder are cross members positioned to support individual section molds.

Main rails and end pieces for a cruising boat strongback should be made of 2 × 12-inch floor joist lumber. Ask the lumberyard to allow you to pick through the stack to find the straightest pieces. Discard any warped wood or joists with excessive or loose knots. Standard 2 × 4-inch studs can be used for the section mold cross members and spalls. Again, ask permission to pick through the stack to get

This simplified drawing shows the major components of the strongback, which supports the station molds. The side rails and ends should be heavy enough to resist warping during construction. Lighter timber can be used for the cross members. Note that the center wire runs beneath the cross members the entire length of the strongback.

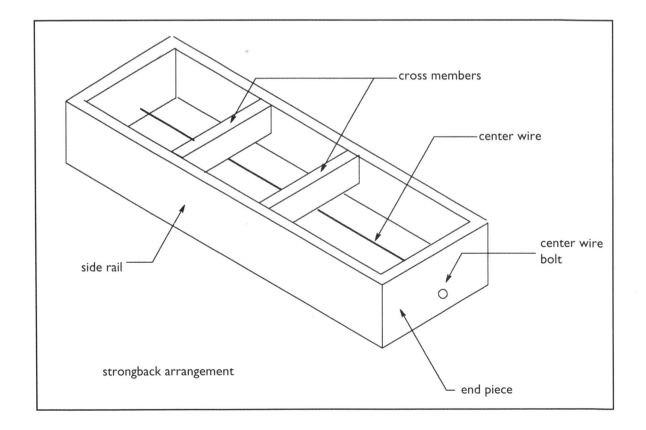

cross members

center wire

center wire bolt

side rail

strongback arrangement

end piece

studs that are straight and clear. The size of the strongback must be scaled to the boat. Heavier timbers are needed for a very large boat. Likewise, lighter materials are called for when building a dinghy. Strongbacks for multihull floats are diminutive compared to those for monohulls of the same overall length.

Assemble the strongback with care. It must be square and true. The tops of the rails and cross members must be absolutely level once the strongback is erected. Screws, lag bolts, and carriage bolts should be used to ensure the strongback stays true during construction of the boat. Avoid relying on nails, which tend to loosen over time. Epoxy glue the strongback together to ensure that it won't change shape. The amount of glue needed is so small that it won't be noticed in the overall cost of the boat.

Cross members are placed either at every mold section, every second one, or some other repeating pattern. Mark the midships station on the strongback, then work forward and aft, marking sections on the side rails at the intervals shown on the lofting. Exact positioning of the cross members must allow the center of the particle board molds to lie on the section lines when they are erected. Cross members are normally installed *inside* the strongback with their top edges flush with the tops of the rails. On a female mold, the cross members are often laid *across the tops* of the rails.

The strongback may be narrower than the beam of the boat, especially when building dinghies and smaller vessels. However, on large boats it is customary to make the strongback several feet wider than the boat's maximum beam. This allows placing catwalks on either side of the hull. Catwalks raise workers off the shop floor, making it easier to reach the keel during planking. They should be far enough away from the hull not to interfere with planking along the sheerline.

(left) *A substantial strongback constructed by students at the Marine Trades Center (Washington County Technical College) in Eastport, Maine. Horizontal planks have been placed along the outside edges to serve as catwalks for the workers during planking.* (Courtesy WCTC)

(right) *This closeup of the Maine school strongback shows the strength of construction. These timbers must support not only the weight of the hull, but also the weight of the station molds.* (Courtesy WCTC)

The male mold for the author's 9-foot DuraKore dinghy. A center wire has been placed over the tops of the station molds to supplement the wire in the strongback. Also, a homemade gauge ensures that the waterlines are the correct height above the strongback.

Making the strongback wider than the beam of the boat can also prove helpful during rollover of larger hulls. This will be discussed in Chapter 10.

REFERENCE CENTERLINE

Install an eyebolt in either end of the strongback so that the eyes are on the centerline. Stretch a light steel wire between these eyes. This wire becomes the reference centerline for erecting the section molds, so it must be absolutely tight. A small turnbuckle at one end allows it to be properly tightened. Don't bother with expensive sailboat gear for the center wire. Ordinary hardware store $\frac{3}{16}$-inch aluminum turnbuckles will suffice.

If 2 × 4 studding was used for the cross members, there should be room enough below them for the center wire to run without interference. If not, notch the cross members so that the wire touches nothing for the full length of the strongback.

Many builders add a second center wire over the male mold. This wire should be high enough above the keel line that it won't interfere with planking the hull. Don't make it too high though, because it serves as a handy reference for erecting the section molds and aligning the keel. A couple of 2 x 4 studs bolted to the strongback is generally sufficient to support the upper center wire. Be sure that these supports are far enough away from the stem and transom so they won't interfere with construction.

If two centering wires are used it becomes necessary to verify their accuracy. The center point of a plumb bob dropped from the top wire should lie right over the lower wire over the entire length of the strongback. Any misalignment of the two wires must be corrected prior to erecting the molds. And the plumb bob check should be repeated at regular intervals during the building process to be sure the wires are still aligned. When aligning the wires, consider the lower wire as always being "true" and adjust the upper wire to it.

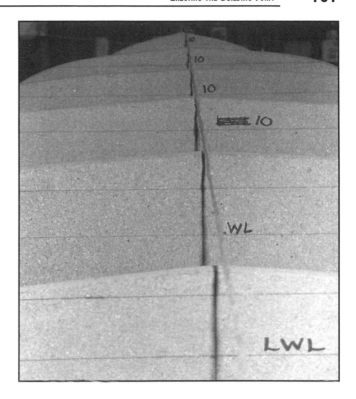

The top center wire is clearly visible in this photo. It crosses each station mold precisely at its vertical centerline. A plumb bob was used to insure that the top wire was located in exact alignment with the bottom center wire in the strongback.

SCRAP LUMBER

Nothing says that the strongback and other support pieces of the building form have to be made from new stock. Considerable savings are possible if acceptable used lumber can be found. Most large cities have firms that specialize in selling studs and joists removed from demolished buildings. This wood is well seasoned and often has fewer knots and a tighter grain pattern than new studding available in lumberyards today.

LEGS OR SUPPORT PYLONS

The need to crawl inside the hull while it's on a male form was mentioned a few paragraphs back. Now is the time to plan for that eventuality by raising the strongback off the floor on short legs. Don't overdo the legs. Keep the hull low enough that most of the planking can be done standing on the shop floor. Working from ladders or scaffolding slows down your progress. Place legs in the corners of the strongback and along the rails as needed to prevent sagging. Secure them with epoxy and carriage bolts. Check for level as you go.

A strongback and building mold for a dinghy or a narrow multi-hull boat may not be heavy enough to keep itself in position during the building stages. Heavier molds for larger boats usually have enough mass to stay where they're put. If movement appears to be a problem, secure the whole structure to the floor. Legs can be nailed to a wooden floor.

CONSTRUCTING THE MOLD

Each section mold is normally cut from a single sheet of material. Ordinary particle board subflooring (also known as "chipboard") is the suggested material for making section molds. In the United States it comes in 4 × 8-foot sheets in a variety of thicknesses. Material ½ inch thick is the logical choice for most boats. This is thick enough to accept the screws used to hold the DuraKore strips temporarily on the building form. Yet ½-inch particle board doesn't add excessive weight to the form. Thicker boards of ¾ or 1 inch are exceedingly heavy for the purpose.

Particle board is the least expensive material from which molds can be made. It seems like excessive cost cutting to build a fine yacht from such cheap material. However, this is not the case. Particle board is heavily saturated with glue, so it does not change size or warp easily. It also accepts drywall screws without the need for drilling pilot holes. Molds can be made of expensive plywood (or even more expensive solid timber), but there will be no improvement in the completed boat to reflect the greatly increased cost of construction.

Except for dinghies and smaller craft, it's seldom possible to build a male mold out of a single sheet. Instead, these molds are made as a "horseshoe" of particle board supported by additional framing. The outside of the horseshoe carries the required shape of the boat.

USING MYLAR PATTERNS

Computer lofting plots the curved shapes of the section molds on paper or Mylar patterns. These shapes must be transferred to the particle board. Remember that the patterns show only one side of the boat because the section view shows the bow on one side and the stern on the other. It's necessary to create a mirror image of each pattern to make a full section mold.

Draw a centerline on the particle board in ink and align the centerline of the pattern over it. Prick through the pattern with an awl on the outer curve to transfer its shape to the underlying wood. Use a lofting batten to join the prick points into a smooth curve and ink it with a pen. This line should go slightly beyond the sheerline. Mark the sheerline before lifting the pattern.

Flip the pattern over and use the centerline pricks to realign it on the particle board. Tape it down again and use the existing prick holes to mark the opposite side of the station curve on the board. Again, use a lofting batten to join the pricks into a smooth curve and ink the line. As before, extend the curve slightly beyond the sheerline mark.

LARGE SECTION MOLDS

Section molds for larger boats are too big to be made in one piece. Splitting molds into sections is often necessary to make the best use

Larger station molds are seldom solid. Instead, they are pieced together with uprights and spalls to support the particle-board shape.

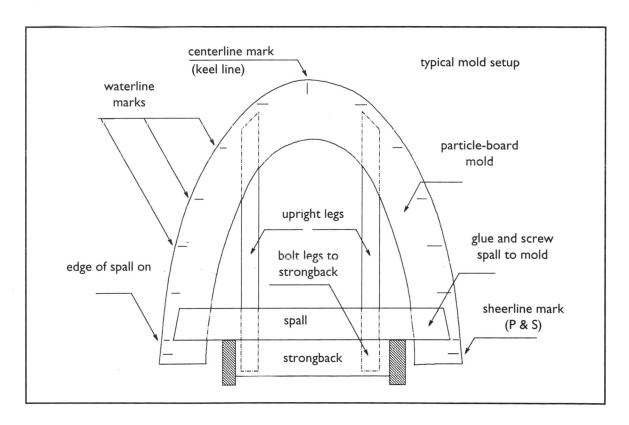

typical mold setup

centerline mark
(keel line)

waterline
marks

particle-board
mold

upright legs

glue and screw
spall to mold

bolt legs to
strongback

edge of spall on

spall

sheerline mark
(P & S)

strongback

of the particle board. The most logical split is on the centerline at the keel, but there are no set guidelines.

The big problem with multi-section molds is aligning the pieces during assembly to preserve the exact lofted shape. One solution is to use the patterns a second time to draw outlines of the mold stations on a sheet of plywood. Use the same technique of pricking marks through the pattern to create the lines. This creates a layout board. Assembly of the molds is done on top of the layout board using the section lines as guides.

COMPUTERIZED MIRROR IMAGE PATTERNS

Computers allow creation of instant "mirror image" views. This allows the blueprint service bureau to print Mylar patterns for both the port and starboard sides of the boat from the same computer file. Cut the two section views on their vertical centerlines. Tape the bow views together to get full-size patterns for all section molds forward of amidships. The same cut-and-tape procedure is used to make stern sections. Printing both sides doubles the cost of Mylar, but the money will prove well spent when the time comes to build multipart section molds.

Once you have full-size loftings of the section molds, it isn't necessary to re-loft a layout board for assembling multisection molds. The work can be done on top of the Mylar lofting as long as you're willing to be scrupulously clean. Epoxy glue drippings can quickly render expensive patterns useless. If you must keep the Mylar pristine, transfer the shapes of the section molds to a layout board using the techniques described above.

CUTTING THE MOLDS

Mark each section number on the particle board before cutting. This mark identifies the *face side*, which may be necessary to know when erecting the molds. Before cutting be sure that the centerline at the keel and the sheerlines are carefully marked on the face side. Mark the load waterline on all molds for future reference. Cut carefully along the lines with an electric sabersaw. Use a fine-tooth wood blade to prevent excessive chipping. Particle board does not cut quickly and it wears out saw blades because of its heavy glue content.

Section molds establish the shape of the finished boat and support the partially planked hull. Neither of these jobs requires great strength. So on larger craft built in male molds it is advisable to remove excess material from the center of the horseshoe shape to increase space inside the building form. This becomes important later when working beneath the hull scraping off excess epoxy glue or seal coating the DuraKore strips. A width of 6 to 8 inches should be sufficient. A large compass can be used to provide the inside cut line by tracing along the outer edge of the mold shape. Use care when cutting out the center section of molds because particle board is quite brittle and likely to break.

Larger boats require piecing up the section molds. The number of sections is obviously determined by the size of the boat. Joints can be anywhere as long as the smooth curve of the section is not disturbed. Butt blocks are needed to reinforce the joints. Trim them well back from the working edge of the mold to avoid a clash with the DuraKore battens during planking. Use the layout board or full-size patterns to solve the problem of maintaining the proper shape of multipart molds.

Some boat designs require the use of timber keels, sheer clamps, or both, that are thicker than the DuraKore strips that will plank the hull. The use of such pieces requires that the molds be notched to accept the appropriate timbers. The locations and sizes of these notches should be shown on the lines drawing from the naval architect. See Chapter 9 for more details.

ERECTING THE MOLDS

A large horseshoe-shaped male mold is entirely too flimsy to stand on its own. The open ends of the horseshoe must be joined by a

An instructor at the Marine Trades Center aligns the pieces of a station mold prior to assembly. This mold is being built on top of a full-size lofting. (Courtesy WCTC)

A closeup of the author's homemade gauge that ensures that all waterlines on the station molds are the same distance from the strongback. The upright supports of the molds were clamped to the strongback cross members and then tapped up or down as necessary to achieve correct alignment. The string from the plumb bob keeps the centerline vertical.

support known as a *spall*. This is made out of dimensional stock (such as a 2 × 4) with at least one true edge. Align the true edge with waterline marks on the mold. Secure the spall with screws and epoxy glue. The true edge on the spall should be oriented so that it is up when the mold is installed on the strongback. A carpenter's level laid on the spall will check that the mold is level. If additional spalls are needed for more support, use the same procedure to install them.

Legs are added after the spall. They support the face side of the mold and help mount it on the strongback. Be sure that the width across the outside edges of the legs is slightly less than the inside width of the strongback to allow the molds to be adjusted slightly during the fairing of the building form. Also, be sure the legs are long enough to allow positioning of the mold at the proper height above the strongback. During the erecting process the top of the strongback performs a similar function to the baseline in the lofting. The legs allow the section molds to be raised or lowered until their waterlines are correctly aligned relative to the baseline.

A plumb bob hung from the centerline mark at the keel should cross the centerline mark on the spall. The section mold is correctly aligned athwartships when the point of the bob lies directly over the centering cable of the strongback. Note that the erecting process has used similar measurements and reference points as were needed to create the lofting. They are:

> ➤ Baseline—This now becomes the top of the strongback. Vertical measurements to level waterlines are taken from here.

➤ Section Distances—As measured along the baseline these are now marked by the cross members in the strongback. These distances establish the locations of the section molds along the baseline.

➤ Waterlines—These are now marked on the section molds. The molds are adjusted vertically until all of the waterlines lie parallel to the top of the strongback and are located the correct distance above the strongback.

Each section mold should be temporarily secured in place as it is erected. Use as few screws as possible and do not drive them all the way home. Chances are, one or more of the molds will have to be joggled during the fairing process. Scrap lumber can be used to brace the molds in position.

FAIRING THE MOLDS

If every line were absolutely correct on the patterns and every cut absolutely true, then the station molds could be erected and planking commenced without fairing. Unfortunately, in the real world such perfection occurs only by accident. Adjusting the section molds is a normal part of fairing the building form.

Construct a DuraKore fairing batten. If possible, it should be long

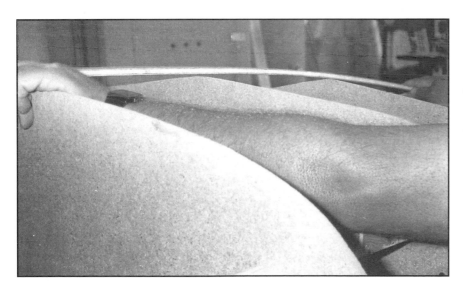

A fairing batten sprung across the outside edges of the station molds quickly shows any unfairness. Here, the batten does not touch the middle station mold, which could indicate that the middle mold is low or that one of the molds on either side is high. Additional checking with the batten will reveal which situation is correct.

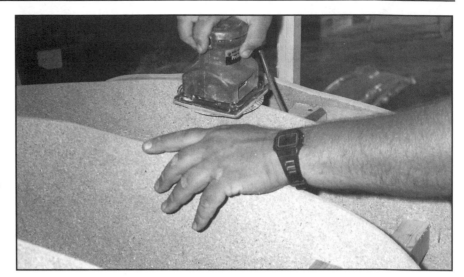

High spots on particle board molds are easily sanded away using 40-grit paper and an electric palm sander. Work a little bit at a time, constantly re-checking with the batten for fairness.

enough to reach from bow to stern with a little overhang at each end. Lay this fairing batten on the hull along the waterlines to detect any misalignment of the station molds. Ideally, the batten should just "kiss" each mold as it wraps around the hull. More likely, however, there will be section molds that don't even touch the fairing batten while other molds push the fairing batten into a sharp bend rather than a smooth curve. Your eye is the best instrument to detect unfairness. Study not only how the molds touch the batten, but also the sweep of the curve outlined by the batten on the hull.

Be cautious as you fair the building form. What seems to be a low spot actually may not be out of fair. The fairing batten may not strike one section mold because an adjacent mold is too high. Keep a log of every adjustment. Note the number (or letter) of the section mold and the type of action taken. This log may save hours of work later when you're trying to figure out how much a section mold was moved. Once you're satisfied that the building form is fair, tighten the mounting screws so nothing will move during planking of the hull.

PREPPING THE MOLD FOR PLANKING

MALE OR FEMALE

Epoxy is wonderful glue but a little stupid. It doesn't know what it should stick to and what it shouldn't. If the mold is not correctly prepared, the epoxy will not only glue the DuraKore strips together, it will also bond the hull to the building form. If this happens, there's only one tool to fix the problem: a kitchen match. Buy a few marshmallows, some chocolate bars, and graham crackers. Any Girl Scout can tell you how to put these ingredients together over a blazing fire to produce a very tasty concoction.

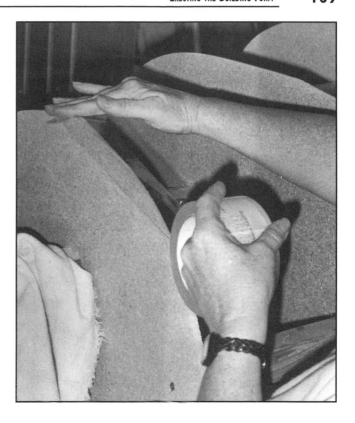

Fortunately, epoxy doesn't bond to various types of smooth plastic. Among these non-bonding plastics are clear package sealing tape and polyethylene sheeting. Package sealing tape is available in several widths. Buy the widest available. Apply tape to all surfaces of the building form that will come in contact with wet epoxy to prevent the hull from bonding to the section molds.

Polyethylene sheeting can be used to wrap the faces of the molds instead of tape. **Do not** line the building form by draping polyethylene sheeting over the section molds. True, this will prevent the hull from bonding to the form, but it will keep you from being able to coat both sides of the DuraKore strips with epoxy resin during the building process.

Clear package sealing tape protects the mold frames from being bonded into the hull. Epoxy does not stick to the tape. The tape is centered over the edge of the mold frame and then carefully rubbed down on the particle board. A single layer of tape provides enough barrier to prevent the epoxy from sticking to the mold.

Chapter 6
PLANKING THE HULL

Strip planking with DuraKore is fundamentally no different from using conventional cedar strips. Anyone who has built a strip planked hull of solid wood will be thoroughly familiar with the technique. The only surprise comes in the speed of planking. Balsa-cored strips are much easier to fit and they do not require difficult coves or beads on the mating edges. This means it is less work to install DuraKore battens on the mold than to do the same with conventional wooden planks.

The theory behind strip planking is that long, narrow pieces of wood allow the builder to create the compound curves of a boat hull. Thin wood strips are flexible enough to bend in two directions at once when required by the shape of the vessel. Long seams between the strips allow tight-radius curves at the turn of the bilge or in narrow "wineglass" sections of sailboats.

The only problem with strip planking is finding the best arrangement for installing the planks. Two factors influence applying DuraKore strips to the hull. First, the girth of the boat varies continuously from bow to stern. "Girth" is the distance from keel line to sheerline. Typically, girth is greater in the bow and stern than amidships. This means that more strips are needed to plank the bow or stern than the midships section.

The second factor is the actual shapeliness of the hull. Strips laid along the keel line will run almost straight from bow to stern. Along the sheerline, strips obviously curve to follow the sweep of the sheer. Then there's the often forgotten curve imparted to the planks by the turn of the bilge or by hollow bow sections. These curves change the run of the planks from straight to shallow horseshoe shapes.

The shape of the boat makes it impossible to lay Durakore planking battens in straight lines over the entire building form. Except for directly along the keel, all of the planking strips will have some bend. The builder must control this bend so that battens near the midships section do not become horseshoes. This is an art that must be learned. Everyone's second strip planked hull is always better than the first because of the experience gained.

Two methods for arranging planks on the building form have been successful with DuraKore. They are essentially mirror images of each other. One starts with a master plank approximately along the mid-girth line from keel to sheer. The other starts planking at both the sheer and keel lines, working toward the mid-girth line. Although both systems work, inexperienced workers are advised to attempt the master plank technique on their first boat. This prevents the difficulty of joining the planks in a fair transition as required by the double run technique.

MASTER PLANK TECHNIQUE

This technique starts with a "master plank" located on the hull at approximately the mid-girth distance from keel to sheer. Locating it on the building form plays a critical role in determining the amount of curve imparted to all succeeding DuraKore battens. Experience has shown that locating the master plank at approximately the mid-girth point accomplishes the goal of keeping plank bend to a minimum. However, the exact mid-girth point is not always the best location for the master plank. Making a "best guess" as to the correct location is one of the learned skills of a master boatbuilder.

A crew of professional builders planks the first U.S. powerboat to be built of DuraKore, a 36-footer at Malcolm L. Pettegrow, Inc. in Southwest Harbor, Maine. The hull was completed from scratch in only four weeks using a female building jig.
(Courtesy Baltek Corp.)

Start by marking the mid-girth distance on all of the section molds except for those immediately in the bow or stern where the shape of the hull changes rapidly. There's no mystery to the mid-girth point. It lies halfway from the keel to the sheer as measured over the outside curve of the section molds. A steel tape measure is best for this job. Divide the girth measurement in half and mark the point on the edge of the mold with a permanent black felt-tip marker. For clarity, use a different color marker for the mid-girth than was used to mark the waterlines.

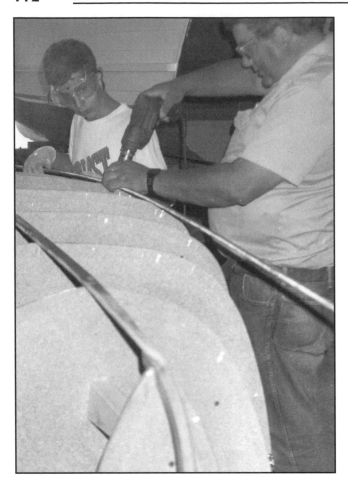

The mid-girth plank goes on the mold of the author's 9-foot dinghy. Adam, the 12-year-old boy in the background, participated fully in the construction of this boat.

Glue enough DuraKore strips together to make a batten longer than the hull. Lay this batten on the mold at the marked mid-girth points. This job usually requires many hands to handle the limber batten. Use care to avoid breaking it. Move yourself from location to location on the shop floor, squinting down the batten to be sure it lies fair to the eye. Look at it from the bow as well as the stern, adjusting out any unfair spots. Fairing by eye is the "art" portion of the job.

Temporarily fix the master plank in place with tape or nails and measure from it to the keel and to the sheerline. Quick mental division calculates approximately how many additional DuraKore planking battens will be necessary to span the distances from the master to the sheer or to the keel line at each section mold. Also, you should be able to envision how these strips will lie on the building mold.

Boats have more compound curves in their bottoms than topsides. Moving the midships portion of the master plank toward the sheer is the standard way to accommodate this characteristic. The unreachable goal is to adjust the master plank so that the number of DuraKore planking battens between it and keel or sheer remains approximately equal over the length of the boat. Accept the best possible compromise. Once the master plank is located, it should be attached to the building form. Planking is then laid on the hull starting at the master plank and working toward keel and sheer.

DOUBLE RUN PLANKING TECHNIQUE

The alternative method of planking starts by installing DuraKore planks simultaneously along the keel and the sheer. This option often works best on exceptionally beamy vessels such as traditional catboats. Planks from the sheer grow toward the mid-girth line as do planks from the keel line. They meet in the midships area, leaving "bird's mouth" shapes at the bow and stern. Tapered DuraKore battens must be prepared to fill these V-shaped openings. Double run planking may produce "hard" spots along the line where the two areas of planking merge. Careful work can avoid this problem, but it takes clear thinking and planning ahead.

ORDER OF PLANKING

Either method of strip planking divides each side of the hull into two sections: sheer to mid-girth, and mid-girth to keel. This results in four quadrants to plank. Normal practice is to plank equal amounts of opposite sides of the keel in order to equalize strain on the building form. For instance, the port side from mid-girth to keel might be done first, then the starboard. There's no magic place to start. One thought is to do the most difficult quadrants first so that the job gets easier as it goes.

A cordless drill drives drywall screws through the DuraKore strips and into the particle board molds. This is the keel plank down the centerline of the boat. Once the clamp was removed the center strip was faired into the timber stem piece.

ATTACHING DURAKORE TO THE MOLD

Until the hull is fully planked and the epoxy cured, a DuraKore hull is just flexible strips and goopy glue. Planking battens must be firmly attached to the mold while the glue cures to ensure the hull takes its correct shape. Temporary fasteners that are easily removed are required. A variety of methods are possible:

➤ Long staples driven through the DuraKore and into the particle board section mold. Removal of staples is facilitated by driving them through a piece of nylon fiber strapping tape. An air- or electric-powered staple gun makes this the fastest way to install planking battens, especially singlehanded.

➤ Double-headed nails are made specifically for temporary use. They are driven until the first head pulls into the surface of the wood. The second head stays well above the wood where it is easy to grab with a claw hammer. Double-headed nails are not widely used, so they can be difficult to find. Unless extreme caution is used, pulling nails with a claw hammer can damage the veneer of the DuraKore strips.

➤ Drywall screws are designed to be driven with an electric screw gun. Use the shortest length that will go through the DuraKore and hold in the particle board mold. A washer can be used beneath the head to prevent it from sinking into the batten, but should be needed only where unusual amounts of pressure must be applied (e.g., near the forefoot at the bow).

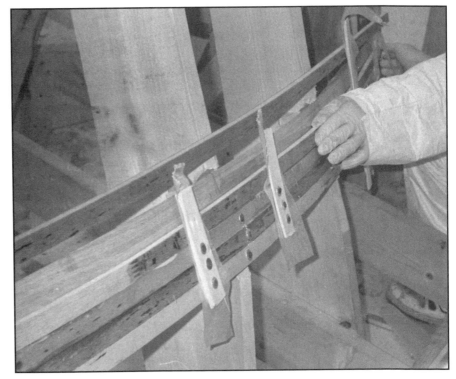

Planking can start at the keel, mid-girth or sheer. Here, planks are growing upward from the sheer of a hull on a male mold. Note the fairing strips to keep the DuraKore aligned while the epoxy cures. Strips of poly film prevent the fairing strips from bonding to the planks. (Courtesy WCTC)

Of these methods, staples are sometimes used by professional builders, while amateurs tend to choose drywall screws. The reason for this divergence of opinion is equipment. Most professionals have compressed air staple guns for use in other jobs around the shop. Few amateurs are as well equipped. On the other hand, most amateurs own a variable speed drill/driver motor. Corded motors work fine, although battery-powered models are much easier to use.

Drywall screws come with either standard Phillips heads or with square drives. Phillips heads do not require special driver bits but have a tendency to "cam out." When this happens, the slots get chewed up and the screw becomes scrap. Square drive heads are less likely to cam out but require special driver bits.

"You have to learn how to use the drywall screws," says trimaran builder Jim Gentry. "If you don't do it right, you'll split the hardwood veneer on the DuraKore. After a while you get the hang of it though."

There is no reason a combination of fasteners cannot be used. Staples work well in areas of little or no hull curvature. Screws with washers are best for holding DuraKore in areas where the DuraKore has to be "tortured" into taking the proper shape.

BUTTERING THE DURAKORE

Each DuraKore planking batten is edge-glued to the previously installed strip plank with a thickened mixture of epoxy glue. How thick to make the glue is a matter of personal choice, although a creamy peanut butter consistency is suggested. Peanut butter consistency glue doesn't drip out of the edge joints, yet is thin enough to wet out the wood. If the glue is too thin, it creates gaps and voids by running out from between the strips. Conversely, if the mixture is too thick, it doesn't "key" into the edge of the DuraKore. Experiment to determine the best consistency by gluing a few sample strips.

Two methods have proven effective for applying thickened epoxy glue to the edges of the DuraKore planking battens. The epoxy can be applied to one planking batten at a time from a pastry bag. Or

multiple battens can be "buttered" using the jig described and illustrated in Chapter 3. Both techniques have their advantages, and builders often use a combination of the two.

➤ Buttering Jig—The best way to apply thickened epoxy when working with a planking crew. Advantage is speed: four to six planking battens can be buttered at one time.

A CLEAN PLANKING OPTION

For those averse to the often messy "buttering" method, I've found something cleaner—and faster.

I found that "buttering" the DuraKore strips was messy and created the difficult and unpleasant job of cleaning off excess glue from inside the male mold. "Why not," I reasoned, "plank the boat dry using temporary spacers to create space for the glue?" Later, it would be possible to trowel the glue into the joint like a bricklayer tuck points a building.

A local hardware store provided ¾-inch aluminum angle of appropriate thickness. This angle was quickly cut into small pieces about 1½ inches long; these became temporary spacers for planking the boat.

With a spacer on each side of the individual station molds, a new plank could be pushed tightly against the spacers as a temporary drywall screw attached it to the mold. The spacers were then moved on to the next mold.

Using the spacers dramatically increased planking speed. A full quarter of one side of the boat was planked dry in the time it had taken to install just ten "buttered" strips.

(continued on page 117)

Spacers were made from short lengths of aluminum angle cut from a longer piece purchased at a nearby hardware store.

Disadvantage is that glue may begin to cure before batten can be installed on the building mold.

➤ Pastry Bag—This works best when working alone to plank a hull. Put thickened epoxy in a disposable plastic bag. Close the bag and snip off one corner to create a "nozzle." Squeeze the bag to force a bead of glue out of the nozzle and onto the edge of the batten.

(continued from page 116)

After planking from sheer to mid-girth on the starboard side, I moved to the port side of the boat. My assistants began "tuck pointing" the starboard dry seams. We found that the two processes took about the same time to accomplish.

A mixture of epoxy the consistency of smooth peanut butter worked best for filling the seams.

We used ordinary steel putty knives to push thickened epoxy into the seams. It was easy to tell if a seam was filling properly. The glue would seem to "push back" out of the seam under pressure from the knife, and we found it easy to learn the trick of pushing just enough glue to prevent it from coming out the back side of the seam.

The "tuck pointed" seams were extremely clean from the outset. Excess glue was not left on top of the adjoining strips. Rather, it was moved down the hull to be used somewhere else, resulting in much less sanding to fair and smooth the tuck pointed sections than the areas of the hull built with conventional gluing techniques.

At rollover we discovered that the tuck pointed seams were much cleaner and required almost no arduous sanding. A small amount of back filling with thickened epoxy was needed, but this took far less time than sanding would have.

Thinking that I had discovered something, I called Keith Walton at Baltek. "It sounds like a great idea," he said. "The guys out in Australia say they've been doing it for months."

According to Walton, this method of planking should produce an equally strong hull to one done conventionally.

"The epoxy should be mixed to gap-filling consistency," he said. "And it's critical that there be no voids in the seams. You have to fill any empty spaces in the seams from the other side before laminating the reinforcement material."

Aluminum angles worked well but did have some flaws. The angle shape is necessary since a U-shape could not be removed after the plank is screwed to the mold. However, the angles provide nothing to prevent them from being knocked off while the new plank is being positioned. Having an extra supply of angles allowed the planking to continue without us stopping to pick fallen spacers from the floor.

Steel angles might serve better when working high off the floor. They could be picked up with a small magnet on a string, thus avoiding the tiring job of climbing down off the building mold just to get a spacer.

Another way to apply the epoxy: putting it in a plastic bag, where it's then squeezed from a corner of the bag that has has been snipped off. (Courtesy WCTC)

FINGER JOINT WARNINGS

Caution: Never place finger joints on top of molds. Dura-Kore planking battens have finger joints every 8 feet. These joints should never land on one of the particle board molds. Glued joints are considerably more brittle than the rest of the batten. Forcing a staple, nail, or drywall screw through a joint will probably crack the joint and ruin the batten. Also, finger joints should be staggered on the hull. Never allow them to line up on adjacent strips. Good practice is to have a full unjointed strip on either side of a finger joint.

MALE MOLD

When working your way up from the master strip plank toward the keel, apply the glue to the top of each strip plank. It may be less messy to use the pastry bag technique to apply the glue after the plank is installed than to butter the plank prior to installation. When working from the master plank down to the sheer, it's usually easiest to butter the DuraKore batten before installing it on the mold.

There's no requirement to use either approach. "We fit our strips dry and then buttered them with the 'pastry bag' method," says Bret S. Blanchard of Washington County Technical College in Eastport, Maine. He designed a DuraKore powerboat constructed by students. "Due to the number of available hands, we did not have any incentive to develop a shortcut."

FEMALE MOLD

When working upward from the master plank toward the sheer, apply thickened epoxy to the top of each DuraKore planking batten after it is installed in the mold. Use the pastry bag technique. When working below the master plank, apply glue to the batten before installing it in the mold.

INSTALLING BUTTERED DURAKORE

Several things must be kept in mind while installing epoxy-buttered DuraKore battens. Each batten must be "stretched" between the molds to avoid sagging. The glue joint itself must be full of thickened epoxy without gaps or voids. Skins of the DuraKore strips must be aligned between molds, and extra glue must be removed before it cures.

STRETCHING DURAKORE BATTENS

Fastening the DuraKore normally starts amidships and works forward and aft. On some hulls it may be easier to start at either the bow or stern and work toward the other end of the boat. Both methods are acceptable because the work forces any extra material outward and off the boat. Never allow two installers to work *toward* each other from the bow and stern on the same plank. They will push extra length created while stretching the plank toward the midships section, where it will appear as a "bubble" that cannot be pulled tight to the mold. When two people are working, have them start amidships and work toward the ends.

Section molds should be close enough together to prevent appreciable sagging of the DuraKore spanning them. Thus, it should not be necessary (or desirable) to use any great stretching force when installing battens to the mold. Instead, it's more of a smoothing

Planking of the Maine Marine Trades Center boat nears completion. In this case, the boat was "shuttered" along the keel. The ease with which DuraKore strips are bent over the molds is readily apparent.

A line of heads marks the drywall screws holding the DuraKore strips to the molds. Each line is a potential weak spot in the hull if the holes are not carefully filled with thickened epoxy once the screws are removed.

action as you work toward the ends of the boat. Prevent any hollowness between section molds, but don't put stress on the strip.

Individual strips of DuraKore do not need to be attached to every section mold of the building form. Attachments are only needed to keep the seams tight and the strips properly stretched between molds. Since it takes considerable work to remove the fasteners after the hull is planked, the fewer fasteners the better. On most boats the smallest number of fasteners is required amidships above and below the turn of the bilge. More fasteners are needed to hold the strips at the ends or in curved bilge areas. Despite the warning about excessive fasteners, use one wherever necessary.

Working alone requires considerable creativity to come up with the required extra "hands." Long, flexible DuraKore planking battens are a case in point. You'll need to find some way of supporting both ends while attaching the midships section to the hull. One way is to attach temporary wooden supports to the building form using C-clamps. Rubber bands, duct tape, wood props, nails, and lead weights have all been used as "third hands," depending upon the situation.

GLUE SEAMS

Finger pressure is usually sufficient to push the seams between the strips together while fastening them to the mold. Look for an even bead of glue to squeeze out of the joint along the length of the seam. Changes in the size of the bead may signal problems. If no glue squeezes out, you're not applying enough pressure. If so much glue comes out that it begins to run and drip, you're probably using too much pressure.

Pot life of epoxy glues varies depending upon the temperature and concentration of material. A pot of glue kicks much faster than the same glue spread over the length of a DuraKore planking batten. This means that epoxy buttered onto a plank stays workable longer than it does in the pot.

At some point even the thickened glue on the batten begins to show signs of curing. Once epoxy in the pot turns the slightest bit rubbery, it should be discarded and a new batch mixed. If you work fast enough, rubbery glue can be scraped off the DuraKore, saving the strip for later installation. Scrape the curing glue into a plastic-lined trash container for disposal.

No matter what method is used, there is always excess glue to be scraped off the hull. Removing the glue while it is still soft is relatively easy. Once it hardens, however, only laborious sanding will work. (Courtesy WCTC)

Use only *low-density* filler when thickening epoxy glue for seams between planks. Sanding will be necessary to fair the boat after planking, and low-density fillers sand easily, making the job less of a chore. High-density fillers are difficult to sand. Using a high-density filler will cause the sandpaper to grind into the surrounding soft wood veneer, creating unfair low spots.

ALIGNING WOOD VENEER

The hardwood veneer surfaces of DuraKore strips will automatically align over the section molds. But they will occasionally get out of alignment between section molds where they are not supported. Alignment of the veneers should be done as each new plank is attached to the molds and checked again after it is fully screwed into position before the glue kicks. Double attention paid to plank alignment pays big dividends when the time comes to fair and smooth the hull.

Misalignment is fixed by pinning successive strips into alignment with wooden dowels, nails, or long staples. Align the new strip with its sister by hand or with light pressure from a clamp. Drive a pin completely through the new strip and into its sister. A couple of pins between molds should hold the surface veneers in alignment until the epoxy glue cures. A variety of materials ranging from nails to wooden dowels is suitable for pinning strips.

Wooden dowels do not have to be any more than ⅛ inch (32 mm) in diameter. Sharpen them to a blunt point for easy driving with a carpenter's hammer.In place of dowels, one catamaran builder used long bamboo skewers obtained from a store catering to oriental cooking. Pilot holes were drilled, then the skewers pushed in by hand. Extra length was then trimmed off. An advantage of skewers or wooden dowels is that they can be left in place without fear of

(left) DuraKore strips can get out of alignment between station molds. One way of correcting this is to pin adjacent strips with wooden dowels. The process starts by drilling an under-size hole edgewise into both strips.

(right) A wooden dowel pin is pushed into the edge hole. This pin should be equal in length to the width of two DuraKore strips. Friction inside the balsa core holds the pin in place. It does not have to be glued.

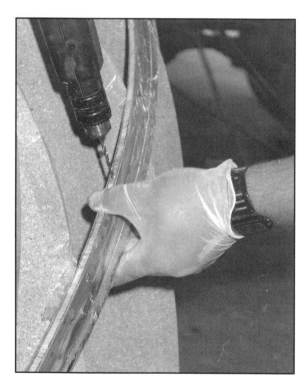
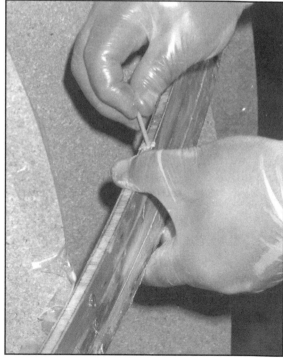

rust or deterioration.

The same is true of aluminum nails. Common steel nails work equally well but raise the fear of rust if water gets into the core. Builders with access to an air compressor can use a pneumatic nail gun to pin DuraKore planks into alignment. Depending upon the size of the gun, nails from small finishing to large studding spikes can be driven. Pneumatic nailers take only finger pressure on the trigger, and the gun used in boat construction can be held in one hand. Pinning planks is just a matter of squeezing the trigger. With a small "pop" the gun shoots a nail deep into the balsa core of the sister strips.

Nails for many of these guns are known as "coil nails" because (logically) they come in long coils that allow a new nail to be fed into the gun each time one is used. The construction trade is the biggest user of coil nails. As a result, virtually all of the nails packaged for pneumatic application are made of ordinary steel. It's all but impossible to find aluminum or stainless nails for these guns. DuraKore boatbuilders who have used steel nails have not reported any corrosion problems. After all, if water gets to the fasteners, the boat has more serious problems than a few rusty nails. A DuraKore strip composite boat built correctly should keep the nails dry and rust-free for its lifespan.

Builders who shy away from ferrous metal inside their hulls do not have to abandon the speed and convenience of pneumatic tools. They can opt for plastic nails that will not rust or deteriorate if exposed to seawater. Information on them is available from Marukyo USA, 511 East 4th Street, Los Angeles, CA 90013, (213) 488-0707.

ALIGNMENT FAIRING STRIPS

Some areas of extreme curvature may require pressure from clamps and temporary fairing strips to ensure alignment. These strips are thin pieces of wood long enough to run between section molds and wide enough to span one or more seams. They are applied over the planking to force it into alignment. A piece of polyethylene sheeting between the fairing strip and the DuraKore prevents unwanted bonding between the two. Fairing strips are held in place by temporary fasteners into the section molds.

REMOVE GLUE SQUEEZINGS

Thickened epoxy squeezed out of the seams during planking must be removed before it cures. When working with a team of helpers, this job is best done after three or four planking battens have been installed on the mold. Scrape the excess glue back into the pot and use it again (as long as it has not started to kick). If you're working alone, it's best to scrape off the squeezings as you go, one seam at a time.

A metal putty knife works well to pick up uncured glue. Once it turns rubbery, switch to a sharp wood chisel. Rubbery epoxy cuts smoothly away from wood. Never let excess glue from the seams harden past the rubbery stage, as the only way to remove cured glue is laborious sanding. Don't forget to scrape off the excess glue from both the outside surface and the hidden inside surface of the mold. While scraping up the glue, examine the seams for gaps and voids. Use recovered glue on a putty knife to fill these areas.

STRAIGHTENING PLANK RUNOUT

Ian Farrier cautions builders of his F-9A and F-25 trimarans that finding the right location for the master plank is difficult. "In the real world this is next to impossible," Farrier admits in his well-written instruction manual. Since there is no perfect location for the master plank, it's inevitable that planks begin to curve as they go around the shape of the boat. The way planks curve around the hull is known as their "runout." Excessive curve in the runout makes planking difficult. "The easiest solution is to recut the strips straight once they start to bend too much when nearing the gunwale or bilge radius," he says.

Farrier wisely counsels builders not to waste time trimming or beveling so-called "stealer" strips to straighten plank runout. He says correctly that it's not important for all DuraKore strips on the hull to run continuously from bow to stern. Cutting the strips already on the hull to a straight line is easily done with a builder's saw set to the proper depth. Mark the cutline with a chalk line or with pencil and lofting batten laid on the partially completed hull. Naturally, trimming can only be done after all the glue between the strips has fully cured. Measure twice, cut once.

Cutting a new straight line for DuraKore planking does not create structural problems as long as the glue joint between the next batten and the cut edge is properly made. The goal of planking is to create a continuous core of end-grain balsa and/or thickened epoxy inside the reinforcing laminates, which will be added later. Long, straight planking battens look good, but are no more effective than battens

The planked hull of the author's 9-foot dinghy is almost perfectly fair immediately following completion of the planking, with no sanding or smoothing.

that have been sliced to an odd shape in accordance with Farrier's instructions.

STRAIGHTENING KEEL AND SHEERLINES

This discussion assumes that a solid timber keel is not being used. Along the keel line the planking from the first side will sweep past the centerline due to the natural curve of the hull. Let this happen, as it will be corrected once the first side is fully planked and the epoxy glue has cured.

Mark the keel line with a batten or chalk line for cutting with a builder's saw. This cut line should be carefully aligned with the stem, the centerlines on the section molds, and the center of the transom. Measure twice, cut once. Adjust the cutting depth of a builder's saw to the thickness of the DuraKore strips being used. Cut along the line and discard the offcut piece. You should now have a straight saw kerf along the keel line, ready to accept the planking from the second side of the boat.

A hand saw and Stanley Surform tool are used to trim planks from the second side where they meet the planking on the first side. The same thickened epoxy glue used for edge gluing battens should be used to bond the trimmed edges of the planks on the first side to those coming up from the other side. Don't worry too much about the sheer at this point. Rough trim any extra-long strips, but leave them extending beyond the sheerline for now.

Chapter 7
INITIAL SEALING AND FAIRING

Strip movement caused by changes in the moisture content of the balsa is a serious problem that can cause a great deal of grief (and expense) to the unwary builder. These variations are the normal result of changes in the weather as well as of heating the building during winter. As with any wood (or wood product), dimensional changes or warping follow significant changes in moisture content.

Fortunately, this is not a difficult problem to solve. Professional builders from around the world have shared the methods they developed for avoiding problems caused by changing moisture content. All of the solutions revolve around seal coating both the inner and outer hardwood surfaces of the DuraKore with unthickened epoxy. Once the DuraKore strips are protected with waterproof epoxy, their moisture content does not change and movement of strips on the mold ceases.

REMOVING TEMPORARY FASTENERS

If the strips were not precoated before planking, they will have to be sealed now. Temporary fasteners holding the hull to the building mold should be removed once the epoxy seams between the strips have fully cured. Gravity should keep the newly planked hull in position over a male mold. This is not always the case with female molds, especially those used for catamaran half-hulls. It is possible for the newly planked hull to slide in a female mold unless it is restrained. One way to restrain movement is to toenail temporary screws into the back of the hull through the mold frames. Screws can be angled through the wooden molds or driven through small blocks screwed to the molds. The same technique can be used on a male mold if the hull wants to squirm around.

SEAL COATING APPLICATION

German boatbuilder Helge von der Linden of Hamburg has found that problems associated with moisture changes in the balsa are easily minimized in two ways. First, he gets the planking installed over as short a period of time as possible—a couple of days or so. Second, he coats both sides of the DuraKore strips with epoxy before placing them on the mold.

"I agree with a very short planking and laminating phase," von der Linden says. "Since this is not always possible (actually never if you want to take advantage of the female frame method and insert all structural items such as bulkheads, floors, etc.), a better way is to coat the outside of the planks with just one coat of unthickened epoxy as you continue planking."

PRECOATING

The easiest way to seal the hull is to follow von der Linden's suggestion and precoat both veneer surfaces of the planking battens with epoxy before installation on the building mold. Planking battens can be precoated as they are installed on the form, but this is a messy procedure. It's much better to coat a day's worth of planking battens ahead of time so that the epoxy has time to harden.

"This (precoating) helps in cleaning excess epoxy from the seams," von der Linden says. "But it does not make the final fairing easier. The disadvantage with precoating is that additional sanding prior to laminating is necessary for good adhesion of the laminate."

Precoating the planking battens avoids one of the big headaches of strip composite construction. It's no longer necessary to crawl under the building form to roll epoxy on the underside of the hull. Working with a paint roller inside the dark recesses of a male mold is one of the messiest jobs of building a boat. This isn't necessary if the underside is precoated with epoxy.

Jim Gentry built an Ian Farrier F-32 in his Clarkston, Washington, shop. He discovered that "The nature of DuraKore is that it warps when you precoat the strips, especially where they sit on a support while the epoxy cures. It's not a great deal of warping, but you have to take it into account when you plank the hull."

Jim Watson of Gougeon Brothers, Inc., has studied the relationship of epoxy resins to materials like DuraKore. He warns that coating only one side of a strip creates what engineers call an "unbalanced panel." The coated side is effectively stabilized against moisture change while the uncoated veneer is not. This can lead to unpredictable distortion of the strip if the moisture content of the uncoated veneer changes.

The only possible solution to the unbalanced panel problem is coating both sides at the same time. This requires building a "curing rack" protected by plastic to prevent epoxy bonding. This rack can be nothing more than sawhorses placed every 4 feet or so. Coating both sides of the strips may not prevent minor distortion of the strips, but this distortion is easily accommodated during the planking of the hull.

SEAL COAT APPLICATION

A polyurethane foam paint roller is the easiest way to apply a seal coat of epoxy. Pour mixed epoxy into a roller pan and apply it like thick paint. A few minutes' practice is needed to learn how to apply a thin, even coat-

DuraKore strips can be pre-coated at the same time the finger joints are glued together. Apply unthickened glue to both veneer surfaces of the strips. A layer of poly film will keep the epoxy-coated strips from bonding to the table.

ing. Overuse of the roller creates bubbles in the epoxy film. Once the epoxy is applied, the surface should be "tipped off" with a foam brush to break any bubbles and smooth out roller marks. It helps to have a two-person crew: one rolling and the other tipping.

Rolling epoxy downhand on flat surfaces is easy. The same can't be said for working overhead or on vertical surfaces where drips, sags, and runs are common. The only way to minimize these problems is to apply a thin, even coat and tip it out. If too much epoxy is applied, gravity takes over and causes either a drip or a sag. If there's enough excess epoxy, the sag becomes a full-fledged run. Keep this coat as thin as possible.

Really cold epoxy does not flow well enough to give the necessary thin coat. Consequently, it is more likely to sag or run. There's a great temptation to warm the glue so it flows out of the roller in a nice thin coat. Don't do it! Warming the epoxy to improve flow is certain to cause the outgassing problem explained below.

OUTGASSING

Outgassing is the term used to describe the formation of tiny air bubbles in the first coat of epoxy applied to raw wood. This phenomenon is caused by expansion of air held captive in the fibers of the wood until it gets warm. (This air also gives wood its buoyancy in water.) Expanding air tries to force its way through the wet epoxy coating. If the epoxy is thin enough, the air blows through and creates a crater. More likely, though, the epoxy is just thick enough to stop the air from escaping, but not before a bubble is created.

"I was warned about outgassing, but..." trimaran builder Jim Gentry says, his voice trailing off to add emphasis. "If there is a rise of only one degree on my shop thermometer, I get bubbles. I have a bank of south-facing windows in my shop. I cover them with cardboard when I'm doing any epoxy work to avoid the heat from the sun."

Outgassing bubbles or craters have ranged in size from almost microscopic to the diameter of a soup plate. These pockmarks in the seal coating cause lots of extra work sanding and filling before the hull can receive additional finish coats. All of the professional builders contacted acknowledged severe outgassing problems with their first DuraKore hulls. They also reported that solving the problem is easy and costs absolutely nothing.

According to Jim Watson, the relationships of the two hardwood veneers of DuraKore to the end-grain balsa create the outgassing problem. "Light core woods have more air in them. End-grain balsa provides good channels for this air to reach the veneer," he says. "The veneer then channels it horizontally to small openings. This causes more pressure at these openings than along the rest of the veneer."

The student boatbuilders in Maine found their outgassing problems to be worse on the inside of the hull than on the outside. "We had a lot of outgassing on the inside laminate—not on the outside skin. We experienced severe problems over the DuraKore and over cured laminates," says Bret Blanchard, the instructor who designed the boat.

THE HEAT SOLUTION

Air expansion that causes outgassing is caused mostly by heat in the shop and only secondarily from heat generated as the epoxy cures.

The best prevention for outgassing is having the wood slightly warmer than the epoxy. The amount of temperature difference required is quite small. The wood only needs to be a few degrees warmer than the glue.

Warming the entire hull takes creative planning rather than fancy equipment. During the summer months, plan to apply the first coat of epoxy to new wood after the ambient air temperature has reached its high for the day, usually after 3 p.m. Indoors during the winter, your hand on the thermostat controls when the workshop reaches its warmest temperature. Turn up the shop temperature for several hours to warm the wood. Then turn down the heat and begin applying the seal coat of epoxy.

Whether you wait until after the heat of the day or turn down the thermostat, the formation of outgassing bubbles will be inhibited. The reason is simple. Air trapped in the fibers contracts as the wood cools in the declining shop temperature. This reduces pressure on the wet epoxy coating and those pesky bubbles shouldn't form.

However, there is no absolute cure for outgassing, as Blanchard and his students discovered. "We tried to control the problem with temperature variations by lowering the shop temperatures when laminating. This seemed to help, but did not cure the problem."

Warming the epoxy to make it flow better makes outgassing a certainty. Bubbling is worst when the temperature of the materials is above 80°F (25°C). Another easy way to ensure a pockmarked seal coat is to raise the temperature of the shop after coating the hull. This is often done in an attempt to speed up the cure rate.

INITIAL FAIRING

The goal of initial fairing is to get the hull ready for the application of reinforcement material. Fairing is done to both the inside and outside skins of the hull, but most boats are not finished to as high a standard on the inside of the hull as they are outside. Interior cosmetic imperfections are normally hidden by the furniture.

FIXING GAPS AND HOLES

Gaps in the seams and holes left from removal of temporary fasteners must be filled with thickened epoxy prior to the initial fairing of the hull. Mix a bog putty made from easily sanded low-density filler. Work slowly around the hull, filling gaps and holes with a putty knife. You have to learn how to see these problem areas. Don't stare at the hull. Instead, scan your eyes over the surface of the boat in long, easy sweeps. Because of the way human vision works, you'll spot most of the problems out of the corner of your eye, in your peripheral vision. Trowel the putty carefully to avoid unnecessary sanding later. Let the epoxy cure fully before continuing with initial fairing.

INITIAL FAIRING OF THE HULL

Seal coating to prevent moisture-related strip movement makes initial fairing more difficult. Cured epoxy resists sanding. In an ideal world, the initial sanding of the hull would be done before the seal coat is applied. As explained above, however, this is seldom possible with amateur construction due to the need to seal against moisture changes. It is better to endure more difficulty during initial fairing than it is to deal with the problems created by strip movement in the mold.

Fortunately, DuraKore strip composite hulls are extremely fair as built and require very little in the way of laborious fairing. Professional and amateur builders have both expressed surprise at the fairness of their first DuraKore hulls. This characteristic of the technique greatly reduces the mind-numbing work of sanding and grinding.

Still, as Bret Blanchard and his students found, there is always work to be done. "There is no doubt in my mind that this construction system provides a shape very quickly," he says. "But one must be prepared to fill and sand if a product of molded hull quality is desired."

Cured epoxy coatings are always suspect of having amine blush, which is normally removed by scrubbing with water and a 3-M Scotch-Brite 7447 pad followed by wiping down with white paper towels. A water washdown of the initial seal coat is recommended only if it is certain that all exposed DuraKore has been fully protected against moisture intrusion. If there is any doubt about the integrity of the seal coat, abrade the dry hull with a Scotch-brite pad.

Power sanding with 60- to 80-grit paper should be used to knock off any ridges of cured epoxy in the seams. Power sanding with an electric palm sander speeds the job, but beware of too much power. Builders with latent Rambo traits should resist the temptation to

Leveling the glue seams is an important part of initial fairing. Use 40-grit paper on an electric palm sander to speed up the task. A dust-collecting sander makes the job less messy. A professional dual-action air sander cuts hardened epoxy much faster, but can do great damage in the wrong hands.

reach for a belt sander. Belt sanders can do enormous damage when the machine digs into the soft DuraKore strips.

Initial fairing is the process of removing any unfair high spots on the hull and filling in low spots. An easy way to find high spots is with a homemade chalk stick. This is just a piece of knot-free scrap wood at least 6 feet long and ¾ inch square. Rub a good coating of carpenter's chalk on all four sides of the stick, then bend the stick over the hull. Slide the stick back and forth so that the chalk rubs off. Chalk marks on the hull identify high spots that need to be sanded fair. Use the chalk stick as often as necessary during the fairing process.

FLEXIBLE SANDING BOARDS

Whether by machine or by hand, sanding both fairs the hull and gives a "tooth" to the hardened epoxy seal coat. Initial fairing goes quickest with a power sander, but the final work should be done by hand with flexible sanding boards. Make sanding boards out of scrap plywood from ¼ inch to ½ inch (0.6 to 1.3 cm) thick. The thickness

Students working on the Maine boat use board sanders to smooth their DuraKore hull. Flexible boards allow compound surfaces to be sanded smooth without gouging. The white patches are applications of epoxy fairing compound.

of the board controls the amount of flexibility. Attach handles to either end. Board sanders can be any size, but most workers make them to take advantage of the measurements of standard sheets of sandpaper (11 × 7½ inches in the United States). The paper is held in place with sanding disk adhesive.

Small sanding boards are most useful in areas where the hull has a lot of shape. Large, flat areas call for longer boards, often 4 feet or more in length. The width of the board should increase in proportion to its length. As a general rule, larger boats require longer sanding boards. Long boards are operated by two or more people to ensure even pressure throughout the stroke. It is tedious work, but every bit shows up as improved cosmetic appearance of the finished hull.

FILLING LOW SPOTS

All of the fairing compound used to fill low spots or smooth the hull should be of the same density. Either purchase premixed compound (SYSTEM THREE F-9 Fairing Compound) or mix it on the job using epoxy glue and low-density filler. Professional builders prefer to mix their own fairing compound in order to have maximum control over the result.

Safety Warning: Never use polyester autobody compound to fair a hull constructed with epoxy. Polyester compounds do not bond well to cured epoxies. Always use an epoxy-based fairing compound when building a DuraKore strip composite hull.

Low-density thickening agents are required in fairing compound to ensure easy sanding. WEST System's 410 Microlight is an ideal filler for creating a fairing compound. It sands easily to a feather edge. (This compound is not recommended under dark paint or other surfaces subject to high temperatures.) Phenolic microballoon-based fillers also work well, although they can take up to 30 percent more effort to sand. Cabosil (colloidal silica) powder can be added to these fillers to prevent sagging.

Experiment with various recipes for fairing compound before you begin to work on the hull. Keep careful records of the filler-to-resin ratio in each experimental batch. Apply the mixed compound to a vertical piece of plywood to determine its sag characteristics.

Most workers find fairing compound of peanut butter consistency works best. Thinner consistency tends to sag, especially on vertical surfaces. Compound that's too thick is difficult to apply smoothly. Once you've found your personal favorite, post the recipe on your epoxy cart for future reference.

Consistency of the ratio of filler to epoxy is vital for successful fairing. If each batch of compound is different, the hull will not sand evenly. Harder batches of fairing compound will resist the sandpaper, and softer batches will erode away quickly. The more you sand, the more the unfairness grows. So establish your fairing compound recipe and stick to it throughout the fairing process.

Low spots in the planking will be discovered as part of initial fairing and should be filled with fairing compound. Spreading the compound with a soft plastic squeegee leaves the area needing little final sanding.

Apply fairing compound to the hull with a large, flexible plastic trowel. Suitable trowels are available from auto parts stores that cater to professional car refinishers. Jim Watson says he uses a long flexible board to scrape off excess compound fair with the contours of the hull. A board about 3 feet (0.9 m) long is about the maximum for one person to handle.

Fill low spots until the compound is slightly "proud" above the surrounding surface. Sand it fair after it cures. Deep low spots may require two or three thin applications of compound rather than one thick application. This is especially true on vertical surfaces where a thick coat of compound would sag of its own weight before the epoxy cures. Remove amine blush and sand the surface with 220-grit paper before applying additional layers of putty.

SANDING THROUGH THE VENEER

Every effort should be made not to sand through either the epoxy seal coat or the hardwood veneer of the DuraKore strips. Still, it happens. Don't panic because no serious damage has been done. Continue sanding until the entire hull is fair, then go back and recoat all burn-throughs with unthickened epoxy. Do not worry about trying to fix the veneer. Just seal the balsa wood core and forget it. As long as the balsa core remains intact, the finished composite will be strong enough once the outer skins are applied.

The exception is if sanding damage to the DuraKore strip is severe. In this case it may be necessary to remove the damaged material and replace it with new. This is obviously delicate, time-consuming surgery that should be avoided at all costs. Sand carefully!

PREPARING FOR LAMINATION

Fairing a DuraKore strip composite hull is much easier than fairing other types of cold-molded hulls. Large areas of the hull may need little or no attention from an initial fairing standpoint. These areas must still be prepared for application of the reinforcement material by thorough removal of the amine blush and sanding with 80-grit paper to give a "tooth" to the epoxy. The importance of this preparation is critical enough that it bears continued repetition. If the hull is not properly prepared, the reinforcement material may not bond correctly to the strips.

Amine blush removal is so important to one East Coast builder that he uses an initial alcohol wash followed by vinegar and water. The hull is then wiped down with clean white paper towels before being sanded. All sanding dust is vacuumed off before another cleaning with both alcohol and water. He admits that this belt-and-suspenders-and-safety-pin approach is overkill, but he doesn't want to worry about the secondary bond between the reinforcement material and the seal coat on the DuraKore strips. Get the hint?

TRIMMING THE SHEER

Now is a good time to trim the sheerline. Trimming the sheer is not particularly difficult, although it can be time consuming. The work must be done to a high degree of accuracy to prevent the boat from appearing lopsided. Mark the appropriate points on the outside of the hull, using references from the section molds. Join these points with a lofting batten to draw a smooth line on the outside of the hull. Girth measurements taken from the keel line are one way of double-checking that the position of the sheer on one side of the boat is the same as on the other. Use the center wire on the building form to mark the keel line on the hull (if it is not already marked). The distance from keel line to sheer should be the same on both sides of the boat at each station. After measuring at least twice, cut along the marked sheerline with a sabersaw, keeping the saw blade *outside* the line. It's always easier to sand away a high spot than to replace DuraKore in a low spot.

If the deck is to be applied directly to the edge of the hull, the sheer should be beveled to match the deck camber. The section view of the lofting should provide enough information for setting the proper angle into the sole plate of the sabersaw. The outside surface of the hull will appear to be *shorter* than the inside surface. This bevel may not remain constant all around the boat. Change the angle of the sole plate as necessary and smooth transitions between angles with a power sander.

Chapter 8
APPLYING REINFORCEMENT MATERIAL

ow is the magic moment. Applying reinforcement material creates the high-tech laminate that gives a composite hull its exceptional characteristics. From a structural standpoint, applying the reinforcement skin is the most critical process in building your boat. Great care must be taken to ensure that the material—whether it's fiberglass, Kevlar, or carbon fiber—is properly bonded to the DuraKore strips. The importance of removing the amine blush and sanding the epoxy seal coat was stressed in previous chapters. It's mentioned again for emphasis.

Outgassing must also be mentioned again, although it should not occur if the hull was seal coated during construction. However, major outgassing problems can develop if the first application of epoxy to raw wood is in conjunction with fiberglass cloth or other reinforcement materials. If outgassing prevention methods are not followed, bubbles will form between the cloth and the DuraKore

Applying the reinforcement material creates the composite hull. This is a critical step: Trapped air between the DuraKore strips and the epoxy/fabric layer will seriously weaken the completed boat. (Courtesy WCTC)

strips. These bubbles effectively eliminate the strength of the composite laminate. Repairs involve grinding them away and filling the resulting holes with new cloth and epoxy. Even done well, repairs are never as good as a continuous skin.

Because of the outgassing problem, it is strongly suggested that laminating over raw wood be avoided. If it can't be avoided, follow the steps outlined under seal coating to minimize outgassing. Maintaining a constant watch over the temperature of the materials and allowing the shop to cool down slightly as the epoxy cures have proven effective in preventing serious problems. The thickness of the epoxy and glass layer is also a factor. Thicker layers of resin generate more heat as they cure. The more the heat, the more the outgassing problem.

Some professional builders combat outgassing by applying a vacuum bag over the wet epoxy and cloth laminate. Thoughts on amateur vacuum bagging will be found at the end of this chapter. Bagging an entire hull is usually not practical outside of a professional boatshop.

FIBER REINFORCEMENT MATERIALS

All manner of fiber materials—woven and non-woven, common and exotic—can be used as reinforcement materials. While it's fun to talk about those exotic materials used in super-secret military aircraft, there is little point to the discussion. Such materials simply are not readily available to the average boatbuilder or are prohibitive in cost. We'll focus on the fabrics that can be obtained through normal consumer distribution channels.

Choosing the right reinforcement material is one of the most important engineering decisions in building a composite boat. Your naval architect will undoubtedly specify precisely what material to use on various parts of the hull and deck. Follow these specifications exactly, as deviations can be disastrous. Different types of reinforcement materials are often combined in areas of unusual stress or where exceptional strength is required.

FIBERGLASS

Fiberglass products are made up of extremely thin strands of real glass, the same glass as in house windows. The mechanical properties of glass make it almost as flexible as cotton or linen when drawn into a thin fiber. This flexibility allows glass fibers to be wound onto bobbins for use in weaving machines. The first fiberglass products were all woven fabrics similar in construction to cotton cloth used in clothing or draperies. As the technology developed, fiberglass materials became more sophisticated. Today, the best reinforcement materials are non-woven products with stretch characteristics to match engineering specifications of high-tech boat construction.

Drawing fiberglass threads and weaving them into cloth requires lubricating the fiber. If lubrication were not applied, the fibers would break in the looms or cause expensive wear to the machinery. Some lubricant remains in the finished cloth despite the best efforts of the weavers to remove it. Additional chemicals known as "sizing" are added to fiberglass cloth to give it certain handling characteristics. Lubricants and sizing are necessary in the manufacturing process, but they become chemical contaminants in epoxy boat construction.

Biaxial cloth resists stretching in two directions while triaxial also fights bias stretch. Use the cloth specified by the boat's designer.

Chemical contamination is a major reason for epoxy glue failing to bond to some fiberglass cloth. Avoid problems by purchasing only

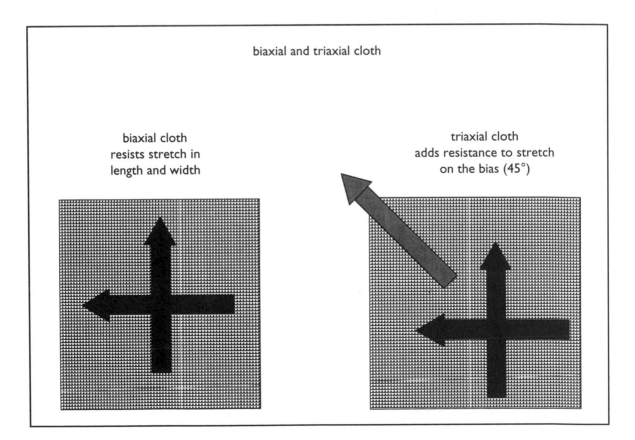

biaxial and triaxial cloth

biaxial cloth
resists stretch in
length and width

triaxial cloth
adds resistance to stretch
on the bias (45°)

fiberglass materials specifically engineered for use with epoxy resins. Never use fiberglass products intended for polyester resins, as the sizing in them is not compatible with epoxies. One way to be sure of purchasing the correct fiberglass material is to get it from the same source as the epoxy glue.

Woven reinforcement materials are created on looms in the same manner as ordinary cloth. Individual threads go over and under each other in a basket-weave pattern. Woven fabrics are relatively stable along their length (warp) and slightly less so along their fill (weft). However, they are quite unstable if pulled at a diagonal (on the bias). In addition, the slight crimping of the threads resulting from a tight weave allows the cloth to stretch in both the length and fill directions when pulled hard enough. These characteristics of conventionally woven fabrics are not desirable in the engineering of a composite laminate.

The solution is non-woven fiberglass materials with specific engineering properties. Of these, the two most common are *biaxial* and *triaxial* cloth. As the name suggests, biaxial cloth resists stretching or distortion in the length and fill directions while triaxial adds bias stretch resistance. Biaxial material is often used in the form of 4- to 10-inch (10- to 25.4-cm) wide tape for tabbing bulkheads or reinforcing corners. Triaxial cloth is one of the best fabrics for composite boat construction and is normally sold in 50-inch wide rolls.

Another specialty fiberglass product is *unidirectional tape*. All the fibers of this material are oriented in one direction. They are held in place by a thin, non-structural scrim. This tape is often specified as reinforcement in corners or areas of unusual concentration of stress.

In the United States, the weight of fiberglass materials is normally described as so many ounces per square yard. The smaller the number of ounces, the lighter the weight of the cloth. Boatbuilding materials vary in weight from 4 to 15 ounces (and occasionally more). Cloth comes in either S-Glass (Structural) or the less expensive E-Glass (Electrical) grades.

XYNOLE POLYESTER

A relative newcomer, Xynole fabric is gaining popularity as a covering material for cold-molded boats. It wets out quickly with epoxy resin and has an extremely high tensile strength. Testing by the manufacturer shows it has approximately eight times the ability of glass to withstand workloads and greater resistance to abrasion and impact damage. At 4.2 ounces per square yard, Xynole is much lighter in weight than equivalent fiberglass materials. Like all "better than glass" materials, however, Xynole is considerably higher in price. It is normally sold in 60-inch widths.

"We use exclusively Xynole polyester fabric as a system for our wood construction," says Reuel B. Parker of Parker Marine Enterprises in Fort Pierce, Florida, the author of *The New Cold-Molded Boatbuilding, From Lofting To Launching* (International Marine, 1990). "Xynole forms a superior barrier membrane, and it flexes with wood as well as accommodating the dramatic expansion/contraction modulus of wood. Time after time we see cracking in fiberglass-over-wood construction, accompanied by water violation and severe damage including delamination (even with epoxy). This simply does not happen with Xynole-polyester/epoxy skins." he says.

Parker goes beyond suggesting Xynole to his customers, he actively discourages the use of fiberglass materials, which he describes as a "brittle, insidiously toxic, user-unfriendly material that historically is a poor companion to wood construction. It has such a vastly different modulus of expansion/contraction with wood that it cannot be considered compatible, except in vastly thick layers."

OLEFIN SPUN POLYPROPYLENE

Polypropylene is another synthetic fiber that is made into reinforcement cloth. Although it is about double the cost of fiberglass cloth of equal weight, woven polypropylene fabric is much more flexible. This means it handles better than fiberglass cloth of equal weight when making compound shapes or tight-radius corners. Standard 4-ounce polypropylene is claimed to have about the same bulk and strength as a 10-ounce fiberglass cloth. It is normally sold in 50-inch wide rolls.

KEVLAR 49 ARAMID

This is the stuff of bulletproof vests, but bullet resistance is not why it's used in composite boats. Kevlar fibers have virtually no stretch and exceptional tensile strength. This makes them ideal for laminating specific high-stress areas. In addition, Kevlar is extremely resistant to abrasion. Kevlar's golden color is indicative of the price, so most designs use this space-age material only in critical areas. It is typically sold as a coarse-weave 4.5-ounce cloth on 50-inch wide rolls.

CARBON (GRAPHITE) FIBER

Carbon fibers are stronger and stiffer for their weight than steel or aluminum. They are often used as a secondary reinforcing material where unidirectional strength is desired. Particular uses include stiffening centerboards, rudders, and composite masts and spars.

LAMINATING RESINS

All conventional marine epoxy glues and hardeners can be used as the laminating resin. West System's 105 epoxy resin combined with either 205 or 206 (slow) hardener is perfectly acceptable. From the SYSTEM THREE offerings, choose the Phase Two Epoxy resin, which was formulated for composite construction.

Warning: Under no circumstances should polyester resin be used to laminate a DuraKore strip composite boat. Only marine-grade epoxy materials should be used. Read and follow the epoxy manufacturer's instructions.

No matter what resin and reinforcement fabric combination is used, there are only two methods of application: *wet* or *dry*. Most amateur builders prefer the dry method, which allows easier positioning of the fabric and is less messy for the workers. Fiberglass products are far and away the most popular reinforcement materials, so in this discussion the term "fiberglass" will refer to all types of reinforcement fabrics. The procedures are essentially unchanged with more exotic fabrics such as Xynole or Kevlar.

MEASURING FOR QUANTITY

The square footage calculation done in Chapter 3 to determine the amount of DuraKore necessary for the hull is equally valid for purchasing the reinforcement material. A quick doublecheck can be done by measuring the maximum overall length of the boat and the maximum girth from keel to sheerline. Multiply these measurements to get the area of one side of the hull. Double this amount for the whole hull. Add to it the area of the transom plus an allowance for overlapping seams. Finally, add enough extra cloth to account for normal wastage and mistakes.

Determining the amount of epoxy necessary to wet out the cloth is a bit more difficult. Different weights of cloth require different quantities of epoxy. And there are differences in the amount of glue required for fiberglass, Xynole, or Kevlar. The accompanying table is adapted from the guidelines of epoxy and fabric manufacturers. It is intended only as a guide and not as a specific recipe for applying one coat of resin to dry material.

ESTIMATING EPOXY NEEDED

PURPOSE	SQUARE FEET PER GALLON OF EPOXY
Coating Wood & Veneer	
DuraKore Strips	
First Coat	250 to 325
DuraKore Strips	
Subsequent Coats	325 to 400
Laminating Reinforcement Fabrics	
4 oz. Cloth	
(Wetting Out)	130 to 150
6 oz. Cloth	
(Wetting Out)	115 to 130
All Cloth	
(Subesequent Coats)	200 to 300

DRY METHOD OF APPLICATION

Unroll the fiberglass, position it over the planked hull, and smooth out the wrinkles. This cloth is somewhat slippery, so it may be necessary to hold it in position with temporary staples or masking tape. Pay attention to how the various axes (biaxial or triaxial) of the material are oriented on the hull. Consult the building plans to be sure this orientation is proper because it plays an important part in the overall strength of the finished boat. Trim the pieces to fit, leaving a few inches hanging beyond the sheerline or ends of the boat.

Piecing together the fiberglass is often necessary because the cloth is only 50 inches (127 cm) wide. Some exotic reinforcement fabrics come in narrower widths. Edges of biaxial or triaxial cloth should never be butted together. They *must* overlap by 2 to 3 inches (50 to 75 mm) to create a continuous skin of cloth. As with the first piece, use tape or temporary staples to hold this one in position and then trim it a bit long. Continue cutting and piecing until the entire hull is covered with reinforcement material.

Some designs call for unidirectional reinforcement applied so that the fibers run across the keel line from sheer to sheer in a continuous strand. Unidirectional material should not be overlapped when applied. A simple butt seam will do; however, It's critical that the pieces be butted tightly with no gaps.

Collect the necessary tools and organize your assistants before mixing any epoxy. Once you have "hot" glue there will be little time to search for a missing squeegee or to argue over who is doing which job. Set up a fan to circulate fresh air through the workshop. Make sure everyone has appropriate protective clothing, especially gloves and safety glasses. Let those who smoke take a final cigarette break and encourage everyone to visit the necessary room.

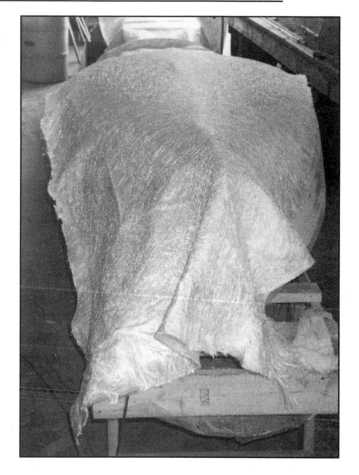

Unroll the reinforcement material over the hull before applying any epoxy. Shape and cut the material to fit. Gloves and long sleeves will prevent "glass itch" if using fiberglass cloth.

WETTING OUT

Assign one person the job of glue guru. This worker needs at least a half dozen plastic mixing containers of equal size. Decide in advance how much resin for the first "pour," usually four to six pumps. Batch size can be increased as experience squeegeeing it into the fabric is gained. Use the alternate pumping technique: one resin, one hardener, etc., to avoid confusion over the resin-to-hardener ratio. It's vital not to lose track of the number of pumps of resin and hardener in each container.

Never short the mixing step. Resin applied to the boat will cool enough that it shouldn't kick before the next batch is properly

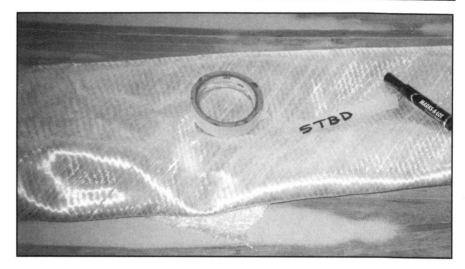

Roll up the cut cloth and label it to prevent confusion, using masking tape and a felt marker. The labels are peeled off and discarded before applying the cloth to the hull.

mixed. There should never be a rush except when working on exceptionally hot days.

Pour mixed glue into the center of the cloth being coated and squeegee it outward. Use a flexible plastic squeegee and just enough pressure to move the glue around. Don't press so hard that you move the cloth or begin shooting wet glue around the room. Some people prefer to use a roller to do the initial spreading of the glue. Special all-metal laminating rollers are available, but a polyurethane foam paint roller does an excellent job at a lower cost.

Final movement of the glue is done with a squeegee because this tool is also best for removing air bubbles. Firm pressure should be used, but don't be so enthusiastic that you squeegee a froth of air back into the resin. With unidirectional materials, squeegee only in the direction of the fibers, *never* across them. Squeegeeing removes excess epoxy that could cause the fabric to float off the surface. At the same time, use care not to create dry spots by squeegeeing too hard.

Properly squeegeed fabric has a somewhat matte appearance. Dry spots usually appear dull or slightly white. (The color of dry spots is affected by the reinforcement fabric being used. For example, they may be brighter gold if using Kevlar.) Continue mixing, pouring, and squeegeeing until the entire hull is completely laminated.

PLANE YOUR SQUEEGEE

Flexible plastic squeegees used in laminating often develop small nubbins or burrs. These can catch on the reinforcement fabric, causing it to move unexpectedly or wrinkle. The easiest way to remove these burrs is to smooth the working edge with a block plane.

WET METHOD

In the wet method, the fiberglass is applied onto uncured (still wet) epoxy resin. This technique is trickier than the dry method because once the cloth gets into the goopy resin, it becomes difficult to move or reposition. However, the wet method is the only way in which fiberglass can be applied to some vertical surfaces and all overhead surfaces.

Start by unrolling the cloth over the dry hull and fitting it in the same manner as described for the dry method. Pre-fit the entire hull with dry cloth. After all sections have been pre-fitted, remove each piece of cloth, label it, and roll it up. Set the rolled pieces aside carefully so you can identify them and apply them in the proper order.

Use a polyurethane foam roller to apply a heavy film of unthickened epoxy to the DuraKore surface. Wet out only as much area as can be laminated comfortably within the gel time of the epoxy. (Remember, the gel time of the film on the hull will be longer than the gel time of glue in the pot.) Cover an area equal to one of the rolls of pre-fitted fiberglass.

A crew of two people can do a dry application, but it usually takes three people to apply fiberglass over wet epoxy. Unroll the first segment of cloth well above the wet epoxy. Don't let it touch the hull until you are sure it is properly positioned.

Lower it slowly onto the epoxy. In most cases, surface tension will snatch the fiberglass once it comes in contact with the glue. When working on a vertical or overhead surface, it may help to wait until the epoxy film becomes tacky before applying the cloth. Work out wrinkles by lifting the edge of the cloth and smoothing from the center with a new plastic squeegee, using long strokes with light pressure.

Apply a second coat of epoxy on the fiberglass with a foam roller. Put down enough glue to thoroughly wet the weave of the fabric. Remove excess epoxy with long, overlapping strokes of a flexible plastic squeegee. Check for dry areas and rewet as necessary.

In the wet method, the hull is first coated with a layer of epoxy, which is easily done with a chemical-resistant, short-nap roller cover.

 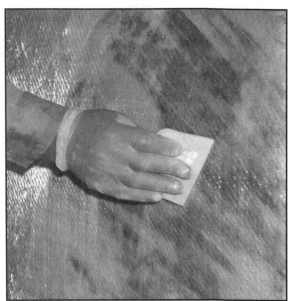

(left) *Mixed epoxy is poured onto the cloth and spread with a roller. Note this Maine student builder is fully protected with a chemical-resistant suit, eye goggles, and rubber gloves. Rolling epoxy can be messy, so such protection is not excessive. (Courtesy WCTC)*

(right) *Use a new flexible plastic squeegee to move excess glue to dry areas of the reinforcement fabric and to eliminate small air pockets and dry spots. Its working edge must be free of roughness that might catch on the fibers of the fabric.*

TRIMMING THE LAMINATE

Professional builders often trim the reinforcement material as soon as the epoxy goes into its first stage of cure. This is when the glue turns rubbery. If the right moment is chosen, the rubbery, glue-laden fabric cuts with a sharp utility knife. Trimming too early results in pulling the fiberglass away from the DuraKore. Wait too long and the laminate is too hard for a knife to cut. Don't expect all of the laminate to cure at exactly the same rate. Some portions will be ready for cutting ahead of others. Always cut *toward* the hull so the force of the knife does not pull the cloth away from the DuraKore.

Once the epoxy has cured beyond the rubbery stage, a knife won't trim the excess. Let the glue cure completely before trimming with either an electric sabersaw or a small "keyhole" hand saw for difficult areas. Use a special fiberglass-cutting blade in the sabersaw. If one is not available, try a coarse-tooth metal-cutting blade.

Whether you are using a knife or a saw, exercise care when trimming the laminate. Inattention will almost always result in cut fingers. Wear protective clothing including work gloves and safety goggles.

Ragged edges of reinforcement cloth can be trimmed with a knife when the epoxy is in its "rubber" stage of cure. An electric sabersaw works well once the epoxy fully hardens. Use caution to avoid cutting into the DuraKore sheer plank.

ADDITIONAL REINFORCEMENT LAYERS

Scantlings for larger boats call for two or more layers of fiberglass reinforcement. It's best if the second layer is applied before the glue of the first layer has completely cured. This allows a primary bond between the layers of the laminate instead of a potentially weaker secondary bond. It's necessary to plan ahead if primary bonding is to be attempted:

➤ Pre-fit all layers of fiberglass ahead of time in the dry. Be sure none of the seams in the second layer lies on top of the seams of the first, etc.
➤ Roll up and identify each section of cloth so that it can be applied in the correct position.
➤ Have enough epoxy resin and hardener on hand for all layers.

Applying the second layer over a gel-state first layer may be impossible on large hulls. There will be no "dry" places for workers to lean or stand on while applying the second layer. Also, a second layer should never be applied if the two layers will be so thick that they create excess heat during curing.

If the second layer cannot be applied directly over the first, the problem becomes creating a good secondary bond between layers. The first layer must be allowed to fully cure. Remove the amine blush and sand with 80-grit paper to ensure a good bond. Once the cured surface has been prepared, the second layer of fiberglass can be applied either dry or wet as required.

Using Release Fabrics

Peel Ply is the most common brand of special *release fabrics,* which have a variety of uses in epoxy laminating. These fabrics are made of finely woven nylon treated in a way that prevents epoxy from bonding to it. Release fabric is smoothed directly into the wet epoxy with a squeegee. Once the epoxy cures, the release fabric is pulled off, leaving behind a clean, matte surface ready for the next operation. A release fabric is said to eliminate the need for removing amine blush or sanding prior to application of additional laminations. (Some professionals use a release fabric but continue to wash off the amine blush and sand. Belt and suspenders . . . but it works.)

Cost often prevents amateurs from using a release fabric. After all, it isn't absolutely necessary and release fabric is relatively expensive. Some of the cost can be avoided by using the material carefully. More than one "peeling" is possible with the same piece of material. Despite the cost there is one time release fabric more than pays for itself: on the last lamination prior to final fairing. The surface left behind is extremely smooth and requires much less labor to sand.

Jim Watson gives this hint for easier lamination of fiberglass or other reinforcement materials to the hull. He lays a piece of release fabric on top of the wet glass cloth after rolling resin into the cloth but before the final squeegeeing of the glue. The release fabric allows the squeegee to move smoothly over the cloth without creating wrinkles or bubbles. Once the glue is properly dispersed, the release fabric is left in place until the epoxy cures.

Vacuum Bagging

If there's one technique associated with high-tech boat construction, it's vacuum bagging. Some boatbuilders are so secretive about this technique they refuse to let visitors see (or worse, photograph) their equipment. These builders are being secretive because they don't want everyone to know how simple it is to use air pressure as a giant "clamp." If you have a shop vacuum, you're more than halfway to doing your own vacuum bagging.

The concept behind bagging is simple: air pressure. Everything on earth is exposed to about 15 pounds per square inch of air pressure (at sea level). That amounts to roughly a ton of pressure per square foot! This pressure is spread absolutely evenly over every square inch of everything. Compare that with a conventional C-clamp with small jaws that pinch only a couple of square inches. Not only does air pressure not mar the surface of soft wood, but it also clamps complex shapes that would be impossible to clamp with metal devices.

A simple sheet of 7-mil polyethylene sheeting is all that's needed to harness air pressure. Cover any surface with this plastic and suck out the air beneath it, and you've theoretically created a one-ton-per-square-foot clamping pressure between the plastic and the surface. There's no force exerted on the underlying substrate by a vacuum bag. Air pressure pushing against the back side of the substrate exactly balances that on the top side of the plastic.

Polyethylene sheeting is not 100 percent airtight. Some air leaks through, lowering the vacuum inside the bag. Adding a second layer of polyethylene helps, but is cumbersome when hot epoxy is well on its way to kicking. Bigger air losses occur around the perimeter of the bag or at the vacuum inlet. A bag in an amateur shop seldom achieves even a third of the full clamping potential contained in normal air pressure, but that's still about 700 pounds per square foot.

The biggest advantage to vacuum bagging is controlling the resin-to-glass ratio in the laminate. Pressure from the bag squeezes extra resin out of the fiberglass. Not only is the resulting laminate stronger, it's lighter in weight because heavy excess resin has been removed. Another benefit of bagging is that it effectively eliminates outgassing problems. Pressure from the bag prevents gas bubbles from forming in the wet epoxy.

THE VACUUM BAG SANDWICH

A successful vacuum bag is more complex than a simple sheet of 7-mil polyethylene plastic. It consists of multiple layers. Starting from the top they are:

➤ The Bag Itself—Professionals use a modified nylon resin film that does not stretch and is virtually impervious to air. Seven-mil polyethylene film is far less expensive and will do an adequate job for most amateur projects. Always buy the best and thickest film available.

➤ Breather Layer—A lightweight nonwoven polyester blanket to provide plenty of air passage for evacuating the bag. As with impervious nylon film, this professional breather material is expensive. Ordinary bubble pack used to protect goods during shipment is an excellent home shop substitute that often can be obtained for free.

➤ Release Fabric—Always use a commercial release fabric to obtain a smooth, easily sanded surface. Bagging will work without a release fabric, but the resulting surface is exceptionally rough and requires hours of grinding to get fair and smooth.

➤ The Laminate—Usually fiberglass set in epoxy resin. Prior to bagging, lay up this laminate using either the dry or wet technique. Bag after final squeegeeing and pull a vacuum before the glue kicks. This technique works well when laminating complex shapes such as skegs or for flat surfaces like decks.

➤ The Substrate—This is the material to which the laminate is being bonded. In most applications, the substrate forms the "back" of the vacuum bag. Obviously, the substrate must be nearly impervious to air transfer.

Each layer of the sandwich is installed in turn, starting with the substrate and working up. The final step is sealing the edges where the polyethylene film meets the substrate. This is a job for that 20th-century miracle, duct tape. Use it generously to create a nearly airtight seal between the plastic film and the substrate. Smooth out as many wrinkles in the bag as possible before taping it into place.

PULLING A VACUUM

Somewhere near the middle of the bag use a razor blade to cut a small hole and insert the suction end of the shop vacuum hose. Seal the hole with more duct tape. Turn on the machine and watch the bag draw down on top of the laminate. Sometimes the bag seals off the vacuum hose as it draws down. If this happens, shove small pieces of wood through the plastic film to create a hard "cage" around the hose nozzle. Tape the holes shut with more duct tape and continue sucking down the bag. Listen for air leaks around the joint between the bag and the substrate. Once again, it's duct tape to the rescue.

The bag is fully sucked down when the tone of the vacuum motor changes. At the same time, discharge air from the vacuum machine is sharply reduced and becomes much warmer. These are signs that something must be done to prevent the vacuum motor from burning out. Crack open the connection between the hose and the body of the machine to let in just enough air to cool the motor. A ¼-inch opening is usually sufficient. Secure the hose with—you guessed it— more duct tape to keep the crack from accidentally closing.

Safety Note—Never leave an operating vacuum alone in the shop. Continuously monitor its operation to be sure the motor is not overheating. To avoid a fire hazard, disconnect the vacuum from electric power if the motor shows signs of overheating.

A portable vacuum gauge used by auto mechanics when tuning up cars is suitable for measuring the vacuum in the bag. Cut a cross of saw kerfs into a small square piece of 1-inch (25 mm) plywood. Drill a hole for the gauge hose barb at the point where the kerfs cross. Set the wood square inside the bag between the top film and the bubble pack with the kerfs down. Then punch the stem of the gauge through the polyethylene and duct tape around the hole to seal it. The saw kerfs in the wood channel the vacuum to the gauge.

A vacuum bag setup takes on a bit of a Rube Goldberg appearance, but it works. If its appearance embarrasses you, don't invite your neighbors to watch. While monitoring the vacuum motor you should see rivulets of epoxy being sucked out of the laminate toward the vacuum nozzle. This is excess glue being forced out of the fiberglass by pressure from the bag. Keep the bag under vacuum until the epoxy inside has gone into its first stage of cure (rubber). Then shut off the machine and let the whole contraption rest until the epoxy completely cures when the bag can be peeled apart.

HOME SHOP CONSIDERATIONS

A single shop vacuum is not powerful enough to bag the whole hull of a large cruiser. An industrial-size vacuum pump is needed for that.

Of course, two or more vacuums can be connected to larger bags, but there is a practical limit to this approach. That's why vacuum bagging in the home shop is generally limited to smaller projects or specific areas of the hull where the benefits outweigh the drawbacks of the complicated setup. The vacuum cleaner technique has worked successfully on several types of projects:

➤ Additional Reinforcement—Some designs call for patches of Kevlar, carbon fibers, or other special-purpose reinforcement materials to be applied at areas of unusual stress. In this case the fiberglass laminate becomes the substrate. Vacuum bagging ensures that the special patch stays in full contact with the substrate while the epoxy glue kicks. This gives a maximum strength secondary bond.

➤ Individual Pieces—Such as hatch covers or deck sections, which are small enough to fit into a single bag. This technique is particularly adaptable to composite pieces with difficult shapes.

➤ Areas of Unusual Shapes—Occasionally a hull or deck has a shape where it is difficult to get the fiberglass to lie in full contact with the substrate. A small bag taped to the surrounding substrate will keep the cloth in full contact until the resin cures.

➤ Decorative Veneers—A bag works well when laminating a decorative veneer such as Formica, especially to a curved surface. Do not bag thin wood veneers, as the vacuum will tend to pull the epoxy glue through the veneer, making it difficult to achieve an acceptable bright varnish finish.

➤ Wood Planked Decks—The weakest vacuum bag beats all other methods of clamping wood planks tightly to the deck while the epoxy glue kicks. Use the bag to ensure 100 percent contact between plank and deck. Staples or screws should be used to hold exact alignment of the planks, especially if they are sprung.

➤ Laminate Repairs—A vacuum bag is an excellent way to ensure that repairs to a composite laminate achieve maximum strength. The bag forces the patch and the original laminate to be in full contact so that full secondary bond strength can develop.

LAMINATING WITH POST-CURE RESINS

Both SYSTEM THREE and the Gougeon Brothers produce laminating resins designed for post-curing. The purpose of these resins is to increase the mechanical properties of the laminate and its ability to withstand higher temperatures without distortion. Some extremely advanced designs may require the additional strength or resistance to fatigue from vibration provided by post-cure resins. For the typical boat, however, the gains from using these materials are outweighed by their higher cost and the complexity of post-curing.

Laminating resins have different ratios from conventional epoxy glues. Special dispensing pumps calibrated for these ratios must be used. Otherwise, mixing and application are the same as with conventional epoxies. Laminating resins often exhibit a sudden onset of gelling at the end of their pot life. The initial cure to the glass-like "B Stage" takes 5 to 7 hours, but a complete cure can take up to a week at room temperatures.

Once these resins have cured, their mechanical properties can be enhanced by heating them to very specific temperatures. This process is known as "post-curing." A few professional shops have autoclaves large enough to hold an entire hull. This is impractical for amateur builders, who must rely on far less expensive methods.

The simplest but least accurate method of post-curing is to cover the boat with black polyethylene plastic and set it in the sun. The plastic absorbs energy from the sun, heating the boat inside to surprisingly high temperatures. This method is not recommended because there is no way to control the post-cure process. Some areas of the hull may be completely post-cured while others are unchanged because of insufficient temperature.

"It's critical to control the ramping up of the post-cure temperature," says Jim Watson. ("Ramping" is technical jargon for the speed at which a material is raised from one temperature to another.) "You don't want it to go up too fast. Nor do you want the final temperature to be too high," he says. Ramping speed and optimal post-cure temperatures are specified by the various resin manufacturers.

CONTROLLED HEAT APPLICATION

A bank of electric heat lamps can be used to slowly raise the temperature of a section of the hull for post-curing. Suitable fixtures are either not available or extremely expensive. However, a homemade one is easily built by mounting ceramic bulb receptacles (called "cleats" by electricians) to a board. Use at least AWG 16 wire or heavier. The heat lamps do not need to be extremely close together. It may be desirable to hinge the board so that it can conform better to the shape of the hull.

In use, the bank of heat lamps warms only a narrow band of the hull at a time. The distance from the lamps to the hull determines the "ramp up" speed as well as the ultimate temperature. Once a portion of the hull has been post-cured for the required time, the lamps are moved to the next section. This continues until the entire hull is post-cured. The process for a large hull can take days to complete.

"The problem with post-curing a material like DuraKore is the high R-value of the balsa wood," says Jim Watson. (R-value is the ability of a material to insulate against heat or cold.) "The outside of the hull which is being heated by the lamps may get warm, but that heat doesn't penetrate the core. The inside stays cool and doesn't always post-cure properly."

Maintaining the correct temperature of the laminate is critical to successful post-curing. An easy way to do this is to put self-stick liquid crystal thermometers at regular intervals on the surface of the hull. Low temperature versions are available at pet stores, where they are sold for monitoring the temperature of fish tanks. A wider selection of self-stick thermometers is available from Edmund Scientific, 101 East Gloucester Pike, Barrington, NJ 08007.

Post-curing requires close attention to detail over extended periods of time. It should not be attempted unless you are willing to make a full commitment of time and effort to the project. In most cases, a perfectly adequate vessel can be constructed using conventional epoxy materials.

Safety Warning—Care must be exercised against the dangers of fire and electrocution when post-curing with heat lamps. Never leave heat lamps unattended. Constantly monitor the temperature of the laminate and all surrounding materials. Observe proper electrical safety precautions, including polarity and grounding. Have a fire extinguisher handy and post the phone number of the fire department near the telephone.

Chapter 9
STEMS, STERNS, AND DIFFICULTIES

The chapter on planking made boatbuilding seem easy. And, in truth, the planking does go quickly. But like any technique, DuraKore composite strip construction has a few unique problems. You may not encounter any of them, or you may face all of them.

PERMANENT MOLD FRAMES

Our discussion so far has focused on building the hull over temporary section molds that are discarded after construction. While this is the typical situation, some boats require permanent section molds that remain in the boat after construction. Permanent mold frames of this type are commonly used as interior bulkheads or furniture. They remain in the hull to give it strength during rollover and as part of the completed interior.

So-called "permanent molds" are more complicated to construct than disposable male mold frames. Here's why: DuraKore strip composite technique requires a continuous inner structural skin of fiberglass reinforcing material. Permanent mold frames prevent application of the inner skin as a continuous strip. The solution suggested by Baltek is a tab of reinforcement material and epoxy attached around the outer perimeter of the permanent mold. This tab becomes the inner skin after the hull is planked.

Measure the girth of the permanent mold from sheerline to sheerline around the keel. Add about a foot to this measurement to determine the length of tabbing needed. Cover the work surface with polyethylene sheeting smoothed to remove wrinkles. Use duct tape to hold the polyethylene down. The length of the tab usually forces the work to be done on the floor. Unroll a length of fiberglass reinforcement fabric equal to the length and width of the required tab. Smooth it out on top of the work surface.

RESIN APPLICATION

Mix a small quantity of epoxy and pour it into a pool near the center of the fabric. Spread this epoxy evenly over the surface of the fabric with a foam roller. Follow the roller with a flexible squeegee to remove puddles of excess epoxy and eliminate air trapped in the wet fabric. Drag the squeegee in overlapping strokes. Use firm, even pressure, but too much force will cause the fabric to squirm around on the slippery polyethylene sheeting. It may also create dry spots if too much resin is pushed away from a particular area.

Continue mixing and pouring batches of resin until the entire surface of the fabric panel is saturated. Check for dry areas as you go. Rewet these areas with a small amount of resin applied with the squeegee. The layup schedule of this strip should be the same as that for the inner skin of the hull. If more than one layer of cloth is called for in the skin, it should be applied on top of the first layer of the tab while the glue is still wet. Orient the weaves of the cloth correctly and apply more resin. Roll and squeegee as above.

When the entire length of the tab is coated, clean up your tools and go for coffee. Let the resin cure before going on to the next step.

FINISHING THE TAB

Allow the panel of fabric to fully cure. Remove the amine blush and rough sand both sides with 80-grit paper. Use a chalk line to "snap" straight lines along each edge. The width of the finished tab should be at least 12 inches (30 cm) plus the thickness of the permanent mold. This allows a minimum of 6 inches of tab to extend on either side of the bulkhead when it is installed in the hull.

Trim the panel using an electric sabersaw equipped with a special fiberglass-cutting blade. If this type of blade is not available, a coarse-toothed metal-cutting blade may be substituted, but expect it to wear out quickly as it chews through the glass inside the laminate. Changing blades several times may be necessary. Bond the trimmed tab to the outer edge of the permanent mold frame using thickened epoxy. This is easiest to do after the permanent mold has been erected in the building form. Attach the prefabricated tab to the mold with staples, nails, or plastic fasteners while the thickened epoxy bonding resin cures.

During planking, the DuraKore strips that go across permanent mold frames are bonded to the tabs using the same thickened epoxy mixture used to bond the DuraKore strips together. Later, when the hull is rolled over, the inner reinforcement skin will be laminated over the tabs to create a continuous structural skin beneath the bulkhead.

SPECIAL CONSIDERATIONS

A word of warning about tab thickness. Adding a tab to the permanent mold increases its circumference by the thickness of the tab. An unfair spot in the hull results unless the permanent mold is reduced by the thickness of the tab. This reduction is in addition to the normal reduction for skin thickness. Reducing the size of the mold must be done when it is cut, prior to attaching the bonding tab.

Some permanent molds have shapes that are too highly curved for attaching a tab of cured resin and fabric. In this case, it may be necessary to install the tab on the mold while the resin is still in the "rubbery" stage of cure. The edge is trimmed after the tab is bonded into position and all of the epoxy involved has fully cured.

KEEL TIMBERS

An actual timber keel is not required in a DuraKore strip composite boat any more than it is in a standard FRP boat. At the risk of repetition: A high-tech cored hull gets its primary strength from the total laminate of exterior skins separated by the core, and not from structural timbers. Yet installing a timber keel does have two significant benefits for the amateur builder: (1) It defines the centerline of the boat, giving a visual reference for planking the bottom; and (2) a timber keel provides noncrushable support for external fin keels or ballast.

A timber keel can be made of a single piece of wood or laminated from several thin strips. Laminating is the preferred method, especially if there is significant shape to the keel. Unlike the stem, the keel does not require a special lamination jig. The work can be done directly on the building form prior to installation of the stem or transom. The width of the keel timber may not be the same throughout its length. For instance, on a fin keel sailboat the timber keel widens out amidships to provide support for the full "footprint" of the external fin.

If the timber keel is the same thickness as the DuraKore planking,

Notches were cut into the station molds of the Marine Trades Center boat to accommodate a full-length solid timber keel. Note that the keel is rabbeted to accept the DuraKore strips. (Courtesy WCTC)

there will be no notches in the mold frames to hold it. The keel piece is temporarily installed like any other plank while the DuraKore strips are bonded over the mold. If the keel timber widens for structural reasons, it may be necessary to create a "flat spot" on the molds to allow the keel to sit properly.

If the keel timber is thicker than the DuraKore strips, you must cut notches into the section mold frames. Normally, the notches are made deep enough to allow the outside of the keel to lie flush with the outside of the DuraKore strips when the hull is planked. Notches in permanent mold frames should have provision for limber holes.

Drywall screws can be used as temporary fasteners to hold the keel timber in place during planking of the hull. Fit everything dry first. If there is considerable rocker to the bottom of the boat, the keel may be laminated from thin layers of wood. This work is done on the building mold prior to any planking. Extend the laminations beyond both the stem joint and the stern so that bracing can be used to pull these extensions into their proper shape. The ends of the keel are trimmed once the glue has kicked.

Laminate the keel timber using epoxy glue. Start on the midships frame first, then work toward the bow and stern. Drywall screws can be used to hold the wet stack of wood, but additional C-clamps will be needed between section molds to maintain even clamping pressure. Pad the jaws of the clamps with scraps of wood to prevent marring the wood. Small squares of polyethylene sheeting will keep the pads from bonding to the keel timber. Be sure that notches in all temporary mold frames are also protected with polyethylene. Scrape off glue that squeezes out of the joints before it cures.

After the glue has fully cured, the laminated keel timber should be removed from the mold to the workbench. Use a disk sander to smooth the sides and remove any excess gobs of glue. The keel timber is then replaced on the mold and bonded to all permanent mold frames with thickened epoxy. Double-check that limber holes are not filled with glue during bonding.

KEEL BEVELS AND SHAPE

Conventional wooden boat construction requires complex bevels on keel timbers. Similar bevels are needed in traditional cold molding. Conventional construction demands complex shapes because structural keels have large dimensions to give the required longitudinal strength. In strip composite construction, strength comes from the mechanical relationship of the inner core (DuraKore strips) and its reinforcement skins. Heavy structural keel timbers are no longer needed. If they exist at all, keel timbers of a DuraKore hull serve as non-crushable core materials rather than structural members.

Relieved of the necessity of bulk for strength, keel timbers in DuraKore boats can be reduced in size. In thickness, the goal is to have a smooth transition between the edge of the timber keel and the DuraKore planking battens. A sharp change in thickness creates a problem that engineers call a "stress riser." Laminate failures are common at stress risers. Also, a sharp change in thickness makes it extremely difficult to install reinforcing materials properly. Being fabric, these materials do not adhere well to sharp bends. Keep in mind the I-beam nature of composite construction. All engineering must be aimed at maintaining the integrity of the relationship between the external skins and the internal core of the laminate.

Composite construction also eliminates the need for the long beveled bonding surfaces required in cold-molded construction. DuraKore strips can be butted against the keel timber using thickened epoxy as glue. This is a major advantage of strip composite construction for the amateur builder. The difficult job of cutting complex bevels on the keels and stems is avoided. This eliminates a lot of expensive mistakes and lost time.

The longitudinal stiffness of DuraKore strip composite construction is substantial, as one East Coast builder of powerboats discovered. His triple-diagonal planked cold-molded hulls proved acceptable to speeds above 35 knots. But cold-molded hulls were too flexible for the job when customers demanded 50-knot boats. High speeds caused them to flex so much that welds on aluminum tuna towers broke apart. This builder could have added additional thickness to his cold-molded hulls, but extra weight would have reduced boat speed. By switching to DuraKore, he solved his flexing problem without increasing weight. His DuraKore strip composite boats exceed 50 knots without straining the towers or upper cabin works. These boats do not have keel timbers as such. They rely on the DuraKore planking and internal stringers for longitudinal stiffness.

Some designs may require (or you may feel more comfortable with) a heavier keel than described above. There is no engineering reason that additional thickness pieces cannot be added either inside or outside of the hull (or both) once the reinforcing skins have been applied. Laminate the thickness pieces on top of the skin using thickened epoxy glue. Bevel or taper the laminations for installation of an epoxy/fabric skin over the thickness piece. Putting a skin over the thickness piece encapsulates it for protection against water or other damage. It also creates a box beam section for added strength.

MAINE BOATBUILDING SCHOOL

Many of the photographs in this book were made by students at the Marine Trades Center of the Washington County Technical College in Eastport, Maine. This is a hands-on school for professional boatbuilders and mechanics. Graduates have gained a national reputation for excellence.

The hull under construction is a New England-style workboat similar to those used for lobstering. Designed by Bret Blanchard of the college's staff, it is 20 feet long. With typical "Down East" conservatism, it has a hefty timber keel and stem piece as well as timber sheer clamps.

JOINING KEEL TO STEM

Stem and keel pieces should be joined in an 8:1 ratio scarf joint. It may be easiest to cut the scarf on the keel timber first, then match the stem piece to it. Hand sawing is the safest approach to scarfing for the inexperienced. Mark cut lines on both sides of the piece to guide the saw. Keep the saw kerf *outside* of this line at all times, leaving a small amount of extra material for removal by sanding or planing. Offer the joint up, checking total alignment of the pieces and making careful adjustments until the dry fit is perfect. Apply epoxy glue to both surfaces of the scarf and install the stem piece in the building mold. C-clamps should be used to provide clamping pressure directly on the joint until the glue cures. As usual, wipe up any squeezings before they harden.

STEM TIMBERS AND BOW SHAPES

In theory, a strip composite hull doesn't need an actual stem piece any more than it needs a keel timber. In fact, professionals building in female molds usually don't include a stem piece in their boats. This omission is permissible because DuraKore planking from each side of the hull meets exactly along the centerline of the bow. This allows the inner and outer reinforcement skins to be continuous through the V-shape of the bow. The I-beam concept remains unbroken. Professionals have the skill to accomplish this technique. It is not suggested to the inexperienced.

DuraKore strip composite construction is still new enough that there is no clear agreement on the best way to build stems. However, two techniques seem to be dominating amateur construction. One, the *stem cap*, works best on multihull floats built in female molds. The other, a conventional *laminated stem timber*, works best on monohull sailboats and powerboats built over male molds. It should be noted that both of these techniques also can be used for the sterns of double-ended hulls. However, the laminated timber method is required when the vessel is to receive an external, stern-hung rudder.

LAMINATED TIMBER METHOD

A great advantage of planking a traditional wooden boat is that the stem piece gives a physical place to "land" the planks. Building a laminated wooden stem into a strip composite boat carries this concept into the high-tech world. A laminated stem creates the required profile of the bow, and it gives a solid timber onto which the DuraKore battens can be glued. This method is highly recommended when constructing a hull over a male mold.

Start by drawing the stem profile on a suitable sheet of plywood. This profile should be equivalent to the "rabbet line" of conventional boatbuilding and not the exterior profile of the stem. Attach clamping blocks to the plywood pattern so they are tangent to the outside of the drawn shape. Spacing of the blocks will vary depending upon the amount of curve. Tight radius curves require more blocks than long, gently curving stretches. Use only as many blocks as necessary to obtain the desired shape.

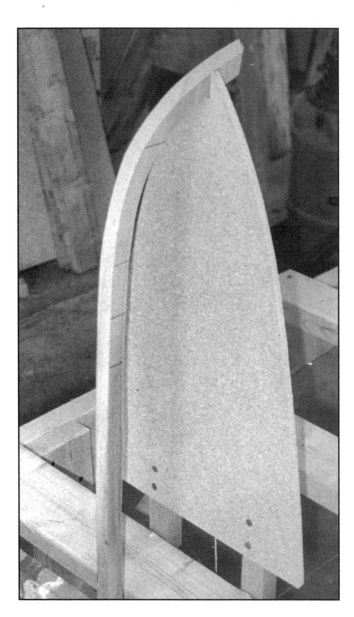

Thin strips of boat-quality mahogany are ideal for laminating a stem. They are easily re-sawn out of lumberyard dimensional stock, or have them milled to your specifications. Cut them as wide as the finished stem and thin enough to allow the wood to make the required bends. The finished stem should have five or more laminations. Re-saw one strip and try it in the bending jig before getting out the entire stack.

Protect the plywood and clamping blocks of the bending jig with sheet vinyl to prevent the laminations from bonding to it. Coat all mating surfaces of the strips with epoxy glue before assembling them into the jig. This will be messy, so be sure to wear rubber gloves. Use steel C-clamps to hold the strips in the jig. Pad the jaws of the clamps with a scrap of wood and a small square of sheet vinyl to prevent sticking. Place additional clamps between the blocks as needed to obtain even clamping pressure. All of the glue seams should be the same thickness their entire length.

Once the strips are bent to shape, use a soft mallet to square up any edges protruding from the laminated bundle. Clean up as much of the excess epoxy as possible while it's still soft.

Don't be surprised if the laminated stem does not quite retain the right shape after the epoxy cures. Most laminations experience "springback," a relaxing of sharp radius curves. Check the piece against the lofting. If necessary, glue extra wood where required, then saw or plane it back to the correct shape.

The sides of the laminated stem are somewhat rough at this point. The easiest way to dress them is with a thickness planer, although the hardened epoxy is hard on planer knives. A disk sander also makes quick work of this job if it is kept absolutely flat against the work and at 90 degrees to the sides of the laminates. Anyone skilled with hand tools should also be able to get the job done with a hand plane, although not without a bit of elbow grease. Cured epoxy loves to take the edge off a sharp plane blade.

INSTALLING THE STEM

Provision must be made for mounting the laminated stem on the proper section mold and on the strongback. In most cases, the sec-

(left) *Extra layers of reinforcement material may be necessary across the stem. A roller helps wet out the fabric and smooth down the inevitable wrinkles. Final smoothing is done with a squeegee.*

(right) *Reinforcement fabric from the sides and bottom of the hull should be carried "around the corner" at the transom. Fabric for the transom is laid over top, which ensures that the reinforcement layer is continuous from side to transom.*

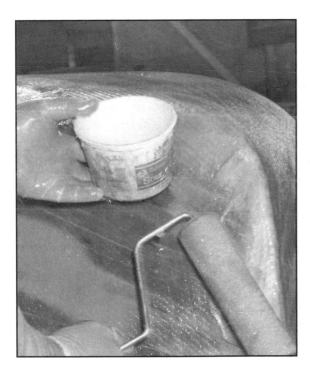

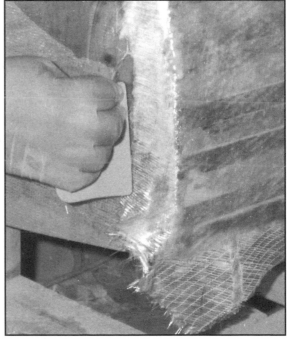

tion mold will be notched so that the outside of the stem lies flush with the outer veneer of the DuraKore planking. Extra length is normally allowed on the stem piece for attaching it to the strongback. This extra length is trimmed off prior to installation of the deck. (Note: If a keel is to be installed, the stem requires additional extra length past the first section mold for a scarf joint.)

Hulls with steeply raked stems usually require extra section molds notched to accept the stem piece. Drywall screws are excellent for attaching the stem to the building form. Keep in mind that they have to be removed before the completed hull can be removed from the building form. Also, it may be necessary to install additional temporary bracing to ensure that the stem remains properly aligned with the centerline of the hull during planking.

ATTACHING THE PLANKING

If planking is started at the bow, there should be little trouble in getting the DuraKore battens to "land" properly on the stem. Simply cut the end of the batten to roughly match the angle at which it will strike the laminated stem. Minor adjustments can be made with a Stanley Surform tool.

On some hulls, it's advantageous to attach the DuraKore amidships first and work toward the bow and stern. This requires slightly more difficult fitting, although it can be done with hand tools. Most workers can "eyeball" the proper angle, especially after the second or third try. Remember to leave the strip a bit too long after the first cut and trim back as necessary. If the piece is cut too short, no matter how many times you trim it back, the batten will still be too short.

Thickened epoxy glue is used in the seams to bond the planking to the stem. Hold the strips in place with drywall screws, staples, or double-headed nails while this glue cures. Some work can be saved by using Monel staples or plastic fasteners, which do not require removal before applying the reinforcement material.

FINISHING THE STEM

Once the epoxy has cured, the wooden stem can be sanded to the desired contour. The final step on the exterior is application of the reinforcing material set in epoxy resin. Inside, the sharp V-shaped channel on either side of the stem where the planks attach must be filled with a thickened epoxy fillet. This fillet adds strength to the bond holding the DuraKore to the stem and fills these grooves to make applying the inside reinforcing material easier. Without fillets along the stem it's difficult to get a continuous layer of reinforcement across the inside of the stem.

ADDITIONAL THOUGHTS

A laminated stem is best from a strength-to-weight standpoint. There is no reason, however, why the stem could not be made of sawn pieces in a traditional manner. These should be glued together with epoxy before being installed on the building form. Small craft such as dinghies may get by with one-piece sawn stems. Choose the method that gives an absolutely true stem without warping or twists.

In theory, the stem (laminated or sawn) need only be as thick as the DuraKore strips and as deep as the bearding line. This is because the boat gets its strength from the sandwich construction of outer reinforcing skins around a core. Such a small stem piece would be difficult to construct and nearly impossible to keep properly aligned on the building form. From a practical standpoint, a timber stem has to be somewhat larger than necessary just to accept the DuraKore strips. But how much larger? There is disagreement here, but a safe rule of thumb is to make it at least heavy enough to support itself without distortion.

SHEER CLAMPS

A sheer clamp is an internal timber that runs right along the top of the hull at the sheerline. It both strengthens the topsides of the hull and provides support for the deck. A sheer clamp is a critical timber in a conventional wooden boat, but may be dispensed with in composite core construction. The sheer clamp is not necessary if the designer takes full advantage of both the nature of DuraKore construction and the strength that can be gained through the shape of the hull-to-deck joint. There are, however, some solid reasons an amateur builder may want to include a sheer clamp:

> ➤ For Maintaining Shape—A sheer clamp laminated in place on the mold frames provides considerable assurance that the topsides will not change shape after the molds are removed.

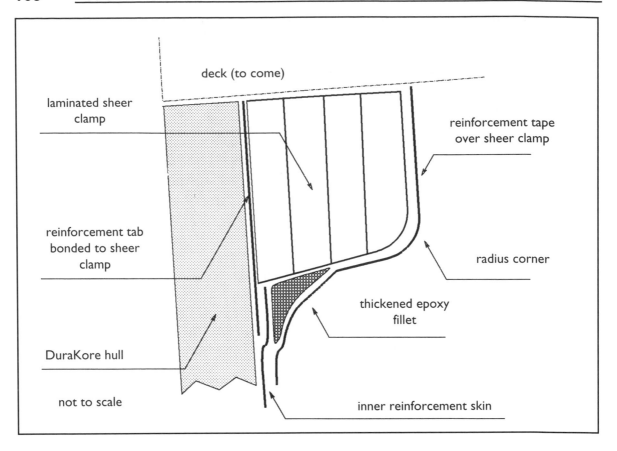

deck (to come)

laminated sheer
clamp

reinforcement tape
over sheer clamp

reinforcement tab
bonded to sheer
clamp

radius corner

thickened epoxy
fillet

DuraKore hull

not to scale

inner reinforcement skin

A sheer clamp can be laminated of DuraKore and then installed. The number of laminations should be part of the scantlings supplied by the boat's designer.

➤ For Attaching the Deck—The sheer clamp provides a wide, flat "flange" along the sheerline on which to bond the deck. A timber clamp also may be notched to support deck beams.

LAMINATED TIMBER

This type of sheer clamp is laminated in place on the building mold. The mold frames must be notched to accept the individual timber laminates. Any standard boatbuilding wood can be used, although mahogany provides a good combination of strength with affinity for epoxy glue.

Get out the pieces to be laminated from the timber stock. Put them together "dry" on the building mold. Use drywall screws and washers to hold the stack of laminations together. Trim and fit the pieces, then disassemble the stack. Number each piece as it is removed from the mold. These numbers are used to ensure that each piece goes back on the mold in its correct place.

Be sure all notches in the mold frames are protected against epoxy. Apply unthickened epoxy glue to all mating surfaces of the timber laminations before reinstalling them on the mold. Tighten the drywall screws until the glue squeezes out. Additional clamps may be needed between the temporary screws. Clean up as much of the glue squeezings as possible before the glue kicks.

If the cleanup went well, the laminated sheer clamp may not require additional finishing if it does not show in the completed boat. If the clamp shows, remove it from the building form for sanding and shaping. Reinstall the laminated timber sheer clamp on the building form before planking the mold.

The I-beam concept of DuraKore strip composite construction requires a continuous relationship between the balsa core and the reinforcement

skins. Just as with permanent mold frames, a timber sheer clamp can receive a tab of reinforcement fabric before the hull is planked. This tab allows the inner skin to be continuous from keel to sheerline. Adding a tab to the sheer clamp requires increasing the depth of the cutout in the mold, or the thickness of the tab may create unfairness during planking.

Some boats have successfully been built by bonding the DuraKore planking directly to a laminated sheer clamp. The inner reinforcement skin was then bonded over the timber as shown in the drawing.

Solid wood is the most practical material for the sheer clamp of a small dinghy. Here, solid mahogany strips are being installed on the author's boat. The wood was bedded in polyurethane caulking and screwed every 3 inches. Black-colored thickened epoxy was used to fill the gap between the inner and outer wood strips.

BALSA-CORE SHEER CLAMP

The problem of notching the building form molds can be avoided by installing the sheer clamp after the hull is planked. In this case, the use of timber (laminated or solid) is not suggested. Rather, the sheer clamp is built up from DuraKore strips cut from planks. These strips are bonded along the inside of the sheerline using thickened epoxy.

Once the glue dries, the top of the clamp is trimmed to match the sheerline. At the same time, it should be given the required bevel to support the deck.

This type of sheer clamp should be installed after the inner reinforcement skin has been installed. After it is trimmed, reinforcement fabric should be laminated over the clamp.

TRANSOMS

First-time builders are urged to choose a design with the simplest possible transom. Flat transoms with little or no rake are the easiest to loft and install. While there is no doubt that a curved and raked transom is far more "eye sweet," the aggravation involved in building one has stopped more than one amateur boatbuilder's career. However, if you're in the hair shirt crowd, DuraKore strips are perfect for creating complex transom shapes. The process is identical to that used in planking the hull.

A transom effectively becomes a permanent mold frame if it is installed before planking begins. Transoms are normally not installed on hulls being built in female molds until all of the planking has been hung. The planking crew uses the opening created by the missing transom for access into the mold during the planking process.

FLAT TRANSOMS (SMALL POWERBOATS)

The typical powerboat transom is either straight up and down or raked a few degrees. Most builders using male forms prefer to install the transom on the strongback before planking the hull. The difference between a bulkhead used as a permanent mold and a transom is that the transom does not require the glass tabbing used on the bulkhead. The reason goes back to the engineering concept behind cored laminate construction.

A midships bulkhead glued to the wood veneer of the DuraKore interrupts the continuity of the inner reinforcing skin. Tabbing on permanent mold frames is just a way of pre-installing the inner skin between the bulkhead and the DuraKore strips. However, the transom is not a bulkhead. It's part of the hull core and will receive reinforcing material on both sides. Thus, the transom doesn't need tabbing, just a good epoxy glue joint where the DuraKore lands.

MATERIAL CHOICES

Deciding what material to use for a flat transom depends on whether it will bear weight. Transoms of conventional inboard boats carry little more than their own weight, so they do not need to be any stronger than other portions of the hull topsides. It's a different story with outboard or sterndrive powered boats, where the transom supports considerable weight of machinery and is the structural member that receives thrust from the propeller. These jobs require a great deal of strength.

The easiest way to build a flat, non-loadbearing transom for a conventional inboard powerboat is to use 4 x 8-foot sheets of DecoLite. If the transom is too large for one sheet, several can be lap or spline joined together. Loft out the shape directly onto the DecoLite surface, or transfer it from the full-size Mylar computer loftings.

Weight-bearing transoms are best made out of the highest grade marine plywood available. True, Baltek produces a high-density balsa-core material made specifically for powerboat transoms, but the cost is seldom justified in amateur construction. If plywood of the required thickness (as specified by the boat's designer) is not available, two sheets can be laminated together using epoxy.

To laminate your own plywood, start by spreading a 10-foot square of polyethylene film on the floor and laying both sheets of wood on it. Use a long-handled roller to apply the mixed epoxy to the upper sides of both sheets. Then flop one sheet onto the other, glue to glue. Fold the poly film over this "sandwich" and apply as much weight as possible. Cement blocks work well, as do old anvils and other heavy objects. Make sure the weight is spread out evenly

This transom is made of one piece of DecoLite. On the building form it serves as a permanent station mold. Note that the supports are angled to give the transom its proper slant in the completed boat.

over the surface of the sandwich. Let the epoxy kick for at least 24 hours before handling the resulting laminate.

TRANSOM BEVEL

Study the lines drawing for a few minutes before warming up your sabersaw to get out the transom. Note that the DuraKore planking seldom lands on the transom at a 90-degree angle, particularly if the transom is raked. The difference between a right angle joint and the actual angle between the transom and the side planks is known as the "transom bevel." In planing hulls the bevel is most pronounced in the bottom planking on either side of the keel line.

This bevel must be reproduced on the appropriate edges of the transom as it is cut out of the DecoLite or plywood stock. Adjusting the sole plate of the sabersaw is the easiest way to cut at a consistent angle. If you are working from the outside face of the transom, the inner surface (facing down) will seem to be *longer*. The reverse is true if your cut line is on the inside of the transom.

Keep in mind that the transom angle varies continuously from keel to sheer. It may be necessary to cut the transom in stages, each with a slightly different angle. Once the bevel is cut, it can be smoothed out with a power sander. Don't worry too much about perfection, since minor gaps can be filled with thickened epoxy during bonding.

ATTACHING PLANKS (MALE MOLD)

Hood ends of the DuraKore planking attach to the transom with thickened epoxy in the same manner as the rest of the hull is glued together. Depending upon the shape of the hull, it may be necessary to hold the planks against the transom while the glue kicks. Temporary screws into a plywood transom will hold nicely, but this solution can be dicey with balsa-cored DecoLite. Use creativity: weights, a Spanish windlass, or light lashings from the ends of the planks to the strongback are all possible ways of holding the strips in position.

It is easiest to leave the hood ends long at the transom until the glue has cured. Then trim the planks fair to the transom with a saw. (A sabersaw is fast, but a hand saw is less likely to cause damage.) Coat the exposed ends of the DuraKore strips with epoxy to seal them.

CURVED TRANSOMS

A curved transom is most easily built on a special mold separate from the main hull. Large ones are done on the shop floor, but smaller transom molds can be set on sawhorses for a more comfortable work height. Loft and fair the transom mold in the same manner as the hull, but don't worry too much about the outer shape until after the DuraKore has been applied. Planking is done in the same manner as the hull, using glued-up battens and thickened epoxy glue. Clean off the squeezings and seal coat the transom blank in the same manner as the hull.

It's customary to plank transoms horizontally, but DuraKore strips can just as well run vertically. In fact, vertical planking may be the better choice for a curved transom. Back in the chapter on lofting we learned that architects develop curved transoms from a section of a cylinder. Naturally, it is much easier to build a cylinder with nearly straight vertical strips (like the staves of a barrel) than horizontal ones that have to be bent into shape.

The stern of the Freedom 35 prototype lies on its male mold. Workers have trimmed it to shape prior to laminating the reinforcement fabric.
(Photo by Billy Black courtesy Baltek Corp.)

Once the epoxy has cured, lay out the lofted shape of the transom right on the glued-up blank. Use a sabersaw to trim the blank to create the transom. Just as with a flat transom, it is necessary to bevel the edges of this curved piece ("transom bevel").

Install the finished transom (still on its special building mold) onto the hull mold strongback. If you have planned ahead, framing of the transom mold will attach to the hull strongback and hold the piece in position. Obviously, the temporary fasteners holding the transom strips to the building mold should not be removed at this point. They remain in place until the transom is glued into the hull and is ready for application of the exterior skin.

Kerf-bending a panel involves cutting a series of saw kerfs about two-thirds of the way through the material. These kerfs allow the panel to bend around a tight radius without breaking. They are filled with thickened epoxy for strength.

FANTAIL STERNS

From a construction standpoint, a fantail stern is similar to a bow, especially below the "knuckle." The only major difference may be internal strengthening to carry the strain of rudder and propeller.

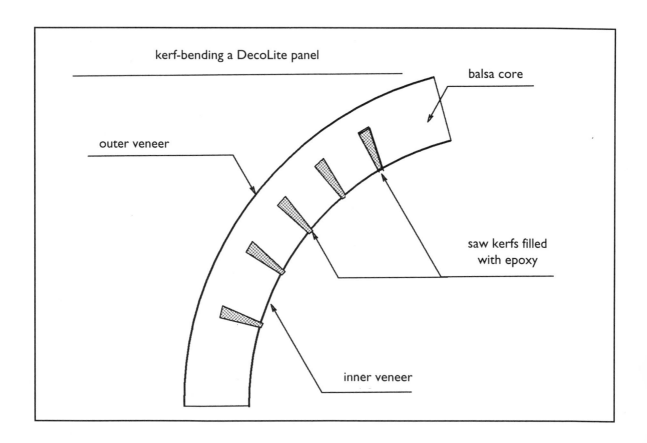

kerf-bending a DecoLite panel

balsa core

outer veneer

saw kerfs filled with epoxy

inner veneer

The "knuckle" is the sharp change in shape where the upsweep of the underbody meets the circular bulwark around the stern. It disappears as a structural shape forward of the stern quarter, but may be carried forward as a trim strip.

Planking below the knuckle is done exactly as it would be at the bow. Some "joggle" planks may be necessary at the knuckle where planking running in different orientations meets. Bending DuraKore strips around a tight-radius stern requires careful workmanship and lots of vertical pins to keep the outer veneers aligned. Many fantail sterns, however, have a radius smaller than can be accomplished with a standard strip.

In this case, make saw kerfs through the inside wood veneer and just *partway* through the balsa core, but not through the exterior veneer. The exact width and depth has to be found by trial and error, but it's best to cut no deeper than two-thirds of the way through the strip. These kerfs remove enough material to allow the strip to bend in a tighter radius. The number of kerfs needed varies with the ratio of radius of the bend to strip thickness. In general, the tighter the radius, the more kerfs needed. Fill saw kerfs with thickened epoxy as the stern is planked.

Kerf bending is the preferred method until the radius of the curve becomes extremely confined. Then, better results can be obtained by vertical planking.

SKEG AND DEADWOOD

Skegs and deadwood pieces of traditional hulls are built up as part of the structural keel. This type of construction can be echoed in strip composite construction by laminating a stack of DuraKore cut from planks to the appropriate shape. Cover this stack with a reinforcement skin after it's bonded to the hull. It sounds simple, but several things must be kept in mind:

➤ The grain of the DuraKore veneers should run in a fore-and-aft direction.
➤ The balsa grain (inside the DuraKore) should be oriented vertically to best absorb impact (such as an unexpected grounding).
➤ The outer reinforcing material of the hull should run continuously *beneath* and *around* the skeg.

➤ Additional outer reinforcing material may cover the skeg and be bonded into the skin on the hull.

LAMINATING THE SKEG

Unless the boat has an absolutely straight keel line, the skeg has to be laminated on the overturned hull to ensure that it has the right shape along its length. This is a two-step process. The stack is laminated on the hull, then removed for final shaping and smoothing. While it's off, the outer layers of fiberglass are applied to the hull. Then the skeg is reinstalled on the hull and bonded with thickened epoxy.

Placing a layer of polyvinyl sheet between the hull and the skeg while the Durakore stack is laminated keeps the two from bonding

A skeg can be laminated out of DuraKore strips. The grain of the balsa should be oriented as shown for maximum strength.

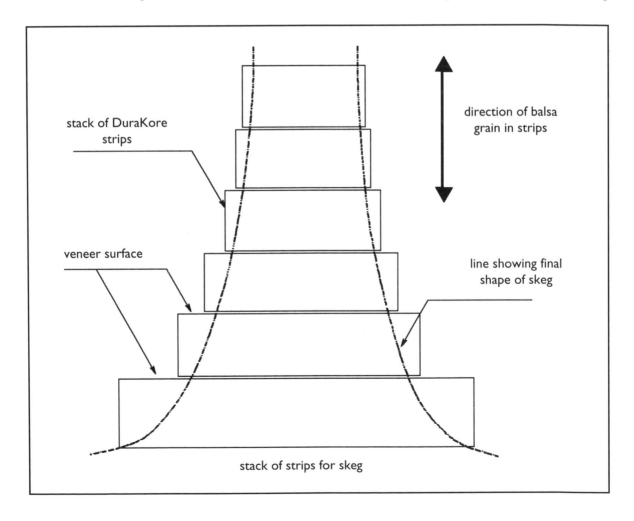

stack of DuraKore strips

direction of balsa grain in strips

veneer surface

line showing final shape of skeg

stack of strips for skeg

prematurely. Cut the plastic sheeting wide enough to catch the glue drips or spills that are inevitable during the layup of a multi-layer laminate. Position the sheeting on the hull with temporary staples, thumbtacks, or duct tape.

Depending upon the width of the skeg, it may be laminated out of the same DuraKore strips as used in the hull. Or the widest layers can be cut out of DuraKore planks lapped together into the required length. As in planking the hull, make sure to stagger joints in the lamination stack. The width of each piece in the stack should only be enough to allow for grinding or sanding to the required cross section. In most cases, the layer in the stack closest to the hull will be the widest, with each succeeding layer a bit narrower. Use thickened epoxy to glue everything together, and remove any excess that squeezes out before it hardens.

Once the epoxy has cured, the laminated stack can be trimmed to the required shape, a job done more easily off the boat. The completed skeg is then laminated to the hull.

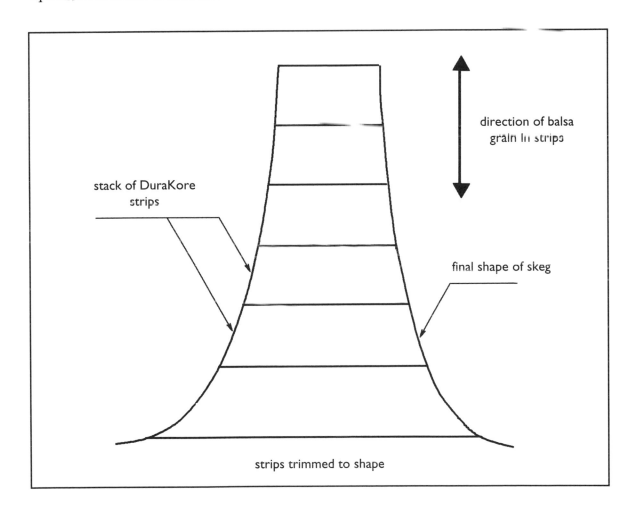

direction of balsa grain in strips

stack of DuraKore strips

final shape of skeg

strips trimmed to shape

SHAPING THE SKEG

Once the epoxy has kicked, the laminated skeg is removed from the hull for final shaping on the workbench. Old-timers might reach for a coving plane with its rounded sole plate to give a smooth transition from the widest to thinnest sections of the skeg. Modern workers get the same job done with an electric die grinder or circular sander. Power tools work faster but are a lot quicker to make big mistakes. Caution is advised. Don't be overly concerned if a bit too much material is occasionally removed, however. It can be replaced with epoxy putty during the final fairing and smoothing of the hull.

Templates based on the full-size lofting or made from full-size computer patterns are needed to guide the shaping operation. Cut them out of scrap ¼-inch plywood, as they will see a lot of use in checking the shape of the skeg during sanding. Paper and cardboard are too flimsy for the job. Number each template with its corresponding section frame.

BONDING THE SKEG TO THE HULL

The outer reinforcing material (fiberglass and epoxy) must be laminated across the keel line before the skeg is bonded into position.

Trimmed roughly to shape, the stack of DuraKore strips is installed on the hull using thickened epoxy. It will be given its final shape after the glue cures. The skeg is applied over top of the reinforcement fabric on the hull. Later, it will receive reinforcement of its own.

Remove amine blush and sand to create a better secondary bond when the skeg is glued in place.

Use the centering wire over the hull to align the laminated skeg. Exercise care in getting it straight, because if the skeg is even slightly angled to the centerline the boat will never track properly. Do the initial alignment "dry," that is, without any epoxy glue in the joint. Once you are satisfied, use a pencil to draw alignment marks on the bottom of the boat around the skeg.

Lay the skeg on its side next to the bonding area on the hull. Mix up a sufficient quantity of thickened epoxy to apply a generous amount to both the hull and the skeg base. This may take two or three mixings to avoid having too much hot epoxy in the pot at one time. Raise the skeg up and set it in position on the hull using the pencil lines as guides. Use the centering wire to check on alignment once again.

The weight of the skeg may be enough to keep it in position and to form a tight glue joint. If not, add weights or temporarily attach the skeg with drywall screws. Check the alignment again and wipe up any excess glue squeezed out of the joint. Allow the epoxy at least 24 hours to cure before removing weights or temporary fasteners.

COVERING THE SKEG

Sharp corners where the skeg joins the hull must be radiused with a bog putty of epoxy before the outer skin of reinforcement material can be applied. Full details on applying the reinforcement material are explained in Chapter 8. The skin of the skeg should extend onto the hull at least 8 to 12 inches (20 to 30 cm) beyond the sides of the skeg. The area of the hull to which this extra material is bonded must be prepared by sanding with 220-grit paper to get a good secondary bonding surface.

Chapter 10
FINAL FAIRING AND SMOOTHING

By now the hull should be quite fair on the large scale, but somewhat lumpy or even rough on the small scale. In other words, it looks pretty good from across the room but roughness becomes apparent as you move closer. While the remaining roughness is relatively small, don't underestimate the amount of work necessary to remove it. Up to half of the time you invest in building the hull will be spent in final fairing and smoothing. Perfection is impossible, but it is entirely possible to achieve a finish that matches any production FRP boat for smoothness. All it takes is work.

FAIRING COMPOUND

As usual, the first step is to remove any amine blush from the cured epoxy resin. This is followed by a light sanding with 80-grit paper. More aggressive sanding may be needed to smooth the joints where layers of fiberglass are overlapped, but don't try to fair them into the hull by grinding away with too much power sanding. The real fairing and smoothing is done with epoxy fairing compound blended just for the purpose. This compound fills the open weave in the fiberglass cloth and smoothes laps.

Premixed epoxy fairing compound can be store bought, but the majority of boatbuilders prefer to blend their own. Everyone seems to prefer a slightly different density or have a personal favorite thickening agent. The two absolutes are that the resin must be epoxy and the thickener must be low density. Polyester auto body filler must *never* be used to fair the epoxy skins of a DuraKore strip composite boat. Fairing compound used in Chapter 7 for the initial fairing works equally well in final fairing.

NOTCHED TROWEL TRICK

Common sense says that applying a smooth coat of fairing compound would be the best way to get the job done. But this is one time common sense is wrong. The right approach defies logic until

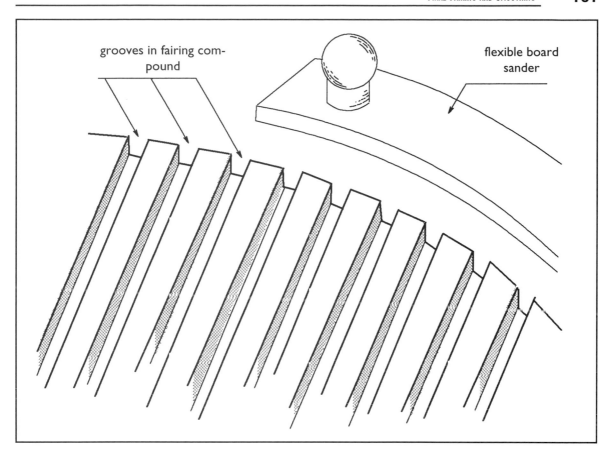

grooves in fairing com-
pound

flexible board
sander

you've tried it for yourself. Apply the first coat of fairing compound with a notched trowel similar to those used to spread floor tile mastic. The hull will be covered with ridges of fairing compound, which definitely seems illogical. After all, the ridges add roughness to the hull when the goal is smoothness.

Ridges in the compound speed up the final fairing, and here's why: The surface area of the tops of the ridges is far less than the total surface area of the hull. Less surface area translates into less material for the sandpaper to cut away. Air gaps between the ridges reduce the contact between the sandpaper and the hull. Less contact reduces friction, which means less muscle power is needed. Grooves between the ridges also give the sanding dust somewhere to go so it doesn't build up between the sandpaper and the hull.

Once the ridges have been faired, the valleys are filled with fairing compound applied with a broad, flexible plastic trowel. Overfilling them a tad is acceptable, but never leave hollows. It takes only rela-

Although exaggerated for clarity, this drawing shows how the grooves produce less surface friction for the board sander. Once the hull is faired the grooves will be filled with more compound and the boat sanded smooth.

Fairing compound should be applied with a plastic squeegee and troweled as thin and smooth as possible to reduce final sanding.

tively light sanding to fair the filled valleys into the ridges and smooth the hull.

There are no absolute specifications for the notches in the trowel used in this process. Ian Farrier suggests using one with ¼-inch notches (5mm) for applying the first coat of fairing compound.

CHALK STICK

Haul out the chalk stick once again during final fairing. Use it in the same manner as during initial fairing to mark high spots and locate low areas. The stick will be used twice during final fairing. The first time is to locate unfairness in the ridged layer of fairing compound. The second time locates problems after the valleys between the ridges are filled. Keep using the chalk stick until as much unfairness as possible has been removed.

It's not possible to create a perfect hull. Even the best commercial hulls have small amounts of unfairness or roughness. After all, every boat is built by fallible human beings. Chances are, however, that the worker who did the smoothing at the boat factory is no more of an expert than you are. This is somewhat dull, dirty work that does not go to the best and brightest employees. In other words, if you're smart enough to build the boat to this point, you're more than smart enough to figure out how to get it smooth and fair. In fact, it's a "no brainer." All that's needed is lots of careful work.

ARE YOU A PRO?

The difference between an amateur-built boat and one from a professional shop is seldom in the gross structure. Home builders do a fine job of putting together staunch hulls. The difference comes in what the automobile industry calls "fit and finish." Professionals know customers will complain about even minor imperfections, so they fair and sand to near perfection. The satisfaction level of amateur builders tends to decline rapidly after the first few hours of work. "So what if it ain't perfect, I'm the only one who has to be satisfied," is the distorted logic that allows home builders to quit before the job is done.

Don't succumb. An unfair boat is forever marked as "homemade." Yard crews never view it as having the same intrinsic value as a factory-made cookie-cutter yacht with its highly polished gelcoat. "Hell, it's only a homemade boat," they'll say when they scratch your expensive paint by forgetting to clean off the boat hoist straps during haulout. In their twisted logic, "homemade" is roughly equivalent to "worthless."

And then there's the way the rest of the boating world treats the skippers of obviously homemade boats. Instead of receiving admiration for accomplishing a major undertaking, the owners of unfair boats are seen as people who almost—almost, but not quite—got it right. These builders get the same deference paid to Englishmen who go out in the noonday sun and other eccentrics. "That's ol' Joe," they say. "He built that *thing* himself." In this case, "thing" is roughly equivalent to "worthless and ugly." So keep at the chalk stick, board sander, and fairing compound until the hull looks as good as any boat from a commercial shop.

SANDPAPER GRIT SEQUENCE

Initial fairing is best done with that old standby, 80-grit paper. Once the overall shape is fair, it pays to move up to a less aggressive 120 grit. This finer paper cuts more slowly, allowing better control in the final stages of fairing. It also creates a much smoother surface. Many builders stop sanding once the hull is faired with 120-grit paper. Finish fanatics move up one more step to 220-grit paper for the final overall smoothing of the faired hull. There's no sense in going beyond 220-grit paper when smoothing the fairing compound. The epoxy barrier coat to follow fills any remaining imperfections.

POWERBOARD SANDING

The tedious work of final sanding led Rich O'Meara to develop an unusual sanding machine called the Powerboard. It's two board sanders mounted in a cross on a hydraulic motor. The two boards rotate at controlled speeds, making this tool ideal for final fairing and smoothing of a hull. A dish-shaped dust collector protects the operator from both dust and the spinning boards.

Hydraulic power is the key to the Powerboard. It allows precise control of the rotational speed of the sanding boards. Low speeds are possible with exceptionally high torque. Papers ranging from 24 to 600 grit have been used successfully on the Powerboard. The large dust extractor dish sends dust and debris down a large hose to a power vacuum unit.

Purchase of a Powerboard unit is not cost effective unless you're building several boats. However, units are available for rent in the United States. For more information, contact ROM Development Corporation, 306 Swan's Wharf Row, Brick Market Place, Newport, RI 02840.

EPOXY BARRIER COAT

Low-density fairing compound sands well, but this is partially the result of the porosity of the filler. Because it is porous, low-density compound can be subject to water intrusion with all of its accompanying problems. That's why fairing compound must get a barrier coat of epoxy after the final sanding. This barrier coat is not just a single layer of unthickened epoxy rolled quickly over the surface. It's at least three applications of material applied in a specific sequence to not only waterproof the surface, but also give a glass-smooth substrate for the linear polyurethane paint to follow.

PREPARING THE SURFACE

Freshly sanded fairing compound should be clean and free of chemical contamination. Vacuum as much of the sanding dust as possible. Don't just brush it off the hull, because it will end up underfoot where you'll continually kick up small clouds by walking. From this point on, getting a quality finish requires keeping the shop as dust free as possible.

For the final visual check, hold a high-power light (e.g., a halogen work light) near the hull so that the beam is nearly parallel to the surface. Low-angle light exaggerates minor imperfections in the surface. Pits show up as dark craters, while high spots give off telltale shadows. Make the necessary repairs before continuing with the barrier coat application.

FIRST LAYER

Pour mixed epoxy into a plastic paint pan and use a polyurethane foam roller to apply a thin film to the hull. Mix only as much epoxy as can be applied during the pot life. As soon as it is mixed, pour it into a paint roller pan to slow the curing time. Load the roller with a moderate amount of epoxy. It takes a bit of trial and error to learn how to get a uniform coat of epoxy all around the circumference of the roller. The epoxy on one side of the roller acts as a counter-weight, making it difficult to dip any other side into the glue.

Roll lightly and randomly over an area about 2 feet by 2 feet (0.6 | 0.6 m). Transfer epoxy evenly to the surface without whipping air into it. As the roller dries out, increase pressure to spread the epoxy into a thin, even film. Dry rolling should extend the coverage beyond the original area. Finish with long, vigorous strokes to ensure the film is thin enough not to run or sag on vertical surfaces. Temperature affects the flow characteristics of epoxy. If the resin is too cold, it will be impossible to get a smooth, even coat no matter how much it is rolled.

Have a second worker follow behind the roller to "tip out" the wet epoxy with a disposable foam brush. Tipping should remove air bubbles created by the roller and should level out any ridges. Use enough pressure on the brush to eliminate roller stipple, but not so much pressure that the brush begins removing epoxy from the surface. Information supplied with West System indicates that a pound of epoxy resin should cover approximately 35 square feet (10 sq. meters) of surface.

Apply a coat of unthickened epoxy after final fairing. This seals the fairing compound and provides a smooth surface for the paint to follow.

Outgassing won't occur at this point because all wood has previously been sealed with epoxy. The epoxy should flow onto the hull in a smooth, even coat somewhat like thick varnish. Horizontal surfaces can take a lot of epoxy, but care is needed to apply just the right amount to vertical hull sides. Too thick a coat sags or runs under its own weight before the epoxy kicks. By now you should have gained enough experience working with epoxy to trust your judgment. If a mistake must be made, err by applying the first coat too thin rather than too thick on vertical surfaces.

SECOND AND THIRD LAYERS

Allow the epoxy to cure and remove the amine blush before using a critical eye to evaluate it. Expect the first barrier coat layer to have pinholes and other imperfections. Low-density fairing compound can be used to fill in holes, while sanding with 80 grit should cure the rough spots. Lightly sand the entire hull with 220-grit paper to give a "tooth" to the surface for better adhesion of additional layers.

Apply a second layer of epoxy using a new foam roller in the same manner as the first. Again, follow the roller with a foam brush, tipping out any bubbles or ridges. This layer should really have a glass-like appearance when you're done. The importance of using extreme care to avoid runs or sags on vertical surfaces cannot be overstated. Care now prevents agonizing hours of sanding later.

The exterior of the hull should get a third layer of barrier coat epoxy. This gives plenty of film thickness for later sanding during preparation for painting. There is no need to sand or remove amine blush between the second and third coats if they are applied on the same day. Interior surfaces need only two layers of epoxy as, in most cases, they will not receive much aggressive sanding from here on. Avoid the temptation to put a fourth or fifth coat on the exterior of the hull. Almost nothing will be gained in terms of abrasion resistance, but the hull will be many unnecessary pounds heavier.

TO PAINT, OR NOT TO PAINT?

Preparation for exterior painting can begin as soon as the last layer of the barrier coat has kicked. This may be the best time to get at least a base coat of paint on a male-mold boat. The hull is still upside down with no cradle in the way. In the days of wooden boats, the hulls were primed while upside down but not finish painted. Those old-timers knew that glossy yacht paint was likely to be damaged during the lengthy process of completing the interior, deck, and superstructure. What was true fifty years ago is still true today: painted topsides are subject to accidental damage wile working on the rest of the boat.

Take a tip from the old-timers and apply a base coat of paint now. That's enough painting for the topsides, which are easily finished later on, but not for the underwater portion of the hull. The bottom of the boat is still fully exposed. Cradle- or jack-stand pads that will hold the boat when it's rolled over aren't causing any problem now. So paint the hull from the waterline down until the required layers have been applied, including antifouling.

For a complete discussion of finishing the exterior, see Chapter 15.

Chapter 11
ROLLOVER AND INTERIOR LAMINATING

f any part of building a boat can be described as scary, it's rollover. Builders using male molds have only one opportunity to enjoy this heart-stopping event. Those who use a female mold can look forward to two rollovers. Because of the wide variety of sizes and shapes of boats, it's impossible to give specific rollover instructions that will work every time. The following suggestions have been gathered from a variety of builders to illustrate the inventiveness needed to get the job done.

SUPPORT THE HULL

In all cases, the hull must be properly supported before, during, and after rollover. Those who have not worked on unfinished hulls are always surprised how "floppy" the sides of the boat are prior to installation of the deck. This is true even of boats with sizeable sheer clamp timbers. The hull needs the support of the deck and, in some cases, of the superstructure to gain its full strength. These have not yet been installed in the upside-down hull, so the sides of the boat are weak during rollover.

Considerable damage can be done to the partially completed hull through improper handling, primarily for two reasons. The first is resting the entire weight of the hull on a small portion of the sheer amidships. This puts all the weight at the weakest point of the unfinished boat.

The other cause of damage is losing control of the hull during rollover. It normally happens just after the boat reaches the vertical and starts over onto its new side. Up to the vertical, all of the lifting and bracing has been done under the hull to raise dead weight. Suddenly, the weight transfers. Gravity, which up to now was working against rollover, tries to finish the job in a crashing instant. Unless preventers (braces, ropes, etc.) have been rigged, the hull slams down, doing great damage to itself.

PERSONAL SAFETY

Personal safety must be foremost in your mind during any rollover. It's always possible to build another hull, but growing a new foot is not so easy. Rollovers should be done slowly, with lots of advance planning. All members of the team must know exactly what's going on at all times. Send home "maverick" workers who do unexpected things on their own initiative. The whole team needs almost military discipline. Nobody does anything without everyone else's knowledge and everybody follows orders from one boss.

There is one cardinal rule during rollovers: *The hull never moves with anyone in harm's way*. If disaster happens, all of the crew should be standing out of harm's way where they can watch the pieces fly. Don't let anyone become a "hero" by trying to catch the boat. Let it crash down. After the dust settles, the crew should go for a beer, not to the hospital.

Work slowly. Professionals with overhead cranes and all the necessary jacking and blocking equipment usually plan at least half a workday for this process. Some rollovers take a full day in a commercial boatshop. Don't expect to get the job done any faster than the guys who do this for a living. In fact, plan plenty of extra time to get the job done safely.

ROLLOVER METHODS

THE BRUTE STRENGTH APPROACH

The light weight of DuraKore strip composite hulls tends to make rollover less formidable than it is with other, heavier construction methods. With boats under 25 feet (7.6 m) it may be possible for a crew to get the job done by old-fashioned manhandling. Calculate the total weight of the hull before attempting to use human muscle power. (See Chapter 3 for information on approximate weights of DuraKore strips and epoxy.)

Because of its odd shape, a boat is difficult to lift and carry properly. Even a crew of weightlifters will have trouble handling more than 60 to 80 pounds (27 to 36 kg) of hull weight per person. Remember, it doesn't matter whether you strain your back lifting a

The author's dinghy immediately after being removed from the building mold. Note the clear tape that kept the molds from bonding to the DuraKore. One person was able to lift the hull off the mold and place it on the sawhorses alongside.

ton of bricks or a ton of feathers—it still hurts. The brute strength approach works reasonably well with the individual hulls of a multihull sailboat or with smaller monohull sail and powerboats. Beyond that, mechanical help is needed.

USING SIMPLE MACHINES

To roll over larger boats, you need to work smarter, not harder. High school physics class introduced the simple machines: the wheel, the pulley, the inclined plane, and the lever. Each amplifies human muscle power. In theory, there is no limit to the size of the object that can be moved by a simple machine. Archimedes is supposed to have said, "Give me where to stand and I will move the earth." Unfortunately, he had a problem finding a fulcrum for a lever big enough to get the job done.

The same is true when rolling boats. At some point the concept of simple machines runs into the hard facts of reality. Boats up to about 35 feet (10 m) can be rolled over using simple machines. Larger hulls develop problems quickly. Even with small boats, success depends upon the equipment at hand, the number and skill of the workers, and the prevailing conditions.

➤ Long Lever—Using a stout 4 × 4-inch (10 cm^2) timber balk is often the easiest way to lift the hull a short way off the building mold. A lever is good for lifting one gunwale just enough to allow the rigging of other devices such as a block-and-tackle or hydraulic jack. Levers are seldom useful past the initial few inches of lift.

➤ Hydraulic Jacks—Those ubiquitous hydraulic "bottle" jacks are excellent for lifting large weights short distances. Use the biggest jack available, since big jacks have larger base plates and are inherently more stable. Tool rental stores catering to professional contractors are the best source. Rent several jacks because it's often necessary to use two or three simultaneously to lift the hull without creating unfair strains. Most hand-pumped hydraulic jacks have a limited lift of 12 inches (30 cm) or so. Raising the boat requires a repetitious series of jacking and blocking. (Note: Rolling garage jacks are not recommended because they can slip sideways at inopportune moments.)

➤ Block-and-Tackle—Sailors are familiar with four- or six-part mainsheet tackles, which give a child the power to control a large sail. The same concept can be used to lift and roll the boat hull, provided there are overhead beams strong enough to support the weight of the boat. Oversized blocks are also necessary, as friction in the sheaves can reduce the effective lifting power. The amount of rope consumed by a six-part tackle can be surprising. It needs a minimum of 70 feet (21 m) of rope for every 10 feet (3 m) of lift.

➤ Chain Hoists—Whether electric or manual, chain hoists are just an improved form of block-and-tackle. Electric hoists offer almost total control over the movement of the boat. Some larger tool-rental stores offer chain hoists. Be sure the beams of the workshop are strong enough to support the boat hull before renting a chain hoist.

PROFESSIONAL CRANE SERVICES

If you're uncertain about your ability to roll the hull, it's too big to lift without professional help. Hiring a professional crane service is normal for large hulls too heavy for manhandling. In the United States, look under "Crane Service" in the yellow pages of the phone book. Call at least two months in advance of rollover day and ask for a crane expert to visit your shop to study the situation and give advice as to what equipment will be needed.

Some hulls can be turned with one crane and lots of timber props. Really big hulls require two cranes, one on either side of the hull. Temporary attachment points may have to be bonded into the hull for these cranes. These attachment points are cut away once the boat is upright. Specify that only modern hydraulic cranes be used on

Lindsay Boatbuilders uses a chainfall to overturn the hull of Cepheus. Two station molds have been left in the hull to add support. (Photo by Mark Lindsay courtesy Baltek Corp.)

your job. Old-fashioned friction clutch (also called "friction drag") cranes do not have the fine control necessary for delicate work.

Hiring a professional crane service is a major expense. You will be charged not only for the time spent on the job, but also for the time it takes to drive the cranes to your shop and back to their yard ("portal to portal"). Obviously, you want to have everything ready the instant the crane arrives on your property. Time wasted after the machine arrives comes out of your pocket in the form of dollars, big dollars.

REINVENT THE WHEEL

No matter whether brute force or a construction crane is used for motive power, rollover is easier with a special cradle designed for the

A rollover cradle should be used to support larger hulls. Some of the supports may be retained to support the rightside-up hull while it is completed.

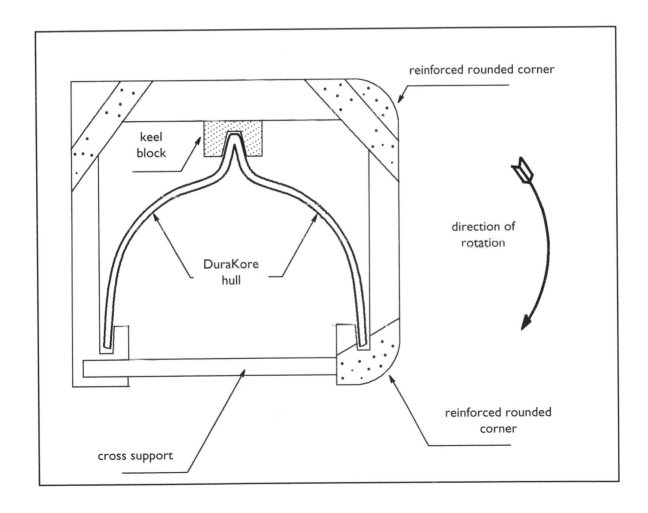

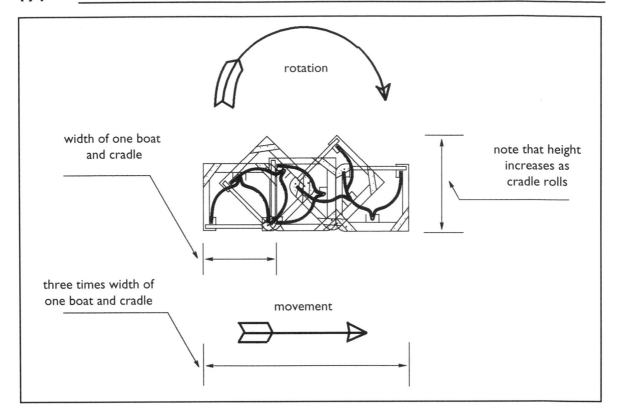

rotation

width of one boat
and cradle

note that height
increases as
cradle rolls

three times width of
one boat and cradle

movement

Using a rollover cradle causes the boat to move sideways as it is turned upright. Note that the height of the boat and cradle also increases as the cradle rolls.

purpose. This cradle consists of two or more semi-circular ring frameworks that support the hull as it rolls sideways until it is upright. Ring-shaped cradles prevent the sides or gunwale of the boat from touching the shop floor. This protects the unfinished hull from unfair strains that would come from resting on its gunwale.

On smaller boats the cradle frameworks may, in fact, be circular to allow rolling the boat over in one smooth motion. With larger hulls it is desirable to do the rollover in steps: first onto the boat's side and then upright. A stop-roll requires a cradle that combines round and flat sections. Rolling the boat in stages allows time to change the position of hoisting cables. It also prevents problems created by the momentum of a large object. If a big boat rolls too quickly, it may just keep going past the upright position and wind up flat on its opposite side. Ouch!

A hull rolled in a ring cradle is displaced horizontally by slightly more than the diameter of the rings. Sideways movement may be acceptable in a large building, where boat construction can continue with the hull in its new location. However, most shops are small enough that the unfinished hull has to be moved back to its original location. Rollers made from short sections of iron pipe make the job of pushing the boat sideways easier. A plumbing shop may be willing to "donate" odd-length pieces of scrap pipe to the project.

ROLLOVER FROM A MALE MOLD

Consider how the boat will be held upright once it is rolled over. The hull needs plenty of support for the remainder of the construction process. It's easiest to build a work cradle now, while the boat is still upside down. Main hull supports (often called the "bunks") are easily spiled off the upside-down hull. Make cardboard patterns first to avoid expensive mistakes. Once the patterns fit the hull, use them to mark and cut the wood.

Another approach is to cold mold the bunks right on the hull, using epoxy and thin strips of wood. Place a barrier of polyethylene between the support and the hull to keep the two from bonding. Weights, a vacuum bag, or a combination of the two hold the strips in position while the glue kicks. No matter which method is used, completed bunks should receive a layer of padding to prevent bruising or scratching the hull.

Ring frameworks intended to make the hull roll easier should be constructed as an integral part of the work cradle. Later, when the boat is upright, the unneeded parts of the rings can be unbolted or sawn away. The ends of the rings should hook over both gunwales to hold the hull firmly during the roll. Apply padding to portions of the rings that touch the hull.

Once the rollover cradle is built, disconnect the boat from all parts of the building form that won't be rolling with the hull. (The strongback may not roll with the hull.) This step seems obvious, but it is often overlooked until there is an ominous crunching sound as something tears apart when the hull lifts. Permanent mold frames (which are now internal bulkheads) must be disconnected from the strongback. Some section molds may be left in the hull as temporary bulkheads to strengthen it during rollover. These, too, should be disconnected from the strongback. Either unbolt them, or saw off the legs attaching them to the strongback. All remaining temporary fasteners holding the hull to other section molds must be removed at this time.

> ### SAFETY WARNING
>
> Warning: Disconnecting section molds from the strongback may allow the hull to settle quite suddenly. Blocks placed at regular intervals under the gunwales and at the bow and stern can prevent damage to the boat and injuries to workers. Put the blocks in place before disconnecting mold frames or braces. Never allow anyone to crawl under the hull unless it is safely blocked. Workers should never go under the hull when it is supported only by a jack, block-and-tackle, or chainfall.

ROLLOVER FROM A FEMALE MOLD

Female molds are most often used for multihull sailboats. Extreme light weight (without compromising strength) is an overriding factor in the design of these craft. As a result, the individual hulls are often easily lifted by hand out of the mold. Even the larger central hull may require only minimal assistance from a block-and-tackle.

Commercial builders are using DuraKore strip composite construction to create offshore powerboats to 65 feet (20 m) in female molds. Industrial overhead cranes coupled with heavy webbed nylon slings are used to roll these monsters. Heavy equipment and a professional knowledge of moving large, heavy objects are required.

LEVEL THE HULL

Although it seems almost an afterthought, leveling the hull is the critical last step in the rollover procedure. Installation of the interior, the deck, and the superstructure cannot proceed until the hull is level both athwartships and longitudinally.

LAMINATING THE INSIDE

Once the hull is safely rolled over, the interior reinforcement skin can be applied. This requires removal of temporary section molds left in the hull as support during rollover. Fairing, sanding, laminating, and barrier coating procedures inside the hull are essentially the same as those used on the outside of the boat. The only difference is that the quality of the final finish does not need to be as high as on the exterior. Furniture, ceiling strips, or decorative laminates usually hide the interior skin of the hull from view after the boat is completed.

Fairing and sanding creates clouds of dust, which collects in the bilge. Human nature lets the mess grow until either the sanding is completed or it gets in the way. Experience in professional shops has shown that the job goes faster and easier if workers stop from time to time to clean up. Keep a shop vacuum in the boat throughout the fairing and sanding so that it is always handy. Vacuum the crud that collects in the bilge and the dust that sticks to the sides of the boat.

It's difficult to find a suitable place to stand inside the DuraKore hull before the reinforcement material is applied. Walking on unsupported DuraKore should be avoided as much as possible. Not only can heavy footsteps damage the veneer surface, but footprints leave behind chemical contaminants that may inhibit bonding of the reinforcement skin. Loose strips of ¼-inch (0.6 cm) plywood can be used as walkways to spread the weight of workers' feet and prevent contamination.

Ladder feet are notorious for damaging unfinished hulls. They should be padded with foam rubber wrapped in rags and duct tape. Even if padded, always sit ladder feet on plywood to spread the strain.

Laminate the reinforcement fabric in the bilge area first. Sand and fair from the turn of the bilge down to the keel. Work from the bow toward the stern when applying the reinforcement material in the same manner as on the outside of the hull. Good planning is needed to have a clean area in which to work. At the stern, leave the last work area unlaminated until the epoxy on the rest of the bilge kicks. Go back into the boat to laminate the final section.

Once the bilge is laminated with reinforcement, it will be strong enough to support all of the walking necessary to laminate the rest of the interior. Reinforcement material may be applied either dry or wet to the interior topsides from the turn of the bilge up to the sheerline. Try the dry method first, but resort to the wet approach if necessary to get the fabric to stay positioned on vertical surfaces.

Using fairing compound on interior surfaces is optional. It is necessary only in those locations where the inside skin of the hull will be visible in the completed boat. If fairing compound is used, it must be sanded and given one layer of barrier coat as was done on the outside of the hull. The entire interior should then receive two layers of barrier coat epoxy.

PERMANENT BULKHEADS

With the hull off the building form and rightside up, what were called "permanent mold sections" take on their true role as bulkheads. Reinforcement fabric must be carefully laminated to the tabs glued on the bulkheads' edges during the earliest phase of construction. Remove amine blush from the tabs and sand the epoxy with 80-grit paper to give it a "tooth" for a strong secondary bond. Reinforcement material should go over the tabs and right up to the bulkheads.

Chapter 12
INSTALLING BULKHEADS AND FURNITURE

There's no sense in building a lightweight, high-tech boat and then reverting to old-fashioned construction for the interior. Heavy timber-framed plywood furniture negates the benefits of light weight gained from DuraKore strip composite construction. Instead of plywood, continue using lightweight balsa composite construction for bunks, settees, cabin soles, and even galley cabinets. Weight savings of 30 to 40 percent over plywood are possible by using DuraKore planks or DecoLite panels.

If you're a solo boatbuilder, the light weight of balsa-cored materials has a major side benefit. They are much easier to carry to and from the workbench or to lift into the interior of the boat. Because they're lighter, you can work longer with less fatigue.

Finger-jointed DuraKore strips can be used to create interior furniture, although they are not cost effective for this purpose. The 12-inch wide planks give more "bang for the buck." DecoLite composite panels are even more economical for large, flat pieces. These balsa-cored materials can be cut and fitted in with normal woodworking tools. Combining them allows construction of complex shapes and curves in the interior furniture.

It's normal to construct the hull and deck of a DuraKore strip composite monohull boat separately. Assembly of these units is usually done when the interior of the hull is virtually complete. This technique allows everything from V-berths to galley stoves to be installed free of confining obstructions. With no deck overhead, the work goes exceedingly quickly. Large pieces of furniture can be pre-assembled on the shop floor and hoisted into the boat. Working in an undecked hull is also easier on the cranium because workers can stand up without hitting their heads.

PATTERNS AND TEMPLATES

Visit any custom boatbuilder and you'll find dozens of patterns or templates being used, particularly for the interior. Professionals know it's a lot cheaper to toss away a misshapen piece of cardboard (or ¼-inch [6mm] plywood) than to discard a far more expensive DecoLite panel. The pros take great care in making patterns right, even for a one-off boat where the patterns will be used only once.

The word "template" usually refers to a plywood or tempered hardboard shape the exact size of the finished part. Made of hard materials, templates can be used dozens or even hundreds of times. "Patterns," on the other hand, are usually made of cardboard or kraft paper. They are suitable for making only a part or two before wear and tear makes them unreliable. In actual practice, spiling patterns are often used to make hard templates. The two terms are often confused with no harm to the boat.

Avoiding expensive mistakes is only one reason for using patterns and templates in professional shops, where time is money. An hour spent in spiling a pattern or cutting a template is always recovered in faster installation of the finished part. In fact, the assembly job goes so much faster that it costs less to go through the work of making patterns than to attempt to fit the parts themselves directly into the hull.

Take a hint from the guys who build boats for a living: make paper patterns for all parts. In critical situations, go the next step and make a hard template out of ¼-inch plywood. Check and adjust the fit of the template, then transfer the correct shape to the final part.

ENGINE BEDS

Boat factories install inboard engines before any of the rest of the interior is put in place. Immediately after rollover is the easiest time for engine installation because there is nothing to get in the way. However, an engine is usually the biggest single expense in building a boat. Thin wallets force many amateurs to defer buying the engine until the boat is nearly completed. This avoids having a large amount of cash tied up for a year or more in a chunk of iron that does little more than gather dust in the bilge.

Installation of the engine beds and supporting structure must still be done prior to completion of the boat's interior. All interior bulkheads, partitions, and furniture must then be designed with an eye toward getting that unwieldy chunk of iron in place. Bulkheads and furniture surrounding the engine compartment must be removable for full access. A hatch must be placed directly above the engine bed so that the iron can be lowered into position using an overhead crane or a chainfall.

Heavy timbers supporting the engine are part of a general class of structural members known as "longitudinals." They run fore and aft, supporting both the machinery and the hull along a line parallel to the keel. The number and placement of these structural members, as well as their construction, are specified by the naval architect. Designs adapted from conventional cold molding usually suggest that longitudinals be installed on the building form prior to planking of the hull. This approach creates serious problems in DuraKore strip composite construction. Longitudinals installed on the building form get in the way of installing the internal reinforcement skin in the same manner as do permanent mold frames (internal bulkheads). They prevent the continuous installation of the material as required.

Because of the inherent stiffness of DuraKore strip planked hulls, installation of longitudinals on the building form should not be necessary. It should be possible to delay installing them until after the inner reinforcement material has been laminated onto the planking. Check with the designer of your boat before making such a large change in the construction process. Follow the conventional procedure unless the naval architect gives the okay.

Builders on the cutting edge of technology are using welded aluminum trusses to spread the weight and strain of the engines in high-speed powerboats. These trusses are engineered to fit the hull and the particular engines involved. Marine-grade aluminum alloys are used and the welding is done with inert gas equipment. For all of the expense and work, aluminum trusses save only a few pounds of weight over laminated wood engine beds. "They aren't worth the cost for an amateur," said a naval architect who requested anonymity. "They're only worthwhile for someone who will pay thousands of dollars for another quarter knot of speed."

Each engine requires two beds, one on the port and the other on the starboard side. A total of four beds is needed in a twin-screw vessel. The following discussion focuses on the installation of just one bed. Repeat the steps as many times as needed for the vessel under construction.

BALSA-CORE BEDS

DuraKore or DecoLite can be used for engine beds, but their use is not suggested except to experts in cored construction. Balsa-core engine beds require careful engineering to prevent their being crushed by the engine mounting bolts.

LAMINATED WOOD BEDS

Engine beds can be laminated out of a stack of non-oily boatbuilding timber such as Honduras mahogany (*Swietenia macrophylla*) or the more expensive white oak (*Quercus alba*). Timber that contains a great deal of sap must be avoided because the oily resin in the wood prevents good bonding of the epoxy glue. Even white oak can present problems. The dense, hard structure of this wood provides a poor bonding surface for epoxy compared to woods with a more open grain structure.

Shaping an engine bed to fit the inside of the hull is a test of your ability to visualize three-dimensional bevels on curves. The top of the bed must be flat and straight to accept the engine mounts, while the bottom must be curved and beveled to fit the shape of the hull. There is no easy way to do this in one-off construction except to cut, fit, and recut until the right shape is achieved.

It may be possible to determine the fore-and-aft shape of the hull in the way of the engine bed from the lofting. If not, spile this shape directly from the hull. In either case, start by making and fitting a cardboard pattern. Transfer that shape to the piece of wood that will lie against the inner skin of the hull. Then measure the athwartships bevel along the length of the engine bed. Set the bandsaw to the *minimum* bevel angle that you measured. Cut along the line transferred from the cardboard pattern. This results in a board that is flat on top for the engine, and simultaneously curved and beveled on the bottom to match the hull.

Final beveling has to be done in a trial-and-error process because the angle changes over the length of the piece. Old-time shipwrights would carefully plane the correct bevel, often working completely from memory. Not many people have that much skill these days, and it's not worth trying to learn the intricacies of the jack plane just to install a couple of engine beds. An electric circular sander with 40-grit paper cuts quickly and doesn't need as much skill to operate. Move the sanding disk in long, sweeping motions with the minimum pressure to keep the sandpaper cutting. Don't let it sit in any one place too long!

Use thickened epoxy to glue this specially shaped base board to the interior of the hull. Once this glue has kicked, add the rest of the wood until the stack achieves the correct height. Glue the stack together with thickened epoxy using non-ferrous screws to hold everything in alignment. Each layer in the stack is screwed to the one below it, with the screw heads staggered. These screws are left permanently in the stack. Clean off glue squeezings before they harden. When the glue kicks, sand the stack smooth. Cover the engine beds with the same reinforcement schedule used for the interior of the hull.

PLYWOOD BEDS

High-grade marine plywood is an excellent choice for engine beds, except for weight. Long plywood beds are too heavy and awkward for one person to handle. This weight is multiplied by the number of times the beds have to be handled during the cut-and-try beveling process.

Plywood beds are also laminated together, but the laminations are vertical instead of horizontal as in the case of laminated timber. Rip the stock into strips slightly wider than the depth of the completed bed. Using epoxy glue, laminate the strips into a long blank. Butt joints are acceptable as long as they are staggered and at least 2 feet, 6 inches (.76 m) apart. If the stock is one-third the thickness of the completed bed, all butt joints will be supported by two additional layers of plywood.

Choose a flat stretch of shop floor for laminating the stack. Put down a layer of plastic sheeting to avoid bonding the stack to the floor. Apply unthickened glue to the facing sides of all pieces, then build up the stack. Carefully align what will become the top edge of the engine bed. The bottom side does not require alignment, as it will be cut and beveled. Apply weight to the stack to ensure good contact between the layers while the glue kicks.

The laminated blank must be cut to shape and the bottom edge must be rough-beveled while it's still on the shop floor. A heavy-duty sabersaw works best, although cutting through thick plywood is never easy. Set the saw to approximately the correct bevel for the bottom edge. Get several friends to help hoist the piece into the boat. Position it carefully to check the bevel. A high-speed circular sander can be used to adjust the bevel as needed. Expect to wrestle that heavy bed into position several times before the bevel is correct.

Bond the plywood bed to the hull with a putty of thickened epoxy. Be generous, as any squeezings can be recycled in the fillets along both sides of the piece. Rig temporary bracing to hold the bed vertical until the glue kicks. Apply the required reinforcement fabric over the plywood, fully encapsulating it in 'glass and epoxy.

SHORTENED BEDS

The best design practice runs engine beds the full fore-and-aft length of the hull. Unfortunately, it's more typical for the beds to begin and end butted against bulkheads or floors that provide athwartships support. If they are shortened in this way, exceptional efforts are needed to maintain structural continuity. Ends of the beds should be firmly set in thickened epoxy glue where they land on the athwartships members. The reinforcement material should overlap a good foot (0.3 m) onto the surface of the bulkheads. Overbuilding is normally a cardinal sin in lightweight construction, but it's expected in engine beds. Even a small sailboat motor can exert tremendous strains.

LONGITUDINALS

Many designs call for additional fore-and-aft support beyond just the engine beds. These supports are known as "longitudinals." Baltek manufactures a variety of shaped balsa materials specifically for this purpose. However, these are expensive for use in nonprofessional

Longitudinals should be installed after the reinforcement fabric has been applied to the inside of the hull. Thickened epoxy is used to both bed the longitudinal and glue it to the hull. Additional reinforcement fabric encapsulates the longitudinal, which has been beveled to make cloth application easier.

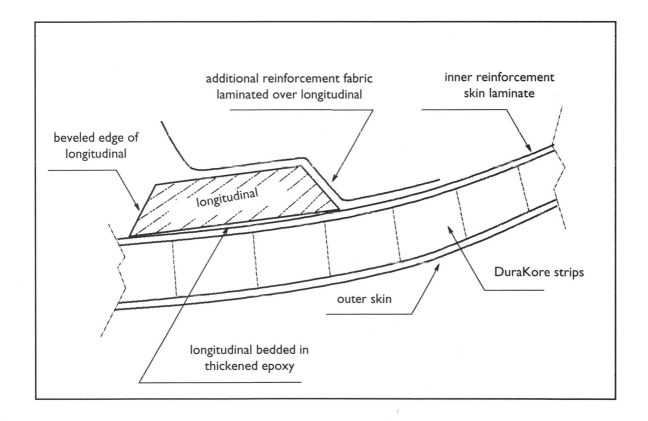

beveled edge of longitudinal

additional reinforcement fabric laminated over longitudinal

inner reinforcement skin laminate

longitudinal

DuraKore strips

outer skin

longitudinal bedded in thickened epoxy

construction. DuraKore planks ripped to width and kerfed for bending are a more cost-effective approach. The sides of longitudinals should be beveled to avoid an abrupt transition.

Longitudinals are installed after the inner reinforcement skin has been applied. Remove amine blush and sand the bonding area before setting the longitudinals into thickened epoxy. Clean up excess glue. A fillet should not be necessary if the longitudinal was properly beveled. After the glue kicks, cover the piece with reinforcement fabric set in unthickened epoxy. Extend this covering at least 6 inches (15 cm) onto the hull on either side of the longitudinal.

FLOORS

In classical wooden boat construction, "floors" are timbers that tie the ribs or frames together across the keel. Since there are no ribs or frames to tie together in a DuraKore strip composite boat, there are no "floors" as classically defined. Yet this term survives in high-tech boatbuilding as the handiest way of describing transverse structural members confined primarily to the bilge area across the keel line. Floors are often used in sailboats to spread the strain of external fin keels, or in powerboats to help support high-powered engines. Another major use of floors is to support the cabin sole. They are essentially diminutive bulkheads with installation identical to that of full-size partitions.

INTERIOR BULKHEADS (NOT PERMANENT MOLD FRAMES)

Some interior bulkheads cannot be installed until after the hull is rightside up, because they would interfere with the strongback during construction or rollover. Bulkheads installed after rollover must be cut to the exact shape of the inside of the hull, then bonded in place with thickened epoxy. A reinforcement fabric tab set in unthickened epoxy is used to tie the bulkhead to the hull.

SPILING TECHNIQUES

"Spiling" is the name for a broad range of techniques that record and then recreate odd-shaped areas of boats. None of these techniques creates a true pattern. Instead, all methods of spiling record

abstract measurements, which are used later to draw a full-size repro-
duction of the shape from which a pattern is made. The measurements to be recorded are usually made with a tool known as a
"spile" or "tick stick." In some cases, a scribing compass replaces the
spile. A piece of light plywood or cardboard serves as the "spiling
pattern" on which the measurements are recorded.

Back in the shop, the spiling pattern is laid on the raw material
and the spile or tick stick is used to recreate specific points around
the perimeter of the required shape. A lofting batten is used to connect these points in a smooth, fair line, which is marked for cutting.
Three spiling methods suggest themselves for use in high-tech amateur boatbuilding:

Computer Patterns may show the required shapes of the bulkheads if the boat was lofted electronically. These patterns will have

A tick-stick spiling pattern is used to fit interior bulkheads into the hull. The completed pattern bears no relation-ship to the actual shape of the hull. Rather, it contains information from which that shape can be re-created.

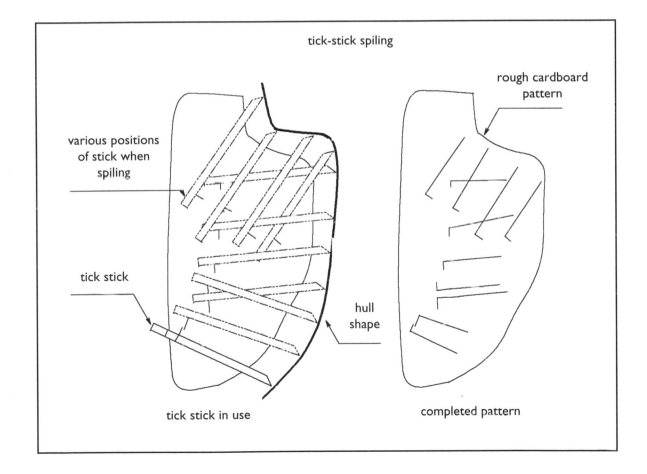

tick-stick spiling

rough cardboard pattern

various positions of stick when spiling

tick stick

hull shape

tick stick in use

completed pattern

to be reduced for skin thickness. (Use the reduction techniques described in Chapter 4.)

The Tick Stick Method is popular when spiling large units such as bulkheads. Suspend the spiling pattern athwartships so that its surface lies exactly where the surface of the bulkhead will be. Use a piece of scrap lumber spanning from gunwale to gunwale to support the pattern. Another support should drop down on the boat's exact centerline to the bottom of the inside of the hull. Clamp everything tightly in place to prevent movement during spiling. It is critical that the face of the pattern be both plumb and at right angles to the centerline of the hull.

Whittle one end of the tick stick to a point. Make marks along the length of the stick at convenient intervals, usually about 6 inches (15 cm) apart. Label each mark with a letter (e.g., "A" through "Z").

Place the tick stick on the face of the pattern with the point touching the hull. Draw a line along the length of the tick stick,

Use simple geometry to find the center of the arcs swung on the spiling pattern in the boat. These centers represent locations on the hull of the boat. Join them with a lofting batten to create the exact shape of the hull.

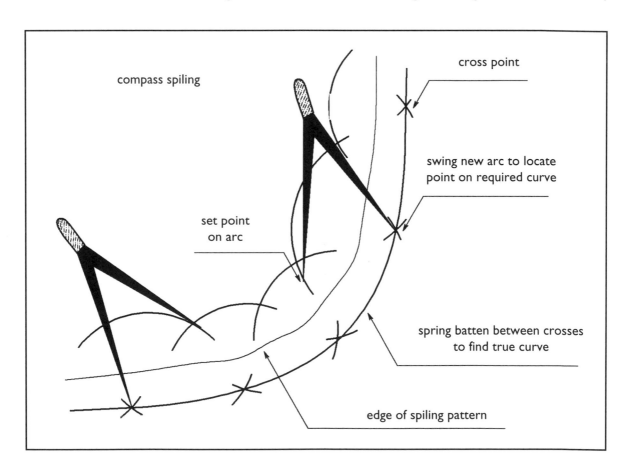

compass spiling

cross point

swing new arc to locate point on required curve

set point on arc

spring batten between crosses to find true curve

edge of spiling pattern

then make a "flag" mark at right angles to this line. The flag mark is made at one of the lettered marks on the stick. Label the flag with the corresponding letter on the stick. Make as many lines and flags as necessary to record all of the significant changes in the shape being spiled.

In the shop, align the pattern on the sheet of DecoLite that will become the bulkhead. Tape the pattern firmly in position. Align the tick stick along the lines on the spiling pattern so that the correct letters are opposite the appropriate flags. Make a mark at the end of the tick stick. Join the marks with a lofting batten and draw the cut line.

Compass spiling can be extremely accurate, but requires a spiling pattern of the approximate size and shape of the bulkhead. Heavy cardboard works well but may need stiffening from a framework of scrap lumber. The edges of the pattern should conform closely to the shape of the hull, although minor raggedness is acceptable.

Compass spiling is based on a geometric principle used to find the center of a circle. For accuracy, purchase a drafting compass with a thumb screw adjustment that is not likely to accidentally change setting. Avoid stamped steel children's compasses, which lack a positive means of maintaining the setting. Adjust the compass to a convenient size and record the exact distance between the points just in case.

Set the pointed leg of the drafting compass tightly against the hull and swing a semi-circle on the pattern. This semi-circle should be as large as possible. Move the compass and mark another semi-circle. The distance between marks should reflect the amount of curve to the hull. Only a few semi-circles are needed on long straight stretches, while marks every 3 inches (7.6 cm) may be needed in tight-radius curves. It is critical that the spiling pattern not move during the marking process.

Remove the pattern from the boat and lay it on top of the panel to be cut. Fasten it firmly to keep it from slipping. Set the point of the drafting compass on any semi-circle mark on the pattern. Swing a short arc on the panel. Move the divider's point to another location on the semi-circle and swing another short arc on the panel. The two arcs will cross, and where they cross represents the exact position of the compass point when the semi-circle mark on the pattern was drawn.

Use a spiling batten to connect the crosses on the panel into a smooth curve and draw the cut line. This line should represent the exact shape of the hull. Use a sabersaw to cut along the line.

Professionals confidently spile directly from their pattern onto the raw material for the bulkhead. If you are not sure of your spiling skills, there's no shame in making a full-size cardboard template of the bulkhead. Hold the template in position inside the hull to check fit before cutting the more expensive DecoLite panel.

CONSTRUCTION TECHNIQUES

DecoLite allows essentially "frameless" construction of interior bulkheads. These self-supporting panels already have a balsa core faced with fiberglass reinforcement. Internal framework is not needed as long as the required thickness of the bulkhead is no more than that of a sheet of DecoLite. Also, as long as the bulkhead (or floor) isn't larger than a single panel of DecoLite, you can just cut out the appropriate shape and bond it into the boat. Bulkheads larger than a single sheet must be pieced together. This can be done either before they are cut to shape or after the shaped pieces are installed in the hull.

Lap Joints—A simple half-lap (often called a "ship lap") can be the quickest way of joining panels. No industry-accepted standard exists for the distance of the cutback along the edge of each panel. The minimum distance seems to be equal to the thickness of the panel, but some people are making the cutback equal to three or more times the thickness. The depth of the cut should be half the thickness of the panel.

Wet the exposed balsa with unthickened epoxy, then use thickened glue to bond the joint in a two-step bonding process. Add a layer of reinforcement material over the joint on both sides. This reinforcement should be at least six times as wide as the thickness of the panel. Set it in unthickened epoxy. After the glue kicks, the bonded and reinforced seam should be as strong or stronger than the original DecoLite panel. The edges of the reinforcement can be sanded and faired into a smooth transition with the panel's original fiberglass surfaces.

Spline Joint—This is a simple and effective joint. Slots are made in the mating ends for the full width of the panels to be joined. A hardwood spline is inserted in these slots during the bonding process. As with a lap joint, there are as yet no industry standards for the size of the spline or the depth of the slots. A starting point might be to make the spline about one-fourth the thickness of the panels. The depth of the slot probably should be no less than the thickness of the panels, and extra depth wouldn't hurt. The width of the spline must be sufficient to fill the slots in both panels. Use a two-step bond, wetting the panel edges, slots, and splines with unthickened epoxy. Slightly thickened epoxy should be used as the glue. Laminate a layer of reinforcement material over both sides of the joint as reinforcement.

Hollow Bulkheads—Built-up bulkheads with a hollow space between the skins offer distinct advantages when the time comes to wire interior lighting or install plumbing. Hollow spaces inside the bulkheads provide natural "chases" for the wires or pipes. Cut out one skin of the bulkhead from thin DecoLite and lay it on the shop floor. If it has two or more pieces, be sure they are held in correct alignment while the interior braces are bonded into place.

Solid wood is used for the internal framework. Philippine mahogany is the most readily available boat wood in most U.S. lumberyards. If found, western red cedar or Sitka spruce will save a few vital pounds. However, if the naval architect specifies oak or some other dense wood, use that and nothing else. Clamps or temporary nails can be used to hold the pieces of the internal framework in position while the thickened epoxy cures. Bond the second skin of the bulkhead onto the framework, using weights to ensure firm contact.

INSTALLATION

A troublesome aspect of bulkheads is the need to bevel them in areas of the hull that are rapidly narrowing (e.g., close to the bow). The accompanying drawing shows why it may be necessary to bevel the edge of the bulkhead where it strikes the hull. The amount of the bevel is often quite small and can sometimes be estimated accurately enough by eye. Cutting a bevel on a scrap piece of DuraKore is a quick way to check your estimate. Once you have the right degree of bevel, set this angle into the base plate of your sabersaw.

Bulkheads are bonded to the hull using a thick bog putty of epoxy. Use the two-step bonding method for best results. There should be glue between the edge of the bulkhead and the hull. A generous putty fillet should run along the joint on both sides of the

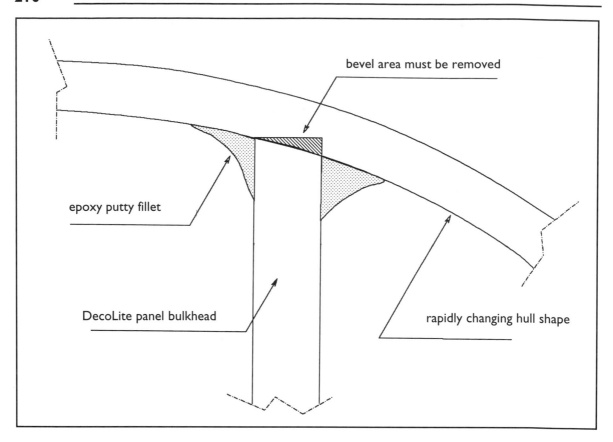

bevel area must be removed

epoxy putty fillet

DecoLite panel bulkhead

rapidly changing hull shape

In areas where the hull's shape changes rapidly it may be necessary to bevel the edge of the bulkhead for a proper fit, though laborious planing is not necessary. Use a disk sander to cut the edge quickly. Any imperfections in the bevel can be filled with thickened epoxy putty used to bond the bulkhead in position.

bulkhead. Jim Watson of Gougeon Brothers, Inc., recommends a large fillet of low-density filler rather than a small fillet of high-density filler. He says the larger fillet of low-density filler will be equally strong, but weigh less—and light weight is a primary goal of high-tech boatbuilding.

While the fillet is still soft enough to permit a primary bond, apply a tape of reinforcement fabric along both seams. Use the dry application method to apply the fabric, and wet it out with unthickened epoxy. Reinforcement tape should be as wide as possible, but must extend at least 2 inches (5 cm) onto both the bulkhead and the hull.

Reinforcement tape can be cut from the same fiberglass material used for the hull skins. Better joints, however, are created from special prefabricated tapes designed specifically for this purpose. A 45-degree biaxial tape is often specified because it easily conforms to irregular shapes. For instance, Ian Farrier calls for 45-degree tape backed with chopped strand matt for use in his trimarans.

Fillets are easily applied with the curved edge of a flexible squeegee. Little sanding is needed to smooth the cured epoxy once the trick of using the tool is learned. The putty should be just thick enough to remain in place without sagging.

LIMBER HOLES

It is possible to bond bulkheads into the hull so well that they divide the boat into watertight compartments. This situation is not always desirable, as it requires separate bilge pumps for each such compartment. Limber holes along the keel line allow water to flow to a common sump where it can be pumped out of the boat. This is the traditional arrangement of smaller (under 40 feet [12 m]) monohulls and some larger multihull boats.

It is easiest to cut limber holes into bulkheads or floors before bonding them in place. There are no hard and fast rules for the shape of limbers, which can be square, triangular, or round. The latter shape, round, is the one to choose when possible because the shape does not create what engineers call "stress risers," because they concentrate any stress in the object. A half-circle notch cut out of the bulkhead at its lowest point in the bilge is sufficient. As with shape, there are no standards for the size of limbers but common sense says don't be stingy. Small holes are easily clogged with the inevitable debris found in boat bilges.

The balsa core inside limber holes through DecoLite panels must be sealed against water intrusion. Two coats of epoxy brushed onto the exposed balsa in limber holes should provide sufficient sealing. A more conservative approach is to cut back the balsa core for about ½ inch (1.3 cm) inside the fiberglass skins. Fill this cutback with epoxy putty thickened with high-density filler, using a two-step bonding procedure.

CABIN SOLES

It's possible to get into great philosophical discussions over whether cabin soles should be bonded into the boat or removable. Those who favor bonding point to the added strength that is gained from this type of construction. They also show that a bonded sole can be lower in the boat, resulting in more cabin headroom. Opponents say that it's virtually impossible to clean the bilge under bonded soles. They also point out that bonded soles can block access to the inside of the hull should repairs ever become necessary. Most builders solve the problem by compromising. They opt for bonded soles with plenty of access hatches.

Think of cabin soles as horizontal bulkheads, and installation becomes the same as for a vertical partition. Use the same spiling and fitting techniques outlined above to create the actual pieces of decking.

Bonding the sole to the hull at its outer edges makes the boat more comfortable for those who sail in it. An epoxy joint prevents bilge water from creeping into lockers above the sole when the vessel heels or rolls. Also, the fillet stops small objects from rolling into the bilge, where they get lost until they clog the pump.

SUPPORT FRAMEWORK

Many custom builders laminate their own deck panels from blocks of end-grain balsa up to 6 inches thick. They use such massive panels to replace the conventional (and heavy) beams and carlins needed to support thin decks. Having balsa custom milled to size is not cost effective for amateur builders. A better approach is to use a grid of floors and longitudinal supports beneath decking cut from additional sheets of DecoLite.

Bilge water is a fact of life. All floors and longitudinal supports for cabin soles need limber holes to allow water to flow to the lowest point of the bilge where it can be pumped overboard. DecoLite panels are suggested for structural members in the bilge because their fiberglass skins are resistant to the water expected there. Hardwood veneer-covered DuraKore planks can be used, but require sealing and coating with epoxy to waterproof them. Because they have fiberglass skins, DecoLite panels do not require this additional step on their flat surfaces. However, the edges where the balsa is exposed do need to be sealed with epoxy.

Bonding the Sole

Use the pastry bag technique to apply a bead of thickened epoxy to the support grid. Lower the cabin sole onto the wet epoxy and apply enough weight to ensure even contact between the grid and the deck. Don't apply too much weight, however, because this can cause a dry joint. Use the thick epoxy that squeezes out to create fillets along both sides of all joints that can be reached. As an alternative to weights, the panels can be held in place with plastic fasteners driven by a nail gun. Fill the fastener holes with epoxy fairing compound.

Apply a bead of thickened epoxy along the outer edges of the sole where it meets the hull. Smooth this bead into a fillet and then apply a tab of reinforcement material set in unthickened epoxy.

Permanent Furniture

Permanent interior furniture such as settee bases or a galley unit should be bonded into the hull during installation of the bulkheads and cabin sole. The exact order in which items are bonded into the hull varies from boat to boat. In some cases it may be easier to install some furniture prior to installing the cabin sole.

Becoming your own interior designer is one of the great joys of building your own boat. Most home builders take full advantage of the freedom to adapt the interior to their personal needs. There are, of course, dangers in this process. One Midwestern builder rearranged the galley in his sailboat to give more space in the main saloon. Unfortunately, being a lifelong powerboater, he forgot that sailboats heel. On one tack everything was fine. On the other tack, however, the gimballed cookstove oven swung into the narrow galley aisle he had created. The cook was trapped by the stove until the captain decided to wear ship.

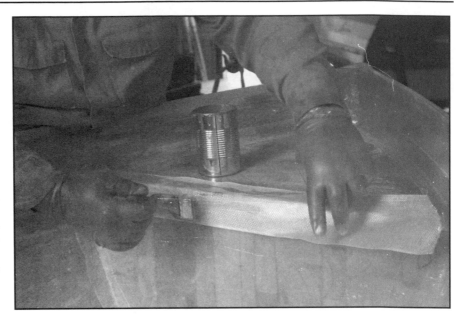

Outside corners of DecoLite furniture should be rounded and then reinforced with fabric set in resin. Here, a foam-filled watertight air tank is being created in the author's dinghy using DecoLite panels. The fabric is special fiberglass tape manufactured for this purpose.

HUMAN ENGINEERING

In recent years the auto companies have transformed the word "ergonomics" into advertising jargon. The word refers to human engineering—making things fit people rather than the other way around. Consideration must be given to the size and shape of the human body in designing everything from bunks to passage doors and galley counters. Here are some ergonomics to consider:

➤ Bunk Size—A minimum length of 6 feet, 4 inches (1.9 m) for the average adult male. Single bunks should be at least 24 inches (61 cm) at the head end. The foot end can narrow down to a minimum of 14 inches (35.6 cm). In the United States, a double bed is 4 feet (1.2 m) wide, and a queen-size bed is 5 feet (1.5 m) wide.

➤ Bunk Headroom—For sitting, the headroom above a bunk should be at least 40 inches (101 cm). If sitting is not critical, the headroom can be reduced. Headroom should be measured from the top of the mattress.

➤ Cabin Headroom—At least 6 feet, 2 inches (1.87 m) is required for "full" headroom, although this may not be enough for some tall individuals. If full height cannot be supplied, it is better to have less than 5 feet, 6 inches

(1.67 m) of headroom. Heights between these two measurements tend to fool people into thinking there is
enough room to stand up when there isn't. A lot of
bumped heads result.

➤ Counter Dimensions—Galley counters should be at least 36
inches (91 cm) and no more than 38 inches (96.5 cm) high.
The cook will appreciate a countertop 18 inches (46 cm)
wide, although this is not always possible. At least 3 inches
(7.6 cm) of toe relief should be provided at the base of all
counters.

➤ Passageways—These can be narrower at the bottom than at
the top. A minimum width of 20 inches (50.8 cm) is necessary at shoulder and hip height. Passageway doorways can
narrow to 14 inches (35.6 cm) below waist height, if necessary.

➤ Settees—The top of the cushion should be at least 18 inches
off the deck, although this is difficult to achieve in small
boats. If the seat height is shorter, more legroom must be
supplied. Avoid seats more than 20 inches (51 cm) from
front to back, as they are uncomfortable.

CARDBOARD MOCKUP

Even professionals have difficulty envisioning furniture inside a boat
hull. Drawings can be deceiving because the shape of the available
interior space of a boat changes from cabin sole to deck sheerline.
Most large boat companies make cardboard mockups of boat interiors before constructing them of "real" materials.

Large sheets of corrugated cardboard can sometimes be purchased
from box manufacturers. Look under "Boxes—Corrugated & Fiber"
in the yellow pages. An even better material is Foam Core, a lightweight board used by artists to support photos and paintings. It
comes in 4 by 8-foot (1.2 by 2.4 m) sheets, although most art supply
stores cut it in half for easier handling.

Use a sharp knife or scissors to cut the cardboard to the approximate shape of the interior furniture. Connect pieces with wide masking tape. Install the furniture in position inside the hull, then walk
through the boat to test the layout. Once you approve of everything,
use the cardboard mockup pieces as rough patterns for the actual
pieces.

Two men easily handle this DecoLite cabinet front for the 67-foot Deerfoot. The white balsa can be seen along the exposed panel edges.
(Photo by David Soliday courtesy of Baltek Corp.)

BUILD OUTSIDE THE HULL

Construction of furniture is most easily done outside the hull. The light weight of DecoLite panels makes it possible to build a settee or a galley counter on the workbench, then lift it into the hull. Working on the shop floor allows faster, more accurate construction.

Individual furniture units are bonded together with thickened epoxy. Simple temporary jigs can be built of scrap lumber to hold pieces in position until the glue kicks. Be sure not to squeeze all of the epoxy out of the joints during assembly. Create fillets of thickened glue along all joints on the inside where they will not be seen. Before the putty hardens, laminate reinforcement tabs over these fillets using fiberglass tape and unthickened epoxy.

Outside corners are difficult to laminate with reinforcement material without making the joints obvious. Use the thinnest reinforcement material available to reduce the "bump" at the edges. Once the epoxy cures, apply fairing compound and sand the surface smooth, using the same techniques as on the hull.

CREATING CURVED FRONTS

Flowing curves can add elegance to the interior of a boat when used as part of galley units or settees. Curved fronts also provide the builder with a lot of praise from visitors, who never suspect the simple manner in which they were created. They are easily made by the technique of kerf bending discussed earlier.

Use a table saw to make a series of cuts about two-thirds of the way through the panel to be bent. Make the cuts from the back so no evidence of these saw cuts shows on the front. Each cut leaves a kerf the width of the saw blade. Kerfs allow the panel to bend into a tight radius. Some experimentation is necessary to discover the correct number and spacing of saw kerfs to achieve any particular bend.

Thickened epoxy glue is troweled into the saw kerfs. The piece is then bent to shape over a temporary mold or by using band clamps. Once the epoxy kicks, the piece will hold the desired shape with only slight springback. It is possible to prevent all springback by bonding integral stiffeners while the clamps are still in position.

The outside radius of a kerf-bent piece should be smooth enough for final finishing. Additional work is necessary before an inside radius bend is ready to finish. The piece will have to be sanded into a smooth radius. An additional layer of reinforcement fabric applied over the saw kerfs gives strength and helps to smooth the surface. Final smoothing uses fairing compound and hand sanding in the same manner as was done for the exterior of the hull.

CABINET DOORS

Cabinet doors can be fabricated by simply saving the cutout from an opening in a piece of furniture. A careful worker who knows how to plunge cut with an electric sabersaw can produce smooth, straight cuts suitable for exhibition to the public. Most people, however, will allow the saw to wobble enough that trim strips and moldings will be necessary to give a professional look.

L-shaped moldings hide both wobbles in the saw cut and the interior core of the panel. Teak and mahogany are the traditional materials for these L-shaped moldings, although there's no reason that aluminum or plastic extrusions couldn't be used if required by the interior decor. Dry fit the door into the opening to be sure there is enough "slop" around all sides to allow easy opening. Once everything fits correctly, bond the moldings in place with thickened epoxy.

Hinge fasteners put considerable strain on both the door and the piece of furniture. Bonding hardwood reinforcement into both the door and the framework is the best way to ensure that hinge screws don't pull out under pressure.

If the exact location of the mounting screws is known, dowels are the quickest and easiest method. Choose dowels that are at least five times the diameter of the screws. Use a brad-point or other highly accurate drill to bore holes for each dowel. Drill from the back side of the panel and exercise care not to damage the outer surface. Cut pieces of dowel the exact thickness of the panel. Apply epoxy to the inside of the holes with a white pipe cleaner. Also apply epoxy to the outside of the dowels. Drive the cut dowels into the holes until they are flush on both sides and allow the glue to cure.

If an absolutely smooth finish is desired on the inside, cut the dowels slightly shorter than the thickness of the panel. During gluing, drive them into the panel so they are recessed below the fiberglass skin. After the glue kicks, fill this recess with epoxy fairing compound.

If the exact location of the fasteners is not known, the solution is to inset blocks of wood in the panels. These blocks should be large enough to accommodate a variety of hardware. Cut away the inside skin of the door or piece of furniture where each wood block will be located. Remove a piece exactly the size and shape of the wood block. Chisel out the inner balsa core, leaving the outside skin

The DecoLite panel in the center of this photo will become an interior door. It has been notched at the top for solid wood blocks to support the hinges. A similar cutout in the lower left corner allows installation of a wooden handle pull. The wooden strips around the perimeter will be used as final trim. (Courtesy of Baltek Corp.)

intact. Bond the wood block into the hole with thickened epoxy. Epoxy fairing compound and sanding should restore the inside surface of the door so that it can be painted.

FINISHING THE FURNITURE

Fiberglass surfaces of DecoLite furniture can be finished to match the gloss of any factory boat built in a mold. All that's required is painstaking attention to the details of smoothing, fairing, and preparing the surface for two-part urethane paint. Of course, glossy smooth paint is not correct for all surfaces. Other possibilities include:

➤ High Pressure Laminates (e.g., Formica or Pionite)—These come in a wide variety of decorative colors and textures. They make excellent galley countertops since their primary use ashore is in kitchens. Wood grain laminates can be used as easy-care surfaces on bulkheads or table tops. Laminates can be glued in place with epoxy, but it's probably best to use one of the nonflammable adhesives intended for the purpose. That way, the laminate can be removed if repairs are necessary or when redecorating.

➤ Vinyl Wallcovering—Another household product, this one is intended for use in bathrooms and other high-humidity areas. The selection of colors and patterns is almost endless. Do not purchase the pre-pasted versions, as the glue on them is not waterproof. Vinyl wallcoverings must be held in place with mastic-type adhesives intended for installing marine vinyl decking on plywood decks. Test a piece first to be sure the adhesive won't damage the vinyl wallcovering. Install over DecoLite panels with PBO surface.

➤ Marine Carpet—Not "nautical" in the traditional sense, but often quite practical, especially in V-berths. Gluing carpet directly to the rough-finished inside skin of the hull eliminates a lot of time-consuming sanding and fairing. It also provides a warm touch and a visual break with surrounding glossy wood or fiberglass surfaces. Use only marine-grade carpet glued in place with special nonflammable adhesive.

Reserve solid teak, mahogany, or other woods for decorative accent. Wood is heavy. Putting a lot of it into the interior defeats the purpose of building a DuraKore strip composite hull. That was the thought that opened this chapter and it's the thought that ends it. Always keep weight in mind during the interior decorating process.

FABRIC FURNITURE

Many attractive and serviceable interior components can be built without resorting to difficult or expensive jointerwork. It is not necessary to create locker or cabinet doors out of solid material. They can be sewn from the same synthetic canvas used to construct dodgers and bimini tops. This material comes in a wide variety of colors and is readily available through mail order catalogs and local canvas shops. Some possibilities include:

➤ Hanging Locker Door—Make a single panel the same shape as the locker opening cutout, but about 3 inches (76mm) wider on all sides. Hem around the panel, then sew a plastic zipper (the bigger the teeth, the better) down the centerline so that the open end is at the top. Install in the boat with button snaps. Normal access is by unzipping the opening, but full access to the locker is gained by removing the panel from its snaps.

➤ Trap Locker Bag—The contents of trap lockers are always difficult to retrieve. Make a canvas bag the size and shape of the locker. At the top put four brass grommets, one in each corner. Sew nylon webbing handles on the two widest sides of the bag. Install small brass cup hooks inside the rim of the locker opening on which the grommets can be hooked. Access to all of the contents of the locker is a simple matter of lifting the bag off its hooks and carrying it to a convenient table.

➤ Shoe Storage—Solve one of the most vexing storage problems aboard ship by studying shoe bags sold commercially for use in the home closet. Use the same design to make your own out of marine canvas. (Avoid domestic shoe bags at sea as they are often sewn with cotton thread, which eventually rots and comes adrift.)

➤ Dish Storage—Bags similar to shoe bags are excellent for storing dishes. Each size dish should get its own pocket. Attach the bags to a convenient bulkhead with turnbuckle-style canvas fasteners. One dish can be removed at a time, or the entire set can be taken off the bulkhead and carried ashore for a picnic.

The uses of synthetic canvas are as varied as the imagination of the person running the sewing machine. Unlike hard locker doors or storage fixtures, those made out of cloth are relatively inexpensive and easy to build. There's little grief in disposing of them if you decide to change the interior layout. On a high-performance boat, canvas has the additional benefit of being extremely lightweight. Be sure to use synthetic canvas intended for the marine environment. And avoid cotton thread. Dacron or polyester thread lasts years longer.

Chapter 13
BUILDING DECKS AND SUPERSTRUCTURES

A multihull sailboat built in female half-molds requires no additional work to build the decks. They are built "as one" with the hull in the mold. Conversely, hulls and decks of powerboats and most monohull sailboats are built separately and assembled later into a complete vessel. Hulls and decks are "mated" only after the majority of the interior and deck hardware has been installed. Even though they are constructed separately, hull and deck are assembled into true monocoque construction by bonding them together with epoxy.

Because the goal is a monocoque boat (or nearly so), the deck and superstructure of a completed boat should not be thought of as separate units. From an engineering standpoint they are part of a single unit that we'll refer to as the "deck/superstructure." This type of construction is easiest to do on modern sailboats with their low cabin trunks, which blend into foredecks and cockpit coamings. It's not

Arnie Duckworth, left, and Steve Shidler aboard Shidler's 40-foot trimaran powerboat. Built of DuraKore, the Yanmar Endeavor completed the 2,250-mile voyage from California to Hawaii in just 8 days, 22 hours, and 54 minutes without refueling. (Courtesy of Baltek Corp.)

Driving easily to weather is the prototype of the Freedom 35, used as a factory demonstrator for several months before being sold to a satisfied owner. In effect, the buyer got a custom boat at production prices.

quite as easy to create a monocoque deck and cabin for a powerboat, particularly one of traditional sedan or sportfish design.

Two methods suggest themselves for building the deck/superstructure. The first is to follow wooden cold-molded boat construction by installing laminated wooden deck beams and carlins. A DecoLite panel deck is then bonded to this wooden supporting grid. The second procedure is to build the deck, cabin trunk, and sedan deckhouse as a single unit using a mold. In this procedure, the entire assembly is built up of DuraKore strips in the same manner as the hull. Once on the boat, this type of deck/superstructure is supported by the internal bulkheads and by its own mechanical strength.

It is significant that the majority of professional DuraKore builders use the latter procedure or a modified version of it.

THE DECK/SUPERSTRUCTURE MOLD

A male deck/superstructure mold is essentially the same as a male hull mold, except that the deck is built rightside up. A female mold builds the deck upside down. Either type requires the same strongback, center wire (or wires), and mold stations as a hull mold. Computer-lofted Mylar patterns can be used to cut the mold stations, or the work can be done manually on the loft floor. As with the hull, male mold stations must be reduced by the thickness of the DuraKore planking.

Since the deck/superstructure must mate precisely with the hull, the shape of its perimeter is critical. It must be exactly the same as the shape of the outside of the hull at the sheerline. Don't rely on lofted patterns to get this shape, because the physical hull will undoubtedly vary slightly from the perfection of the lofting. One side of the boat probably won't be an exact mirror image of the other. Take measurements off the real hull at each mold station to determine the shape of the boat. Use these measurements when building the mold to ensure everything fits.

Constructing a deck is much less tiring if the mold is approximately standard workbench height of 32 to 34 inches (81 to 86 cm). Provision must be made for the workers as they install the DuraKore on the mold, especially when they're working close to the centerline. It may be possible for them to stand on the shop floor inside the framework of section molds, or temporary scaffolding may be necessary. This can be arranged by laying a sheet of ½-inch (13mm) plywood across the section molds. Naturally, the molds must be built strong enough to support the weight of both the plywood and a worker crawling around on top.

Male or female, which type of deck mold is best? The male mold offers the decided advantage of building in positive space. Deck and superstructure rise naturally, exactly as they would if built out of conventional plywood and timber. In a female mold, the deck is built upside down into negative space. It's an unnatural way to work, but may turn out to be the most efficient way of building. Before deciding which type of deck mold to build, be sure to read the section below on Laminating the Deck. Problems associated with setting reinforcement material overhead in wet epoxy may force the choice of a female over a male mold.

Sailboat decks are easily built on a female mold because they have relatively low cabin profiles. Jersey-style powerboats, on the other hand, call for high deckhouses and perhaps even substantial cabin trunks. This type of superstructure may require a male mold simply to avoid the difficulty of rollover.

Fair the deck molds using long battens in the same manner as was done for the hull mold. Cover the edges of all section molds with package sealing tape or sheet vinyl to prevent the epoxy glue from bonding the DuraKore strips to the building form. A layer of sheet vinyl on the shop floor makes final cleanup a lot easier.

PLANKING THE DECK

Apply DuraKore strips to the deck mold in exactly the same manner as on a hull mold. Glue up long battens from finger-jointed strips in advance, then apply the first batten along the centerline of the deck. Build outward from the center, gluing each succeeding batten with thickened epoxy. As with the hull, clean up any squeezings before they harden.

It's often a surprise to first-time composite strip builders to discover that the thickness of DuraKore strips in the deck often exceeds that of the hull. Technical reasons for this apparent paradox are complex but center on the different types of loads expected. The hull is evenly loaded over its entire length when afloat, while the deck must support concentrated points of weight. One of the easiest ways of making a light but strong deck is to replace weight with mass. Some custom high-speed yachts use balsa cored decks more than 6 inches (15 cm) thick. Follow the naval architect's specifications for your boat.

Allow the strips to extend slightly beyond the sheerline while planking the deck. After the glue has kicked, a lofting batten can be used to draw the correct sheerline. Use a sabersaw to trim off the excess material. Apply two coats of unthickened epoxy to the newly exposed balsa core immediately after trimming to prevent water penetration.

Seal coat both sides of the deck with unthickened epoxy to prevent moisture changes from causing strip movement on the mold. Observe precautions to prevent outgassing. Seal coating is particularly important with decks, which may not receive their top and bottom fiberglass laminations for weeks or months while the cabin trunks or deckhouses are built. Whether done immediately after planking or later, initial fairing of the deck is identical with the procedure used on the hull.

TRUNKS, DECKHOUSES, AND FOOTWELLS

DuraKore strips are most effective for building the actual deck because they easily accommodate the camber. However, using strips to create flat, vertical cabin sides is time consuming and expensive. DuraKore planks and DecoLite panels make for faster construction at considerable savings in cost. Large panels are cut to shape and bonded into position using thickened epoxy and fiberglass tabbing. Prior to bonding, large panels can be held in position on the building form with temporary drywall screws. A simple ship lap joint is all that's necessary where panels join. Full reinforcement of the joint comes when the inner and outer fabric laminates are applied. DuraKore planks are also excellent for creating the footwell of a sailboat cockpit.

RADIUS JOINTS AND CURVES

DecoLite sheets and DuraKore planks can also be used in the seats, seat backs, and cockpit coaming. Sharp inside corners where flat panels meet should always be radiused with a fillet of thickened epoxy. This fillet strengthens the joint and smoothes the transition between surfaces for application of the reinforcement material.

Outside sharp corners should also be radiused slightly. Use an electric sander to "break" the sharp edge and round it slightly. Sharp corners are stress risers. Stress, of course, causes cracks or failures in the laminate. In addition, it is much easier to get epoxy and reinforcement fabric to bond to a soft corner than to a sharp one.

Big panels allow fast construction of box-like shapes. Modern boats tend to have rounded shapes and flowing transitions between horizontal and vertical surfaces. Duplicating the popular "Euro-style" look of today's boats can be accomplished through a combination of panels and DuraKore strips. The panels fill in larger flat areas, and the strips are used to fashion curves.

Strips are necessary when the shape curves and bends at the same time. Such a shape cannot be developed out of a flat sheet. Be creative when using DuraKore strips to create unusual shapes. There is no law that requires the strips always to be horizontal or to follow the keel line. Stand them on end to create a vertical curved surface.

Some shapes curve in only one direction at a time. These are known as "developable" by engineers because they can be formed out of a flat sheet of material. Kerf bending (explained in the chapter on furniture) allows a DuraKore plank or DecoLite panel to be bent to the desired radius.

TALL CABINS

Difficulties associated with applying the reinforcement laminates may force construction of the deck to be done in two stages. This is especially true on powerboats that require high sedan deckhouse walls. Rather than attempt to build the deck and house as one piece, it may be advantageous to build only the deck, leaving a large opening for the house. This allows the deck to be built upside down on a female mold. The exposed underside of the deck is laminated with reinforcement material before rollover. Once rightside up, the deckhouse is installed and the inner and outer laminates applied.

PLANNING FOR HIGH-STRESS DECK HARDWARE

Cleats, stanchion bases, winches, sail tracks, and other pieces of hardware that come under high strain require special treatment of the deck where they bolt down. Timber, plywood, or epoxy-glass plugs must replace the balsa core in these areas. These plugs prevent crushing the core when the bolts are tightened. They also block water intrusion into the balsa core of the composite laminate.

TIMBER OR PLYWOOD PLUGS

High-grade marine plywood is the traditional first choice when wood is used for hardware plugs. It has a built-in resistance to decay and the multiple plies give strength along both length and breadth. Plywood has another advantage over timber: pieces can be formed to match the camber of the deck. Whether timber or plywood, the thickness of wood plugs should match that of the DuraKore strips they replace. This ensures a "no bump" transition between core materials.

Wood plugs are easiest to install during the planking of the deck. Locate the areas that require plugs by using the deck play blueprint. Most naval architects indicate the location of plugs, especially for high-load pieces of hardware such as sailboat winches. Even if the exact outlines of the plugs are not shown, they are easy enough to create. Plugs need to be slightly larger than the area covered by the hardware. A 2- to 3-inch overlap (5 to 7.6 cm) should be sufficient.

If the exact location of deck hardware is not shown on the blueprints, install a plug large enough to allow choosing any location in the general area. Avoid highly curved locations on the deck for

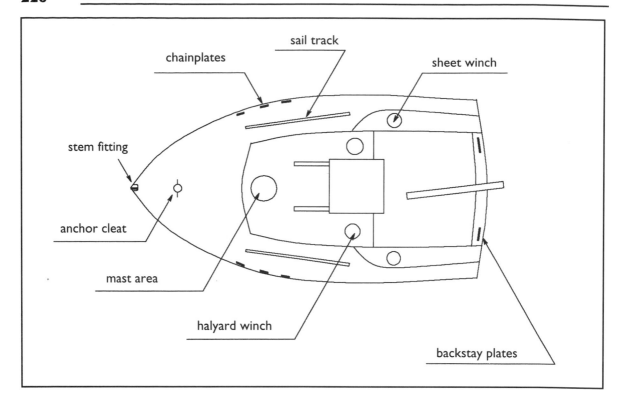

chainplates

sail track

sheet winch

stem fitting

anchor cleat

mast area

halyard winch

backstay plates

Typical deck areas that require additional reinforcement on a sailboat.

mounting hardware. Plywood can only accommodate so much bending. Flat or nearly flat areas of the deck are best for mounting all hardware, but particularly items subject to high loads.

Wood plugs are installed on the building form with temporary drywall screw fasteners. Cutouts in the section molds are not necessary since these pads are only as thick as the core of the deck. Small pads may require some inventive bracing to keep them from falling between the molds. Install pads everywhere a piece of deck hardware might be installed, even if you don't plan to do the installation before launching. Putting a wooden plug into the core is easy before the boat is built but becomes extremely difficult later.

Lay the DuraKore strips right up to the plugs, bonding the strips and plugs into a single unit with thickened epoxy. Smooth the wood plugs into the overall shape of the deck during the initial fairing, prior to installation of the top laminate of reinforcement fabric. Work carefully so that no trace of the junctions between the solid timber plugs and the DuraKore strips shows in the completed deck.

EPOXY-GLASS PLUGS

The following procedure assumes the deck is being built upside down on a female mold. This allows work to be done downhand on the inside skin of the deck after both the top and bottom laminates of reinforcement fabric have been installed, but before final fairing and finishing.

Mark the shape of each plug on the inside laminate, which is now facing up. A permanent black marker should be used because pencil lines get erased. These lines will be removed during the process of installing the epoxy-glass plug, so they won't show through the finished paint job.

Install a combination panel cutter bit in a portable electric router. This is a special router bit for the house building trade designed to drill through the surface, then rout cutouts in plywood panels or floors. It is used by electricians when installing branch outlets in existing buildings. Set the cutting depth of the router so the drill portion of the bit does not go through the laminate on the other side. Plunge the bit into the top surface of the upside-down deck. Follow the outside of the lines to rout a groove the shape outlined on the deck. The router blade should cut away the outline. Plunge-cutting with a router is easier than it looks, but practice on scrap

Epoxy plugs can be inserted by drilling out the balsa core with a spade bit from the inside of the hull. The cavity thus created is filled with thickened epoxy, which squeezes out through the mounting holes. Excess epoxy is removed and the plugs are allowed to cure. Then, the mounting holes are redrilled through the epoxy plugs.

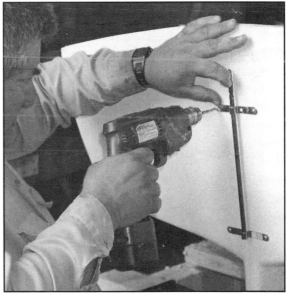

material if you haven't done it before. Eye, face, and ear protection must be worn at all times when routering.

Use a chisel to gently pry the top laminate off the balsa core. Continue chiseling away until the balsa core has been removed from the inside of the lower laminate, creating a cavity the size and shape of the plug. Use a portable disk sander (an air dual-action sander works best) to "feather" the edges of the laminate. Starting about 2 inches (5 cm) from the edge of the cavity, reduce the thickness of the laminate in a gradual slope that reaches zero at the inner edge of the opening. This taper serves the same purpose as a tapered scarf in joining pieces of wood.

Level the rough surface of the inner laminate at the bottom of the cavity, using epoxy thickened with high-density filler. Then immediately begin filling the cavity with layers of fiberglass (or other reinforcement material) set in unthickened epoxy. The dry method of laminating works best. With a stiff bristle brush, force air bubbles out of each layer before installing the next.

Work carefully to avoid an excessively rich resin-to-glass ratio. To avoid problems from heat buildup in the curing resin, the plug may have to be built in two or more stages. Each stage comprises several layers of cloth and resin. Do not allow the epoxy in any stage to fully cure before laminating the next. This ensures that each stage will achieve a primary bond with the previous one.

Stop building the plug when the top of the epoxy and glass reaches the level of the edge of the cavity. Cut a piece of cloth large enough to cover both the cavity and the tapered edges of the surrounding deck laminate. Wet the tapered area with unthickened epoxy, then lay this large piece of reinforcement cloth in position over the plug. Wet out the cloth so there is a definite "dish" in it over the cavity. Use successively smaller pieces of material to fill this dish until the top of the plug is slightly proud above the surrounding deck. After making sure all air has been removed from the wet laminate, let it cure at least 24 hours before fairing.

Placing the largest piece of cloth first (as described)

MAKE A DECK DIAGRAM

Take time out before painting the deck to make an accurate diagram of the location of all hardware plugs. Once the deck is painted, it will be virtually impossible to find the plugs except through the destructive process of drilling test holes. The diagram does not have to be to exact scale as long as the necessary measurements are indicated, including the size and shape of each plug and measurements from fixed locations, e.g., distance aft of mast hole and in from the side of the hull.

Take your rough sketch home and make two clean final copies using waterproof inks. Put a permanent copy aboard by laminating it onto the surface of the hull using unthickened epoxy. Place this diagram inside a locker where it will normally be hidden, but can be found easily when necessary. Put the other clean copy of the diagram in the binder holding all the instruction books and manuals for the boat.

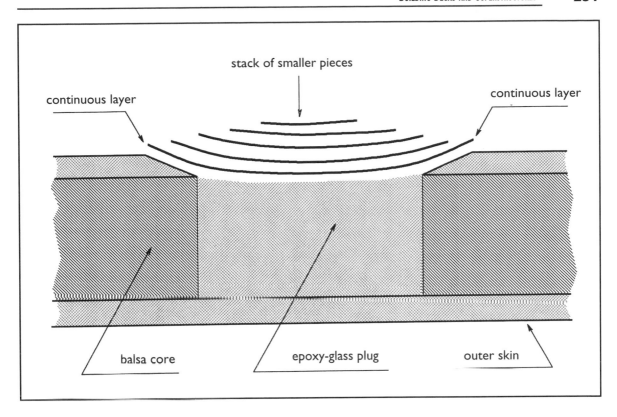

stack of smaller pieces

continuous layer

continuous layer

balsa core

epoxy-glass plug

outer skin

ensures that the entire opening, including the tapered scarf area, is bridged by continuous filaments of reinforcement fabric. Tests have shown this is the strongest way to patch holes in composite laminate surfaces. In fact, this procedure is mandated by the U.S. Air Force for repairs in radar domes and other aircraft parts made of epoxy and fiberglass composites. If the largest piece of fabric were positioned on the top of the stack, it would be ground away during fairing. The result would be a weaker job, because individual strands of reinforcement fabric would not bridge the entire gap.

The inside reinforcement skin must be replaced over large plugs. The first layer should bridge the entire gap of the plug and tapered edges of the surrounding laminate. Smaller patches fill the center of the gap.

DECK HATCHES

Openings for small hatches are most often ignored when setting up the mold or installing the DuraKore strips. These openings are cut out after both the inner and outer skins have been applied to the deck/superstructure. Large hatches require special timber framework to be installed on the mold prior to planking and covering with reinforcement material. The framework becomes a part of the composite deck structure. Naturally, provision for the framing must be made on the building mold. It is often set into notches cut in the station molds and held in place with temporary drywall screws.

The majority of factory-made deck hatches (e.g., Bomar, Lewmar, or Beckson) are designed to sit on flat mounting flanges and not on crowned decks. This allows a standard hatch to fit boats built by any number of manufacturers. Each boat company is free to choose a different radius for its deck camber as long as it constructs the required flat flange on which to mount the hatch. The amateur builder should use the same approach. Make the timber framework around the hatch opening flat to fit the hatch and thick enough to accommodate the curve of the deck.

Bond the DuraKore strips that make up the deck to the framework with thickened epoxy glue. After the initial fairing of the deck, use a bog putty of thickened epoxy to form fillets around the joint of timber framework and DuraKore strips. This fillet gives the joint extra strength, but its primary function is to give a smooth transition and make application of the reinforcement material easier.

AVOID SCRATCHED PAINT

The metal sole plate of the sabersaw often scratches smooth paint. One way to prevent this damage is to apply a layer of duct tape or wide masking tape to the plate. Tape is softer than the paint, so it won't scratch. Remove the tape immediately after completion of the cut. Leaving the tape on too long (even overnight) can make removal difficult. Use mineral spirits to clean sticky residue from the sole plate.

SMALL WINDOWS

Side windows in a sailboat coach house or smaller opening portholes may not require advance planning. Complete the deck, including final fairing and painting, before using a sabersaw to make the necessary cutouts. Use a permanent marker for the cut line. Drill a hole large enough to accommodate the saw blade tangent to this line at a convenient point. Insert the saw blade and start cutting. Expect blades to dull quickly as they chew through tough epoxy and abrasive fiberglass.

LARGE WINDOWS AND DOORS

There are no absolutes, but the general practice is to provide a timber or plywood framework around large openings. This frame does not support the DuraKore or DecoLite, which is strong enough to support itself. Instead, it supports the weight and strain of screws or bolts holding large opening window vents or hinged doors. As with other cases where timber is used as a core, it should match the thickness of the surrounding balsa material. And the wood must be covered by both the inner and outer laminates of reinforcement material and epoxy.

LAMINATING THE DECK

Fabrics used as reinforcement materials on decks and superstructures are the same as used on hulls. They are set in epoxy resin using the same dry or wet techniques. The number of layers and type of fabrics will be specified by the naval architect. Your now-experienced crew of workers should be able to laminate the inside surface with little difficulty.

Anyone who has worked around boats becomes a bit suspicious when things get too easy. And this is one time that suspicion will be rewarded. The side of the deck that's uppermost is easy to laminate, but what about the underside? Ahh, that's a different story. Those supporting section molds effectively prevent application of reinforcement to the underside while the deck is on the mold. Waiting until the deck is off the mold and on the boat will result in a big mess.

The only proper way to apply reinforcement material on both sides of the deck is to roll the deck over. That allows both laminates to be applied downhand, with gravity helping on your side. (Don't even think of trying to laminate overhead unless you've had years of experience working with resins and fabrics.) Obviously, the fewer rollovers necessary, the better. That's why you may choose to use a female form despite the requirement to work in negative space. A deck built on a female mold must be rolled over once. A male molded deck needs two complete rolls. (Note that this is the opposite to the hull where a female mold requires two rollovers while a male hull mold requires only one.)

FINISHING THE UNDERSIDE

While the deck is still upside down, consider what kind of finish the overhead will have in the completed boat. Smooth, fair, and paint the underside laminate if paint will be the final finish. As with laminating, fairing and painting are much easier when done downhand. Carpet headliner is also easier to install when the deck is upside down, and gravity helps keep the carpet in place during cutting and fitting.

Applying either paint or carpet will cause complications in areas where the deck will be bonded to the hull or to interior bulkheads. These areas must be left bare so that the thickened epoxy glue can form a strong secondary bond. Typical areas to be kept free of paint or carpet include:

➤ Edges at the sheerline where the deck will bond to the top edge of the hull.

➤ The athwartships path where interior bulkheads will bond to the underside of the deck.

➤ Fore-and-aft paths where deck carlins or interior bulkheads will bond to the underside of the deck.

Pathways for bonding must be considerably wider than just the thickness of the hull or bulkhead. Cloth reinforcement tabs extend at least 3 inches outward from *both* sides of the bulkhead, or a total width of at least 6 inches. Using thickened epoxy fillets in place of tabs reduces the required width by half.

It is inevitable that some paint will be scratched and the carpet will get dusty during rollover and the finishing of the top of the deck. Neither is a serious problem. Carpet can be vacuumed, and patching a scratch or two is easier than painting the entire underside of the deck once it's overhead in the completed boat. Installation of deck hardware also requires removal of small sections of carpet in the way of backing plates.

FINISHING THE UPPER SIDE

Boat factories normally complete the decks down to the last minor fittings before assembling them to their hulls. This process allows easy access to backing plates and nuts when tightening through-bolts. It also allows working on the deck at workbench height instead of at the top of a ladder. Assembly goes much more quickly, and the work is often done to a higher standard of quality than can be done once the deck is attached to the hull. The interior is being worked on simultaneously with the deck, and once the two are mated the boat is almost ready for shipping to the customer.

It is not always possible at home to subassemble deck and hull separately, especially on boats over 30 feet in length. The pieces get too large to handle without special lifting equipment. However, the advantages of subassembly are great enough to warrant considera-tion of this technique even with extremely large boats.

If the subassembly method is chosen, the upper side of the deck receives its final finish prior to installation of windows, hatches, or hardware. This includes smoothing, fairing, and painting with two-part urethane. (Full details on painting are included in Chapter 15, including methods of applying nonskid materials to walking areas.) Installation of hatches, windows, and deck hardware should not be attempted until the final coat of paint has been applied and allowed to cure completely.

Crawling around on a shiny new paint job can't be done without leaving behind a few nicks and scratches. As with the underside, the work needed to touch up these blemishes is far less than the work saved by completing the deck off the boat. Common sense goes a long way to avoiding damage. Ask a carpet store for pieces of scrap carpet about 4 by 8 feet (1.2 × 2.4 m). Used carpet removed from a customer's house can often be obtained cheaply or free. Clean it to be sure there are no small stones or tacks caught in the nap. Flop the carpet nap-side down on the deck to create a padded work area.

HARDWARE INSTALLATION

Hardware ranging from windows and ports to winches and mooring cleats must be installed so that it is functionally strong and prevents water from entering the composite balsa-cored laminate. Balsa is considerably stronger than most people realize, but it can be crushed by the force of tightening nuts on through-bolts. That's the primary reason for replacing the balsa core with pads of timber, plywood, or epoxy and glass. But keep in mind that wood is wood, whether it's balsa or Douglas fir. Rot is almost inevitable when water and wood get together. Every hole drilled through a composite deck requires sealing against water intrusion.

Bolt holes through timber or plywood should be sealed with unthickened epoxy. An easy way to get epoxy on all surfaces of the hole is with an ordinary white pipe cleaner. Pour a small amount of epoxy glue into a shallow pan. Dip the end of the pipe cleaner into the glue and then wipe it up and down and around the inside of the hole. Bolts should be installed while the epoxy is still wet, but be sure to clean any glue off the threads before running up the nuts. Spray the bolts with release agent to prevent permanently bonding them to the deck.

Two coats of unthickened epoxy are sufficient to seal the exposed balsa edges of openings for lightly stressed windows (e.g., non-opening side windows in a sailboat trunk cabin). Apply the first coat and allow it about ten minutes to soak in before brushing on the second coat. An epoxy seal coat is mandatory even if a polyurethane adhesive/sealant such as 3M's 5200 will be used to bed the window. Through-bolts holding these ports in place should be tightened just slightly beyond hand tight, but not so tightly as to crush the core of the laminate. Never use wood screws or self-tapping screws to hold hardware in DuraKore.

Exposed DuraKore around hatch or porthole cutouts should be sealed. One way is to cut back the wood, leaving the reinforcement skins. The cutback area is then filled with thickened epoxy for strength and to prevent water from intruding into the composite laminate.

Even small opening ports and deck hatches can put considerable strain on their mounting bolts. That's why it's common for these bolts to be torqued to the point where damage may occur to the balsa core. One way to prevent this is to create a ring of thickened epoxy around the cutout. Use a wood chisel to remove the balsa core to a depth of about ½ inch (13mm) all around the cutout. Fill the resulting groove with a bog putty of epoxy thickened with high-density

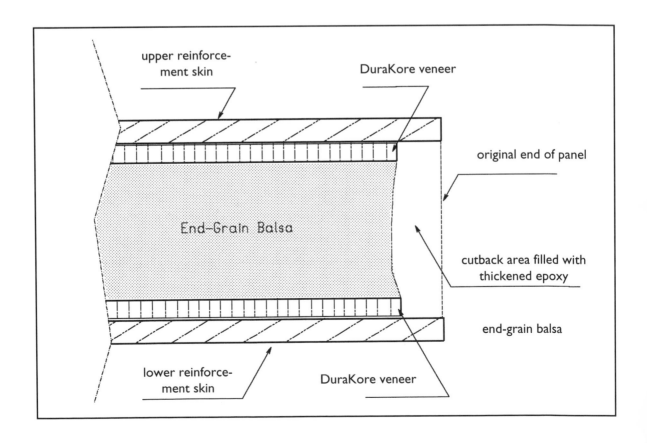

filler. This both seals the balsa core against water and provides a non-crushable ring around the opening. Install the window or opening port according to the manufacturer's instructions.

HIGH-STRAIN HARDWARE

Installing hardware that comes under heavy loading during normal operation of the boat requires special care. A list of high-strain items includes (but is not limited to) such items as:

- ➤ Mooring cleats, especially spring and quarter cleats.
- ➤ Anchor cleats or bitts on the foredeck. These can be the most heavily loaded pieces of deck hardware.
- ➤ Lifeline stanchion bases. The height of the stanchion becomes a lever arm magnifying the strain on the base when a crew member falls against the lifeline.
- ➤ Sailboat winches, turning blocks, and other deck hardware can be extremely heavily loaded when handling large sails.
- ➤ Welded pipe radar arches. A high-speed boat pounding into a head sea creates whipping motions that put considerable strain on the deck and mounting bolts.

The above hardware must have metal backing plates in addition to the wood or epoxy/glass plugs mentioned earlier. Backing plates spread the strain of the mounting bolts over the widest possible area. This prevents mounting bolts from pulling through the deck under severe loading.

Backing plates have been made of almost any metal, although 3/16-inch (5mm) aluminum plate is most popular. Almost any grade of aluminum will do, although copper-bearing alloys should be avoided because they corrode rapidly in salt water. Cut the plate at least 1 inch bigger than the base of the hardware. Drill the holes in the backing plate slightly oversize to allow enough "slop" to align the bolts through the piece of hardware, the deck, and the plate. Always use flat washers and lockwashers under standard nuts. Self-locking aircraft nuts with their nylon inserts eliminate the need for lockwashers but not flat washers.

Through-bolts are recommended for all hardware, whether it is expected to come under load or not. Conventional wood screws or self-tapping stainless steel screws can be used to secure hardware

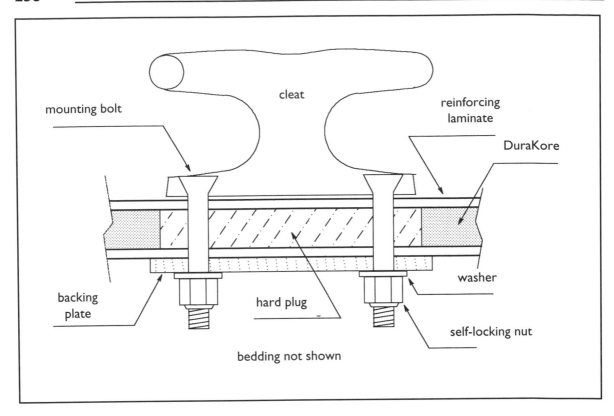

Backing plates and through-bolts are needed for highly stressed hardware such as cleats. The hard plug (wood or epoxy) prevents the DuraKore deck from being crushed as the mounting bolts are tightened. Plenty of polysulfide caulk should be used to prevent leaks.

into timber or plywood in the laminate. Under no circumstances should ordinary wood screws be driven into the balsa core of either DuraKore strips or DecoLite panels. Balsa does not have the ability to hold screws tightly. Eventually, the wood breaks down around the shank of the screw and it loosens or falls out. At that point, there is a potentially dangerous opening for water directly into the core of the laminate.

BEDDING DECK HARDWARE

Hardware mounted on a composite core deck must be bedded in a marine-grade compound. The purpose of bedding compound is to provide yet another barrier against water getting into the wooden core of the laminate. Three types of bedding materials are available:

> ➤ Polysulfide—These compounds form a hard yet slightly elastic barrier between the hardware and the deck. Two advantages of polysulfide are that it is not damaged by teak

cleaners and that joints can be broken when repairs become necessary.

➤ Polyurethane—Favorites below the waterline, these compounds are also excellent adhesives. Polyurethanes should be used only on permanent hardware that will normally not be removed during the lifespan of the vessel.

➤ Silicone—Available in clear, black, white, and a few other colors, silicone compounds are excellent for bedding items that are removed on a seasonal basis. They form only a moderate bond and are subject to old age failure quicker than polysulfides or polyurethanes. Silicone compounds are not highly recommended except for bedding certain plastic portholes and other plastic hardware that may be damaged by polyurethane or polysulfide materials.

Apply bedding compound generously to the base of the piece of hardware. Install it on the deck and push the mounting bolts through. A bit of bedding around the bolts or in their threads does no harm and may actually prevent a leak.

Chapter 14
MULTIHULL CONSTRUCTION

To date, the majority of amateur-built DuraKore strip composite boats have been multihull sailboats, especially cruising trimarans. This type of boat is a perfect match for the light weight and strength of DuraKore construction. In addition, sailors looking for a multihull boat find the offerings from commercial boatbuilders extremely limited. The only way to get some boats is to build 'em yourself.

While the basic techniques for using DuraKore or epoxy are the same, construction of a multihull is fundamentally different from a monohull in several ways. The biggest difference is building the boat in two vertical halves by reversing the station molds for each half. The other major difference is the need for a bridge deck or other structure to tie the outer floats and the main hull together.

HALF-HULL CONSTRUCTION

Ian Farrier's F-25 and F-32 trimarans are undoubtedly the most successful design intended for DuraKore strip composite construction. Amateur builders in the United States, Australia, and Europe have successfully completed boats. The main hull and both floats of these craft are built in two vertical halves using female molds. Building the port and starboard sides of a hull by reversing the section molds is fairly straightforward.

"This method is very suitable for strip planking," Farrier tells builders in his extremely thorough construction manual. "Only half a frame (station mold) needs to be made as a temporary form, it merely being turned around to make the other side. The center hull, the cabin sides, roof and most of the deck can be combined and all made at the same time, avoiding a lot of framing later," Farrier says. "An overlap join is required down the center, but this is exactly where any extra glass/reinforcement should be for stiffness and abrasion resistance."

THE FEMALE HALF-MOLD

Start by cutting as many rectangular pieces of particle board as there will be section molds. These must be absolutely true rectangles with exact 90-degree angles in each corner. All pieces should be identical in height and width. Height should be equal to half of the maximum beam of the completed hull *plus* 20 percent. The width should be equal to the maximum depth (top outside of deck to bottom outside at keel) of the completed hull plus about 20 percent beyond the deck. Allow enough extra material beyond the keel to represent the distance from the outside of the keel to the baseline of the lofting.

(Note: The following layout procedure may conflict with instructions supplied by some kit boat companies. In that case, follow the instructions supplied by the manufacturer or designer of your boat.)

A female half-mold rotates the section view of the lofting 90 degrees so that the vertical centerline becomes the top edge of the section molds. One vertical edge of the rectangular piece then becomes equivalent to the baseline of the lofting. Waterlines should be drawn and labeled on each rectangle to assist in positioning the Mylar patterns. Mark the centerline and baseline on each rectangle.

Lay the pattern for each section on a separate rectangle. Align it with the baseline and centerline edges of the material and with the drawn waterlines before taping the pattern down. Prick through the pattern with an awl to mark the shape of the hull on the particle board beneath. Remove the pattern and use a lofting batten to join the prick marks. Mark the cut line with a sharp pencil. Write the word "face" on the rectangle to identify the side from which you are cutting.

Carbon paper can also be used to transfer the hull shape from pattern to particle board when building smaller hulls. Tracing the line on the pattern automatically creates a similar line on the board beneath the carbon paper. It still pays to check the cut line with a lofting batten before cutting. Minor joggles caused by the rough surface of the particle board can creep into the tracing.

Finally, an alignment control line must be marked on each mold from top to bottom. This alignment control line is strictly for lining up the molds on the strongback. It may coincide with one of the lofted waterlines but probably will not. The purpose is to give you a control line on the mold to align above the center wire of the

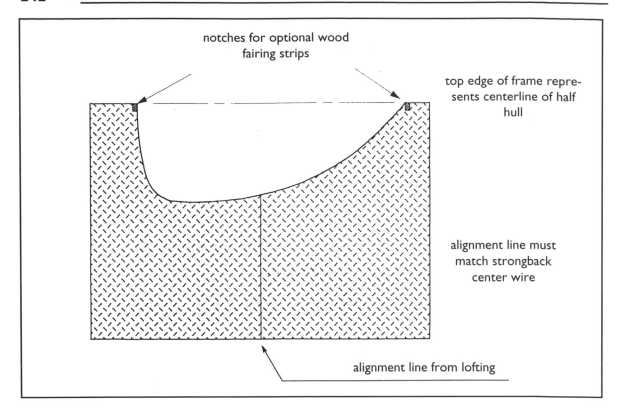

notches for optional wood
fairing strips

top edge of frame repre-
sents centerline of half
hull

alignment line must
match strongback
center wire

alignment line from lofting

Female mold frames are normally used for multihull floats. The shape of the cutout is half a vertical section from keel to the center-line of the deck. Frames are reversed to build both sides of the float. The fairing strips ensure that the joining surfaces of the halves are identical.
(Courtesy Ian Farrier)

strongback. Naturally, the alignment control line must be parallel to the lofted waterlines. Label it "control line" for future reference.

CUTTING HALF-MOLDS

The completed strongback makes an excellent worktable for cutting out the molds with an electric sabersaw. Use a try square to check that the footplate is square with the saw blade before you begin. Then use caution not to rock the saw left or right while cutting. These precautions ensure that the kerf runs at precisely 90 degrees to the face of the particle board. Any deviation from a right angle creates problems when attaching DuraKore battens. Always cut to the *inside* of the pencil cut line so the inevitable joggles can be removed with an electric palm sander and 80-grit paper.

Trimaran designer Ian Farrier suggests that all molds be notched for optional fairing strips. These strips are installed at the deck centerline and the keel. Made out of lumberyard pine, they are used to assist in creating an absolutely straight mating surface of the hull half. If fairing strips are desired, the molds should be notched at this time.

ERECTING HALF-MOLDS

Decide whether you want to build the port or starboard half of the hull first. If it's the starboard, then the baseline edge of the molds should be to your right as you look down the strongback from the bow. Reversing the baseline so that it is to your left will automatically create the port side of the boat. This trick of reversing section molds allows building the whole hull using only one set of half-molds.

Section molds are always attached to the same side of the strongback cross members. Normally, this is the front (bow) side. Clamp a lofting batten to the face of the mold so that its straight edge lies exactly along the baseline side of the alignment control line. Set the mold on the rails of the strongback and slide it until the edge of the batten just touches the center wire. Use a builder's square to make sure each mold stands at exactly 90 degrees to the strongback rails. Work from bow to stern using this procedure to erect all section molds.

Scrap lumber bracing should be used to secure the molds in the

Female mold frames are set up on the strongback in the same manner as male frames. These molds were erected to build the starboard side of a float. (Courtesy Ian Farrier)

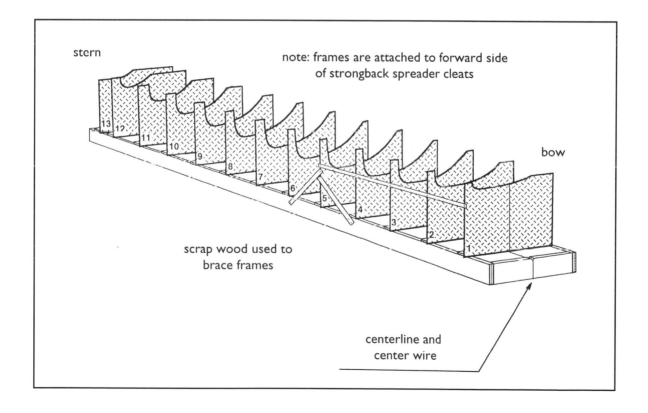

stern

note: frames are attached to forward side of strongback spreader cleats

bow

scrap wood used to brace frames

centerline and center wire

correct position. Diagonal braces from mold to strongback are necessary every fourth or fifth section. Horizontal braces are sufficient to hold the intermediate molds. The mold must be solid, but avoid over-bracing, as excess braces get in the way of planking the hull.

Before tightening everything down, check the fairness of the mold with a long batten of DuraKore. Look for high spots on the molds that pull the batten away from the molds on either side. Likewise, find any low spots where the mold does not quite touch the batten. These problems are normally caused by misalignment of an individual section mold. A bit of creative "ooching" should solve the problem.

Install the fairing strips (if required) along the keel and deck centerline. Cover the edges of the molds with package tape or sheet vinyl to prevent the DuraKore strips from bonding to the building form. The female half-mold is now erected and ready for planking.

PLANKING A HALF-HULL

The following paragraphs outline only the special steps necessary to plank a half-hull. See the appropriate chapters earlier in this book for full details on planking, coating, fairing, and laminating. Pre-coat both sides of all planking battens with unthickened epoxy. Plank the half-hull using drywall screws to hold the strips in position on the mold. Bond the seams with thickened epoxy, cleaning up excess glue before it kicks.

Remove the temporary drywall screws and apply the reinforcement laminate inside the hull. Use unthickened epoxy to seal the exposed edges of the DuraKore strips along the deck and keel where the two halves will eventually mate. Remove the half-hull from the mold and roll it over onto specially built horses to support it at a convenient work height. Carefully perform initial fairing to the outside of the hull. Apply the specified reinforcement lamination using unthickened epoxy.

Two hull halves built in the same molds should be mirror images, but that doesn't mean they will stay that way. One builder constructed a hull half and then stored it in a farm machinery shed while he worked on the other half. The storage period turned out to be a bit longer than planned. When the time came to mate the two half-hulls, something was wrong. The half that had been stored in the shed had changed shape up to 3 inches in some places. Creative thinking saved this builder from disaster. He put the misshapen half

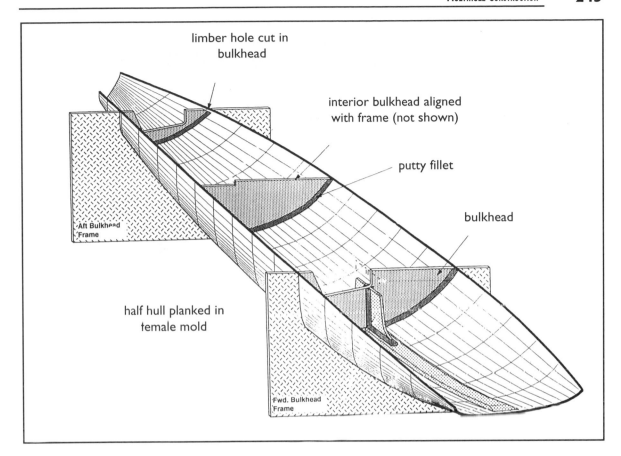

limber hole cut in
bulkhead

interior bulkhead aligned
with frame (not shown)

putty fillet

bulkhead

Aft Bulkhead
Frame

half hull planked in
temale mold

Fwd. Bulkhead
Frame

into a plastic tent and began running humidifiers day and night. Eventually, the piece changed back almost to its original shape and the two hull halves could be joined properly.

There's a threefold moral to this story. First, both halves of a hull should be built as quickly as possible. Don't store one for an extended period of time. The second part of the moral is that the completed half-hull and the materials for building the other half should be stored under the same conditions. That way, if the moisture content of the materials changes, everything will change the same amount. And the third part is that it's possible to fix even huge mistakes if you just keep a cool head and be creative.

Only two female mold frames are shown here for clarity. The bulkheads are aligned with the molds so they will mate with bulkheads in the matching other half.
(Courtesy Ian Farrier)

JOINING HALF-HULLS

Assume that the port side of the hull was built first and the starboard side is still in the mold. Both halves have been laminated with reinforcement material on the inside, and all internal half bulkheads

If the molds were set up with care, the two halves of the float should fit together perfectly, as they did for Canadian builder Colin Haigh. Note that the lower half is still supported by the mold frames.

have been installed. In short, everything is ready to mate the two pieces into a full hull.

Start the final assembly by temporarily removing the second hull half from the building mold. Cut down the top edges of the mold frames by 4 to 6 inches (10 to 15 cm). This clears the area along the hull joint wide enough for the application of the reinforcement tape. These cuts do not have to be neat since their only purpose is to give you room to work. Apply package tape or sheet vinyl to the cut edge to prevent any spilled epoxy from bonding the hull to the mold. Replace the half-hull in its mold.

Note: If two hulls (say two outer floats) are being constructed in the same set of molds, delay cutting down the frames until all four pieces have been built.

Remove amine blush from the mating surfaces of the two parts. Sand the surfaces lightly with 80-grit paper, then lift the port side into position on top of the starboard. Do this "dry," with no epoxy in the joint. Check the fit to be sure there will be no major problems once the bonding begins. When everything checks out, support the port half slightly above the starboard on blocks of scrap wood. The gap between the two parts should be large enough for easy application of thickened epoxy.

Use the same amount of thickener in the epoxy mixture as was used to glue the seams between the DuraKore battens. Apply it around the perimeter of the starboard side using the pastry bag technique or a putty knife. Starting at one end, carefully pull the spacer blocks from between the two halves. Allow the port side to settle gently onto the epoxy-coated starboard piece. Apply glue to the dry spaces left when the spacer blocks are removed. Allow the weight of the top piece to squeeze out excess glue. As with all seams, clean up any excess epoxy that squeezes out of the joint between the hull halves while it is still wet.

Some small misalignment between the pieces is inevitable. Overcome it by screwing temporary fairing sticks across the misaligned section of the joint. These sticks should be about 4 inches (10 cm) wide and wrapped in plastic to prevent their sticking to the hull. Put them in place with temporary screws. The object is to pull both hull pieces into alignment against the fairing sticks by tightening the screws. Once the glue in the joint cures, remove the sticks and fill holes left behind by the temporary fasteners.

After the glue cures, laminate a minimum 4-inch-wide (100mm) strip of reinforcement tape over the joint. This is normally a strip of the same fabric used to laminate the outside of the hull. Clean amine blush and lightly sand the bonding area of the hull before setting the strip in unthickened epoxy. Additional laminations may be specified by the boat designer. These are usually at least 6 inches (150mm) wide and may be 12-ounce (400 gm) unidirectional tape or 8-ounce (270 gm) Kevlar or similar materials. Reinforcement tape must also be laminated over the joint on the inside of the hull, particularly in the bilge area. This inner strip does more than just add strength to the joint, it provides another water barrier to protect the core.

STEM CAP TECHNIQUE

From a practical standpoint, it's nearly impossible to build the stem of a vessel assembled from half-hulls. Instead of planking the exact shape of the stem, Ian Farrier suggests this much simpler technique for building his F 25A trimaran hulls. The hull halves are planked very near—but not quite to—the actual shape of the stem. The ends of the planking battens remain ragged until after the halves are joined. Then a line is scribed around the outside of the DuraKore. This line is used to cut off the ragged ends with a builder's saw. This results in snub-nosed ends to the boat well short of the eventual stem line.

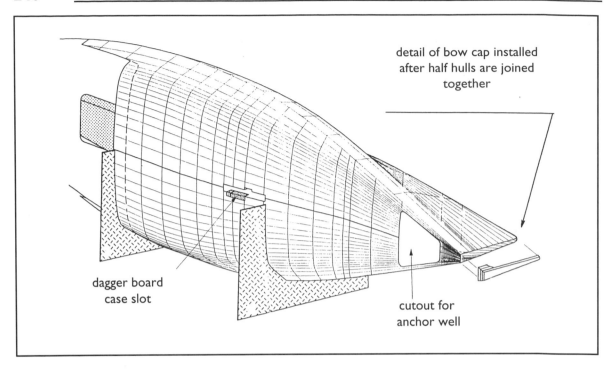

detail of bow cap installed
after half hulls are joined
together

dagger board
case slot

cutout for
anchor well

Ian Farrier uses the half-hull technique for the main hull of his DuraKore trimarans. The halves are joined while one is still in the building mold. A solid cap, sanded to shape before the reinforcement fabric is applied, closes the bow after the halves are joined.

The hull now has an oval opening from keel to deck where the stem should be. The inside corners of this opening are slightly rounded before a strip of reinforcement fabric is applied to seal the exposed balsa. Later, this oval opening is covered with an end panel and capped with a plug carved to the shape of the stem and forefoot.

Plywood or laminated hardwood is always needed to reinforce locations on the stem where hardware such as sailboat headstay tangs or bow eyes of trailerable boats will be installed. A solid wood cap will create the required shape and provides needed reinforcement. Balsa or closed-cell PVC plastic foam may be substituted in nonstructural areas. These softer materials are much easier to sand into shape than solid wood. Both types of cap stems are fully covered by reinforcing skins added after shaping is completed.

Grinding or power sanding is necessary to carve the stem cap to shape. Templates made of ¼-inch plywood should be used to monitor the sanding to ensure the correct shape is achieved. Shapes for these templates can be taken from the full-size lofting or can be printed full size on Mylar by the computer. Once the final shape is achieved, the bow cap must be covered with reinforcing material set in epoxy. Follow the same layup schedule as specified for the rest of the hull.

FINAL FAIRING

Full details are given in the chapter on final fairing. The taping over the hull joint seam requires special attention, as does the stem cap. Sand and fair them into the overall contour of the hull, being careful not to grind completely through the tape.

CROSSBEAMS AND BRIDGE DECKS

Multihulls are just a collection of hulls all going the same place at the same time. Crossbeams or bridge decks keep everything organized. No other part of a multihull requires as much engineering and painstaking construction. If the beams aren't right, the boat isn't right. Considerations in building crossbeams and bridge decks include:

> ➤ Strength—The forces generated in heavy weather can be enormous. Buoyancy of the leeward float pushes upward to resist the heeling pressure of the sails. Add to that the dynamic forces generated by the boat's forward motion through the water. A single weak component can lead to catastrophic failure of the crossbeam or bridge deck.
> ➤ Light Weight—Even though the crossbeam must be strong, it cannot have excessive weight. Most successful designs are trusses built of either aluminum or cored composite materials.
> ➤ Ability to Fold—The sailing width of trimarans under 30 feet (9 m) is usually more than the maximum trailer width allowed on highways. Some method of reducing width is needed if these boats are to be trailered. Folding crossbeams and demountable floats are typical approaches.

Ian Farrier uses a patented folding beam system on his F-Series trimarans. This design is considered the industry leader for both easy construction and simple operation. Larger cruising boats are not trailered, so do not require folding crossbeams. Being permanent, large boat crossbeams are often heavily modified to serve multiple functions. Dick Newick, for instance, uses what he calls "wing akas" on his trimarans. These graceful, gull-shaped structures often have enough interior room for a bunk. However, they are just a modified box beam, which gets its strength from shape and careful use of materials.

BOX BEAM DESIGN

More than thirty years ago Arthur Piver popularized cruising tri-marans. He used laminated timber and plywood box trusses to hold wing floats to the main hull. Kit Cat Designs has updated this concept in its S-28 Sport Cruiser. Panels cut from DecoLite sheets or DuraKore planks are used in high-tech composite construction that is lighter and stronger than earlier designs. The S-28 is currently available in various stages of construction from a basic kit to a complete boat.

Construction of the two S-28 beams is about the simplest boatbuilding possible. Both are essentially flat, square boxes. Panels for the bottom of either box are joined and laid on the shop floor. Because the final product will be a beam, this part is known as the "bottom cap." An identical panel on top is, naturally, called the "top cap." Side walls are called "webs." These pieces are cut to square dimensions. There are no complicated bevels or angles.

Construction starts by dry fitting the webs to the bottom cap. Internal cross members and diagonals are also dry fitted and the positions of everything marked for reassembly. The box is knocked down so the parts can receive a seal coat of epoxy. The parts are then

All square corners and flat pieces, the main beam for a Kit Cat S-28 is both strong and easy to build. The boxy shape is disguised by innovative styling in the final boat. (Courtesy Kit Cat)

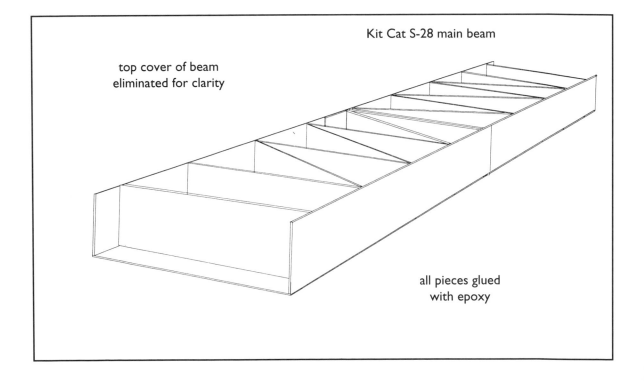

Kit Cat S-28 main beam

top cover of beam
eliminated for clarity

all pieces glued
with epoxy

bonded together using thickened epoxy squeezed out of a pastry bag. Temporary drywall screws hold it all together until the epoxy kicks. Although these beams are essentially oblong boxes, their square shape is effectively hidden in the completed S-28 by a streamlined bridge deck.

LAMINATED TIMBER

It is seldom possible to find solid timber suitable for a crossbeam. Even if it could be found, such a piece of wood would have an astronomical price tag. It is possible, however, to laminate thin strips of wood into complex shapes using epoxy glue. This requires a special jig or a laminating table to hold the strips in the required shape until the glue kicks. Laminated shapes experience a minor change of shape known as "springback" after removal from the jig. One way of accommodating this change is to make the part oversized and then trim it to the exact shape after it's off the jig and has "sprung."

This stern view of the Kit Cat S-28 shows how well the main beam is carefully styled into the twin hulls. Canadian designer Christopher P. Copeland had amateur construction in mind when he drew the plans for this DuraKore boat.
(Courtesy Kit Cat)

ALUMINUM TRUSSES

Aluminum trusses can be quite simple. Round pipe sections are used on smaller catamarans that require demountable floats for trailering. The strength of a tube is related to its diameter and wall thickness. Larger diameter tubes require less bracing than smaller ones. If small diameter is chosen, it is customary to add wire stays from the main hull chines to the outer end of the tubes.

Aluminum crossbeams can also be complex trusses such as those found on high-performance offshore racers. Marine-grade aluminum alloys stand up well in salt water. Welding allows the designer considerable flexibility in putting strength where it is needed while still meeting the demands of complex shapes. The problem with welded aluminum crossbeams lies in the welds, which tend to be weaker than the parent metal. In some cases, welds cut in half the strength of the surrounding aluminum. This may result in premature failure of welds if the designer has not engineered enough strength into the truss.

From an amateur standpoint, welded aluminum trusses are extremely difficult to produce. Aluminum cannot be exposed to the air during welding. Expensive inert gas welding equipment is required, along with above-average welding skills. Few amateurs have the equipment or the experience, so building a truss may require hiring the services of a custom fabrication shop.

FOLDING BEAMS

"Complex" is the best way to describe nearly all folding beam designs prior to Ian Farrier's patented new system. His simple design consists of two central mounting units (CMU) and two sets of beams and struts for each float. All of the parts are prefabricated and shipped to the builder as a unit. Farrier claims that installing his new system allows an F-25A to be built faster than a much smaller Trailertri 720.

The CMUs are fitted into their respective positions in the main hull after the appropriate openings have been cut. Once the modules are leveled and centered, they are bonded into position with epoxy and reinforcement fabric (usually fiberglass). The CMUs contain all of the mounting points and brackets for the float beams and their associated folding struts. Farrier's innovative design allows the CMUs to align the float beams automatically as they are installed. Bonding the floats onto the beams completes construction.

MOUNTING CROSSBEAMS

Crossbeams must be set at the correct angle to the keel line of the main hull and floats of a trimaran (or two hulls of a catamaran). If this angular relationship is not achieved, the boat will be like an automobile with its wheels out of alignment. Many multihulls use internal bulkheads to support the crossbeams, so it's obvious that precise installation of these bulkheads becomes critical to the sailing performance of the vessel.

Because the half-hulls of a tri or catamaran are built in female forms, it is not possible to install the bulkheads on the building form as permanent stations. Instead, half bulkheads are installed in the port and starboard hulls while they are still in the building mold. These bulkheads are placed with extreme care so they mate perfectly when the hull halves are joined. In addition to alignment, attention must be paid to tabbing and bonding these bulkheads into the hulls. Bulkheads come under considerable strain, especially when sailing at high speeds.

Special care is also required when bonding crossbeams to the outer skins of the hulls. Loads should be spread across the largest surface area possible of both the beams and the hulls. Observe all of the precautions for achieving strong secondary bonds, especially removing amine blush and sanding. Somewhat exotic reinforcement materials are often specified for attaching crossbeams. Unidirectional fibers are commonly specified by multihull designers.

Aluminum tube crossbeams may require attaching bolts through structural members of the hull. As with other locations where hardware pierces the laminate, the balsa core should be replaced with plugs of solid wood, plywood, or epoxy and fiberglass.

Chapter 15
FINAL EXTERIOR FINISH

ard and durable as they are, epoxies have an Achilles heel: the sun's ultraviolet rays. Prolonged exposure to ultraviolet causes cured epoxy to break down. This is a minor drawback, however, because two coats of marine paint block ultraviolet sufficiently to prevent breakdown of cured epoxy beneath it. Modern two-part polyurethane paints and their associated clear coats are the perfect finishing touch. They adhere tenaciously to epoxy and have greatly extended lifespans compared to traditional marine enamels.

AwlGrip, Sterling, and Imron are the brand names that come to mind most often when two-part polyurethanes are discussed. All three come in a bewildering variety of colors from plain white to metallic gold. AwlGrip was developed for painting aircraft and still has the reputation as the toughest coating. Sterling and Imron were formulated for the automotive finish market where ease of repair and wide selection of colors are keys to success. All three paint systems are available from stores selling to professional automotive refinishers, if they can't be found at marine outlets.

These paint systems are intended for professional application. Consumer paint companies offer two-part polyurethane coatings designed for amateur application. These are easier to apply, but seem to produce a slightly softer finish. On the plus side, they are easily spot repaired when dinged or gouged. Interlux's Interthane Plus and Pettit's Dura Thane are both two-part systems that can be applied with a brush or roller. The biggest disadvantage of two-part systems from marine paint manufacturers is lack of color choice. The offerings are typically limited to white, off-white, gray, red, and light blue.

Single polyurethanes are even easier to apply or to repair when damaged. And, as might be expected, they have shorter lifespans than two-part coatings. Interlux's Brightside polyurethane offers a wide range of colors from "Seattle Gray" to "Sea Green" and "Fire Red." Pettit's Easypoxy is another low-cost solution. This alkyd paint is offered in an equally wide range of colors.

AwlGrip is definitely the paint of choice if it can be applied by a professional with a spray gun. The long lifespan will more than offset the wages of the painter or the cost of the materials. Imron and Sterling are also best sprayed, although it's possible to get outstanding results rolling and tipping. Boatowners often favor these paints because they are easier to roll/tip and somewhat easier to patch and repair. Two-part offerings from Pettit, Interlux, and other marine paint companies are the best alternative for inexperienced painters. They are more forgiving when applied by roller and brush.

Avoid traditional alkyd enamels for finishing a DuraKore strip composite boat. True, these paints provide both pleasant colors and the required ultraviolet protection. However, these low-tech paints do not have the longevity to match the rest of the high-tech construction. Renewing of old-fashioned coatings will be necessary at least every third season in northern climates and more often closer to the equator. The continuing cost of sanding and painting traditional paint soon outstrips the higher initial cost of a two-part system.

Reflections of the sunset highlight the perfectly smooth sides of a custom sportfish built by Malcolm L. Pettegrow, Inc., in Southwest Harbor, Maine. The hull, deck, and cabin house of this boat were built from DuraKore strips covered with fiberglass set in epoxy. The smooth gloss is the result of hours of careful fairing and smoothing.

There is one application where alkyd enamels are excellent: painted nonskid surfaces. The easiest way to apply an attractive nonskid finish to a deck or cockpit sole is to mix special nonskid granules into alkyd paint of the appropriate color. Shorter lifespan of the paint is of no consequence, because foot traffic eventually wears away the nonskid property of the granules. Regular renewal (every two or three years) ensures that the decks remain colorful and truly nonskid.

SURFACE PREPARATION

Final fairing must be completed and the surface seal-coated with epoxy prior to application of the paint. Remove amine blush and then work up through the grits, sanding the seal coat to ensure it is absolutely smooth and has a good "tooth" for paint adhesion. Runs or sags in the seal coat may require spot sanding with 80 grit before smooth sanding. Otherwise, start with 120 grit dry before moving to wet sanding with 220, 400, and 600 grit.

Use caution not to "burn" through the seal coat. Don't panic if it happens, however. Apply at least two new coats of epoxy over the spot and allow them to harden. Starting with 80 grit, "feather" the edges of this patch into the surrounding area, then smooth sand up through the grits. The same repair procedure is used to fix pockmarks or air bubbles discovered in the seal coat.

Complete all sanding before applying any paint. Take a day to thoroughly clean not only the hull, but also the shop. Vacuum up as much sanding dust as possible, especially from the floor, where it gets stirred up with every step. Wet paint attracts dust like a dog draws fleas. Dust in the atmosphere seems to float directly to a wet surface. The only way to ensure a smooth, glossy look to the finished job is to eliminate as much dust as possible before opening the paint can.

Once the shop is dust free, wipe down the hull with clean *white* rags or *white* paper towels moistened with an approved solvent for the two-part paint system. Never use colored rags or paper towels with colorful ink patterns printed on them. Dyes and inks can dissolve in the solvent and be deposited on the hull as chemical contamination. Allow the solvent plenty of time to evaporate: two to four hours or more.

A trick used by professionals to control dust is wetting down the shop floor. Use a fine spray to dampen dust or small particles that could be stirred up by walking. Damp is fine, but puddles of water should be avoided. Be extremely careful not to wet down the portion of the hull that will receive the paint. Immediately prior to applying the first stroke of paint, wipe the hull down with a commercial tack rag to pick up the smallest motes of dust.

UNDERCOATER

A DuraKore strip composite hull should not need any additional undercoater beyond the seal coat of epoxy. Undercoaters are designed to fill minor imperfections and to allow sanding the surface absolutely smooth. The epoxy does both of these jobs, so a layer of undercoater is redundant. If, however, an undercoater is desired to provide a neutral base color, be sure to pick one that is compatible with the two-part paint system to be applied over it.

FINISH COAT APPLICATION

Two-part polyurethane paints are notorious for being unforgiving. Careless application results in problems or complete disaster. Spend time learning how to use the paint system you choose. Make some test applications on scrap pieces or out-of-the-way sections of the boat. Never attempt to paint the whole hull before learning the unique characteristics of the system you are using.

Two or three thin coats of two-part paint are always preferable to a single heavy coat. This is true on horizontal surfaces, but absolutely true on vertical ones, where thick paint is sure to sag or run.

Two-part coatings must be mixed exactly in accordance with the manufacturer's instructions. The ratio of paint to activator should never be changed from what is specified on the label. However, the mixed coating can be thinned for easier application by using an appropriate "reducer." Some paint systems offer a choice of reducers that alter the cure rate of the mixed paint. This allows the painter to slow down the cure on a hot, humid day or to speed it up in cool, dry conditions. Adding reducer generally extends the cure rate, allowing a longer "wet edge," which makes brushing easier and enhances the flow characteristics.

The chemical reaction that causes two-part paints to cure can't be stopped once the activator has been added. Pot life is from four to six hours at normal room temperature. Mix only as much paint as can be applied during one work session. Leftover paint can't be saved from day to day; it must be discarded. Always mix two-part polyurethane paints in clean metal or glass containers. Avoid plastic containers, which may weaken or melt when exposed to the chemicals in the paint.

> ### SPRAY APPLICATION WARNING
>
> The spraying of two-part polyurethane coatings by amateurs is definitely not recommended. In fact, most paint manufacturers restrict spraying of their products to professional applicators. Fumes and paint dust (small particles of spray that float in the air) from these products contain toxic isocyanates. Mist from spraying can cause severe lung irritation and an allergic respiratory reaction when inhaled. Some paints warn of potential nervous system damage from the solvents. Special clothing and air-supplied chemical respirators are required for safe spray application of two-part polyurethane coatings. Do not attempt to spray them unless you have the proper equipment and training.

MASKING TAPE

Ordinary masking tape is not the best to use with thin paints like the two-part polyurethane systems. These paints easily "creep" under conventional masking tape, leaving a ragged edge. If possible, always use 3M's Fine Line tape when masking. Leave tape on the boat only long enough for the paint to cure. Tape left on too long becomes almost impossible to remove. This warning goes double if the tape is exposed to sunlight.

When extensive two-tone paint schemes are undertaken, it's necessary to use paper to mask large portions of the hull, deck, or cabin structure. Automotive paint stores sell rolls of special paper for this purpose. They also sell a machine that automatically applies masking tape to one edge of the paper as it is unrolled. This machine allows one person to quickly apply long pieces of taped paper. If sanity is important, buy a masking machine. Apply the 3M Fine Line tape to the hull first, then use regular masking tape in the masking machine to apply the paper on top of the finer tape.

PERSONAL SAFETY

Application of two-part paint systems with roller or brush does not present as many potentially toxic hazards to the painter as spraying. Even so, invest in a NIOSH-approved organic vapor respirator for everyone in the shop to wear when paint is being applied. Expensive respirators have soft rubber face pieces and replaceable, screw-on filter cartridges. Less expensive are 3M disposable respirator masks. Both types prevent breathing potentially toxic vapors from the paint. Rubber gloves and eye protection also should be worn.

ROLLER AND BRUSH APPLICATION

The most successful application of two-part paints by amateurs is by roller and brush. This technique requires two workers, one applying the paint with a roller and the other "tipping out" bubbles or roller marks with a brush. Done correctly, roller and brush application rivals a professional spray job for smoothness and high gloss. Special foam roller covers are necessary. They must be compatible with the paint system. Ordinary foam roller covers may be dissolved by the chemicals. A soft, natural bristle (so-called "China bristle") brush is recommended for tipping out. Buy the very best brushes available. Those of high quality are less likely to lose bristles in the work. Good brushes also help the paint flow out with fewer stroke marks.

The first painter rolls the paint onto the hull *in one direction only*. This worker does not use the traditional back-and-forth roller action.

Roll only in one direction—say from left to right. Immediately afterward, the second painter uses the brush to very lightly tip off the fresh paint to remove stipple marks. Never stop in the middle of a long panel. It is virtually impossible to feather new paint into old. Always continue painting to a corner or other obvious stopping point. If it is necessary to stop, wait until you reach a joint or butting edge.

BRUSH APPLICATION

As when rolling, brush application of fresh paint should be done in one direction only. Always start from the dry surface and work back toward the wet edge of the previously applied paint. Load the brush with only a

small amount of paint to ensure the thinnest possible film. Applying too much paint, especially on vertical surfaces, is sure to result in sags or runs. The lap time of most two-part paints is no more than five minutes. Many dry tack-free (when dust will no longer settle into the wet paint) within 15 minutes of application.

Some roller stipple is impossible to avoid. It can be removed by tipping the wet paint with a disposable foam brush. Tipping involves dragging only the tip of the brush across the wet paint with almost no pressure. Done correctly it produces a finish that is nearly as smooth as one produced by a spray gun.

FIXING RUNS AND SAGS

Never try to fix a run or sag by brushing over the wet paint. This only makes the problem worse. Let the sag cure at least overnight before removing it by wet sanding with 220-grit paper. Apply a fresh coat of paint to the entire panel. If the sag occurs in the final topcoat, sand it smooth with 220 grit, then work up to at least 600 grit. All sanding should be done wet. Follow the sanding with mild buffing until the gloss returns. (Note: This technique works with softer two-part systems but is not suitable for AwlGrip.)

TOPCOATING FRESH PAINT

Manufacturers of two-part paints always recommend minimum curing times between application of one coat and topcoating with a second. The typical cure time is 16 to 24 hours at normal room temperature of 70°F (21°C). Longer cure times, up to three days, are recommended in cold temperatures.

Sanding between coats of two-part paints is usually not required if the next layer is applied within 24 to 48 hours. Check with the manufacturer's recommendations. If the next coat must be delayed longer than this time period, wet sand the fully cured paint with 280-grit paper. Remove the sanding slurry with plain water and white rags. Let the hull dry thoroughly and wipe down with a tack rag prior to applying the topcoat.

The completed paint job needs at least five days to cure before the boat is moved or launched. This extended time allows the paint to fully cure and to achieve its final abrasion resistance.

PAINT PROBLEMS AND SOLUTIONS

Polyurethane paints should provide a glossy finish that is often superior to the finest gelcoat on a factory-built boat. Occasionally, however, things go wrong. The following is a list of paint problems and their most common causes:

➤ Sags Or Runs In Finish Coat—Most likely caused by too heavy a coating. Thick layers of wet paint tend to sag. Sagging also occurs if an excessive amount of thinner is added to the paint.
➤ Brush Marks That Do Not Flow Out—Often the result of using a poor quality brush, but may also be caused by applying paint that is not properly thinned or by applying paint on a windy day or in the hot sun.
➤ Wrinkled Or Dull Finish When Dried—Wrinkles often indicate that paint was applied too thick. A dull finish may result when temperature is too low.
➤ Insufficient Adhesion—Almost always caused by improper surface preparation. The surface was contaminated by chemicals. May also result if paint film was too thin or if paint was exposed to weather before being fully cured.

PAINTED NONSKID DECKS

Special nonskid granules can be added to two-part coatings just as they can to conventional paints. Always use the nonskid material recommended by the manufacturer of the paint system. The granules supplied by paint manufacturers are extremely lightweight, so they remain suspended in the paint for a long period of time. Sand is too heavy to remain suspended, and settles quickly to the bottom of the paint can. Even though the nonskid granules remain suspended, they are still heavy enough to settle out of the paint over time. That's why the can should be stirred at regular intervals, say every fifth or sixth brush stroke.

Using a two-part polyurethane to create nonskid areas may not be the most effective method. The nonskid granules gradually wear out of the paint as it is walked on. Eventually, long before the two-part paint is dull and lifeless, the last of the nonskid granules have worn off. The solution is to apply another coat of nonskid paint. Because of the wear factor, it may be more cost effective to use a standard alkyd enamel for nonskid areas. A minimum of two coats of nonskid paint is always recommended.

UNDERWATER AREAS

Despite their great resistance to fading and physical damage, two-part polyurethane paints are not recommended for use below the waterline. This is especially true if the boat will be wet docked, as two-part polyurethane paints do not stand up to continuous immersion. Paint applied below the waterline must be specially formulated to work in the harsh underwater environment. All marine paint manufacturers offer antifouling paints designed to adhere even though under water for extended periods of time.

Chapter 16
MECHANICAL, ELECTRICAL, AND PLUMBING

nstallation of engines, fuel systems, and electrical systems can be the most intimidating part of boatbuilding. These jobs are governed by extensive federal regulations and boating industry practices. It's not sufficient just to get the engine working and the lights lighting. All piping and wiring should be done in accordance with strict guidelines intended to prevent fires and other disasters.

The American Boat & Yacht Council (ABYC) publishes boating industry technical guidelines in a thick notebook called *Standards and Recommended Practices for Small Craft*. Many of the recommended practices have effectively become federal law by being referenced in U.S. Coast Guard safety regulations. Amateur builders can obtain personal copies of this invaluable book by becoming members of ABYC. The cost of membership is $75 (U.S.) per year. The notebook normally costs $150 (U.S.) but is offered to new members at half price. For more information, write ABYC, 3069 Solomon's Island Road, Edgewater, MD 21037-1416. Or phone (410) 956-1050.

The following discussion focuses on installing a single engine, as in a sailboat or New England lobsterboat. Adding a second engine doubles the work involved, but does not appreciably change the nature of the job. Single engines often involve installing propeller shafts through long skegs or "deadwood" timbers. Prop shafts on twin-engine boats usually exit directly through the skin of the hull without complication.

INBOARD ENGINE INSTALLATION

Engine installation actually begins before the first DuraKore strip is applied to the building form. Carefully plan the pathway by which the propeller shaft will exit the hull. Skegs, deadwoods, or other large structural members often need to be redesigned to allow inclusion of the shaft tube. It is always easier to build the tube into the skeg than it is to bore a straight hole after the hull is completed.

PROPELLER SHAFT TUBE, SEAL, AND BEARING

Determine the diameter of the prop shaft to be installed. Then choose the stuffing box or shaft seal and Cutless bearing to match. The shaft seal will specify the outside and inside diameters of the prop tube to which it can be attached. These diameters govern the construction of a fiberglass and epoxy tube for inclusion in the skeg. The tube itself is laminated into the skeg at the correct angle during construction.

Find a length of rigid plastic pipe slightly longer than the desired prop tube. The outside diameter of this pipe should match the required inside diameter of the tube. Schedule 40 plastic drain pipe works extremely well. Coat the pipe with release agent (e.g., non-stick cooking spray) and clamp it to sawhorses at either end. Using the wet method, laminate at least two layers of fiberglass cloth and unthickened epoxy resin around the pipe. Short lengths of pipe will not sag, but longer lengths may need a temporary support in the middle to ensure that the resulting prop tube is absolutely straight.

Allow the epoxy to harden just past the rubbery stage. Set the depth of cut on a builder's saw so that the blade just cuts through the laminate. Slice down the length of the pipe, then carefully peel the fiberglass tube off the pipe. Wrap two or more additional layers of 'glass in epoxy around the tube to seal the saw kerf and give the necessary strength. Support the tube so it remains straight while the epoxy kicks.

Laminate the prop tube into the skeg using thickened epoxy to fill gaps between the round tube and the rough opening in the skeg. The forward end of the prop tube must enter the hull through a hole cut in the bottom of the boat. Because of the angle of the tube, this hole will be a long oval. Seal the exposed balsa core before bonding the tube in place with thickened epoxy and reinforcement fabric.

Shaft logs come in two types. The older style is designed to be lag-bolted into a wooden deadwood timber. If this type is used, mounting bosses are needed at both ends of the prop tube. The interior boss accommodates the shaft seal, and the exterior boss allows mounting of the Cutless bearing. The faces of the bosses must be perpendicular to the prop tube in all planes of reference.

Both the seal and the bearing are bronze fittings with cast "ears" for the bolts that hold them to the boat. Lag bolts should be set into solid material such as timber or a fiberglass and epoxy laminate.

Through-bolts can replace lags if there is sufficient access both inside and outside.

The shaft log or seal must be thoroughly bedded in polyurethane (e.g., 3M 5200 or Sikaflex) to prevent water from leaking into the boat. Use plenty of caulking to be certain of a watertight seal. Fixing a leak around the shaft log is never easy. It requires hauling the boat and pulling the shaft, both of which can be expensive. Do the job right the first time. Caulking should also be used around the bolts holding the Cutless bearing to prevent water intrusion into the skeg.

There is an alternative to lag-bolting the shaft log into the boat. Newer shaft seal designs allow direct mounting onto the end of the prop tube. A short section of flexible hose is pushed over the end of the tube and double clamped in place. The shaft seal is then inserted into the hose and double clamped. This arrangement allows for a small degree of misalignment due to the flexibility of the rubber hose. The only drawback is that the outer perimeter of the inside end of the prop tube must have a smooth circumference to accept the hose. If the tube is not almost perfectly round and smooth, it may be impossible to achieve a watertight seal.

New style or old, correct alignment of the shaft log and Cutless bearing is essential to smooth operation. Many home builders postpone the actual fastening of these parts until the engine is installed and the prop shaft itself can be used as an alignment tool. The log and bearing are installed over the shaft. The shaft is then centered in the prop tube by adjusting the engine mounts.

The shafts of twin-engine boats seldom exit through skegs or deadwoods. Rather, the prop tube stops at the outer skin of the hull. This results in an open-ended, short tunnel from the outside to the shaft log. A Cutless bearing is not installed at the outer end of the prop tube. Rather, it's part of the strut that supports the shaft just ahead of the propeller.

Shaft tubes fill with water once the boat is afloat. If they are short, as in twin-screw installations, no problem results. However, long tubes common on single-screw boats can present a corrosion problem. Stagnant water trapped in a shaft tube has been found to be more corrosive than flowing water. For this reason, the ABYC recommends providing water circulation if the stern tube traps stagnant water. Some shaft logs have fittings that allow cooling water to be pumped down the shaft tube while the engine is operating. Or the tube can be provided with side vents to allow water circulation when the boat is under way.

ENGINE MOUNTS

Engine mounts hold the heavy internal combustion engine in position on the engine beds. Don't confuse good engine mounts with simple bolts. Properly engineered mounts do a lot more than just hold things together. They also allow for adjusting the alignment of the engine and absorb much of the vibration when underway. Most new small diesel engines and marine conversion gasoline engines are shipped complete with rubber insert engine mounts.

Lag screws are often used to fasten engine mounts onto solid timber engine beds. Use minimum 3-inch (76mm) lags through each engine mount. Longer screws are better than short. Drill a pilot hole slightly shorter than the length of the screw. Fill this hole with epoxy thickened with high-density filler. Tighten the screw as normal, wiping up any excess epoxy squeezed out of the hole. The epoxy will bond the lag bolt tightly to the bed and prevent it from being loosened by vibration. If the bolts ever need to be removed, heat them with a soldering iron to soften the epoxy.

Spike Meredith uses marine plywood to build the engine beds of his innovative V-Cat powerboats in suburban Cleveland, Ohio. Plywood is cut to shape, then bonded into the hull and encapsulated in several layers of reinforcement fabric and resin. Spike's patented tunnel hull is designed for high speed, which requires high horsepower. He has developed a system for installing engine mount bolts that prevents vibration and torque from loosening them. Spike uses 8-inch (200mm) long threaded rods bonded into the plywood engine beds with thickened epoxy. Here's how:

Meredith starts by drilling vertical holes the diameter of his mounting bolts down into the beds. He measures down the depth of these holes and marks the bottom of them on the outside of the beds. Using a hole saw, he drills sideways into the engine bed until he hits the vertical bolt hole. This creates an L-shaped passage with the lower end large enough to allow access for a thumb and forefinger. Bolts are inserted dry and double nuts screwed onto their lower ends once in position. Both the vertical bolt hole and the finger access are then filled with epoxy thickened with high-density filler.

INSTALLING THE POWER

Let that cast iron monster sit on the shop floor. Before doing anything, climb into the boat and center the adjusting nuts on the engine mounts. Centering the nuts allows adjustment either upward or downward as required to align the engine and prop shaft. Remove the upper nuts and washers from the mounts and set them aside where they will be handy but not get lost.

The easiest and safest way to put an engine into a hull is with an overhead electric chain hoist. A manual chain hoist also works, but avoid lifting devices that do not have positive control when lowering heavy weights. A runaway engine dropping from only a few feet can come down with enough force to punch its way through the bottom of the boat. Ouch! Most buildings do not have roof beams sufficiently strong for hoisting an engine. It may be necessary to rent a portable crane to get the job done safely.

Raise and lower the engine handsomely. ("Handsomely" is an old sailor's term for slowly, smoothly, and under complete control.) Have at least one assistant on a guy line to keep that iron from turning or swaying as it is raised and lowered. Everyone should stand well clear while the weight is in motion. Hoists fail, and there's no human strong enough to catch half a ton of falling metal. If something goes wrong, let it go.

Chances are, however, that everything will go as planned. Lower the engine handsomely onto the studs of the mounts. Install the top washers and nuts to secure everything. Once the engine is in place, tape sheet vinyl over all intake and exhaust openings, the cooling water intake, and the alternator to prevent dust from getting into the works.

FUEL SYSTEMS AND VENTILATION

A significant number of Coast Guard and ABYC regulations cover fuel tanks and their associated plumbing and fittings. The reason for all of this attention is the very real possibility of fire or explosion. Gasoline (petrol) systems get the most attention, but diesel systems also have safety regulations.

DIESEL FUEL SYSTEMS

(ABYC Practice H-33)
All components of a diesel fuel system must be constructed to withstand the combined conditions of pressure, vibration, shock and

movement encountered under normal operating conditions. Vibration is a serious consideration with diesel engines. Most builders use a flexible "rubber" hose to absorb engine vibration. All flexible hose must be identified as meeting USCG Type A1 or USCG Type A2 specifications. Both of these hoses meet a minimum 2½ minute fire test. Hose clamps are required on all barb fittings. Metal fuel lines should be seamless copper, nickel copper or copper nickel with a nominal wall thickness of at least 0.31-inches (0.81mm).

Filler lines can be hose or metal pipe. Hose will "snake" around the numerous bends between the deck and the tank. Filler hoses should have a minimum inside diameter of 1½-inches (31.75mm). All fuel tanks must be equipped with a vent that terminates outside the hull so that no fuel flowing from the vent will enter the boat. Vents must be equipped with a flame arresting screen. Vent lines must run from the highest point of the tank at normal angles of operation. Due to heeling, sailboats may require two vent lines. No part of the vent system should trap liquid.

Purchase fuel tanks from reputable builders who are familiar with the appropriate legal and technical specifications. Large tanks require internal baffles and must be welded in an approved manner. All tanks must be pressure tested for leaks by the manufacturer. Commercial tank builders can fabricate fuel tanks to fit into spaces of unusual shape. Naturally, such custom fabrication costs more than buying a standard design "off the shelf."

Federal regulations and ABYC practices require commercial boatbuilders to pressure test the entire fuel system after it is installed in the boat. The rules call for pressurizing the system with air to a minimum of 3.5 pounds per square inch. To pass the test, there should be no loss of pressure on a 50-gallon system during the first five minutes. Add another minute of test time for every additional 10 gallons' (or part thereof) capacity. In addition, a solution of soapy water should be used on every joint or connection in the system to detect leaks too small to show on the pressure gauge.

Permanent fuel tanks must be rigidly supported. Straps and supports should be separated from the tank by a non-metallic, non-moisture-absorbent, non-abrasive material such as neoprene or Teflon. Metal tanks installed above flat surfaces must have at least a ¼-inch (6mm) air gap between the tank bottom and the mounting surface.

It may come as a surprise, but the regulations do not require either a water separator or a "crud" filter in the fuel system. Of course, no sane skipper would operate a diesel engine without both. Racor, Stanadyne, and other manufacturers produce excellent units that both filter the fuel and remove any water. Good practice is to install filtration between the fuel tank and the engine fuel pump. Better practice is to install two filters with a crossover valve system. That way, if one filter becomes plugged with crud, operating a few valves takes it out of the system and replaces it with the second filter.

GASOLINE FUEL SYSTEMS

(ABYC Practice H-24)
Gasoline fumes are explosive. That is reason enough to treat them with respect, but in boats gasoline fumes are doubly dangerous because they are heavier than air. They collect in the lowest recesses of the bilge just waiting for a spark to set them off. Coast Guard regulations and ABYC practices are aimed at the same goal, preventing gasoline fumes from collecting in the bilge at explosive levels. A secondary goal is to protect the boat's fuel supply from ignition should there be an accidental fire aboard.

The same regulations regarding acceptable hoses and piping apply to gasoline and diesel. All flexible hose must be USCG Type A1. Also, the entire fuel system must be pressure tested in the same manner. Follow all of the suggestions for a diesel fuel system. Gasoline systems also must meet several additional regulations which do not apply to diesel systems.

Antisiphon protection is the first of these additional requirements. An antisiphon device must be installed at the tank end of all fuel lines. This is to prevent gasoline from being siphoned into the bilge should a break develop in the fuel line. There must be a shutoff valve at the tank end. This valve must be operable from outside the compartment in which the tank is located. (This can mean a shutoff valve located directly below an access port in the deck through which the valve can be operated.)

All metal parts of the fuel system—especially the deck filler plates—must be grounded. The maximum electrical resistance between any metal component and the boat's ground must be less than one ohm.

BILGE VENTILATION

(ABYC Practices H-2 and H-32)
The purpose of bilge ventilation is to remove any potentially explo-

sive fumes. Venting requirements for gasoline-powered boats are naturally more stringent than those for diesel vessels. Even with diesel power, however, it pays to follow the more stringent gasoline regulations which ensure constant exchange of bilge air for fresh outside air. The result is a slightly sweeter smelling boat and less potential for mildew.

Vent systems cannot remove all flammable vapors if the fuel system springs a leak or gasoline is spilled in the bilge. Even with the mechanical blower running there will be a continuous buildup of dangerous fumes as long as liquid gasoline is present.

Powered ventilation is required in all confined spaces that contain a permanently installed gasoline engine with an electrical cranking motor. The powered vent system must be able to exhaust air from the compartment at a minimum rate of 20 cubic feet per minute (cfm) for compartments smaller than 34 cubic feet. As the engine compartment gets bigger, the amount of powered exhaust ventilation also increases. Several exhaust blowers may be required for large compartments.

Electric exhaust blowers must be permanently installed above the normal level of bilge water. The blower intake duct should be permanently fixed in the lower third of the compartment as nearly as practical below the engine which it serves. The opening also should be above the normal accumulation of bilge water. Note that two independent vent systems may be required with dual engines.

Natural ventilation is also required for all compartments that contain a gasoline engine and/or a fuel tank and an electrical component that is not spark protected. This ventilation must be supplied even though the compartment also has power ventilation. Supply and exhaust ducts must terminate in the outside atmosphere. Each exhaust duct must originate in the lower third of the compartment, but above the normal accumulation of bilge water. The minimum internal cross section of any supply or exhaust duct must exceed 3.0 square inches (76 sq.mm). The aggregate cross section of all intake ducts is determined by the formula:

$$\text{Area} = 5 \times \log_e \frac{\text{Compartment Volume}}{5}$$

Using this formula, a 10-cubic-foot compartment would require an aggregate intake ventilation of 3.5 square inches (88 sq. mm):

$$Area = 5 \times \log_e (10/5)$$
$$= 5 \times \log_e 2$$
$$= 5 \times 0.693147$$
$$= 3.4657$$

The aggregate area of exhaust ventilation is calculated using the same formula. Thus, the boat in the above example would require one intake and one exhaust duct of 3.5 square inches each. No regulation prohibits installing more than the minimum required ventilation.

Ventilation openings must be installed so they remain outside of weather enclosures such as mooring or cockpit covers. Cowls and fittings should be arranged to prevent the entrance of significant amounts of water considering the maximum conditions of heel or trim. In addition, cowls should be placed so there is minimal recirculation of engine exhaust. Fuel fills should be as far as possible away from vent cowls, but in no case closer together than 15 inches (0.38 m).

ENGINE AIR INTAKE

High horsepower engines gobble vast quantities of air in order to provide enough oxygen for combustion. The amount of air required is far in excess of the capacity of the Coast Guard–required ventilation system. Safety regulations are not concerned with combustion air requirements of the engines. As a result, it's not uncommon for marine engines to starve for air at high speeds.

Gasoline and diesel engines get their air from inside the engine compartment. In turn, that air enters the boat from the outside atmosphere through ventilators. A handy rule for computing the minimum size of ventilators in square inches for proper engine performance is:

0.5 sq. inches (13 sq. mm) per horsepower

Using this formula, a typical 250-horsepower inboard engine needs 125 square inches of ventilation. This represents an opening about 11 inches square, quite a hole!

Even a hole this size may not be large enough. A 350-cubic-inch engine needs approximately 500 cubic feet of air per minute at 5000 r.p.m. To get that much air through a 125-square-inch hole requires a velocity of 576 feet per minute, or about 7 miles per hour. A mechanical blower may be required for high-horsepower engines. Giving the engine enough air to breathe significantly reduces fuel consumption and increases performance.

ENGINE COOLING AND EXHAUST

(ABYC Practices H-27 and P-1)

RAW COOLING WATER

An adequate supply of cooling water is critical to the operation of gasoline or diesel engines. Standard practice is to supply each engine with its own raw-water pickup. This ensures that if one intake becomes clogged or restricted, the other engine is not affected. There is a tendency among builders of cored composite hulls to stray from this practice in an attempt to reduce the number of through-hull fittings. Some builders put a single large raw-water pickup through the hull, which serves a "sea chest" from which each engine draws cooling water. An engine-cooling-water sea chest is not always practical for a couple of reasons:

➤ A small bit of eel grass clogging the single pickup can shut off cooling water to both engines, possibly resulting in total loss of power.

➤ The single pickup may not be large enough to provide an adequate flow of raw water into the sea chest, especially at higher speeds. Inadequate flow of raw water results in engine overheating.

Installing a separate water intake for each engine is the safest approach. Crush-resistant pads should replace the balsa core in the way of each through-hull fitting. These pads must be completely sealed against water intrusion and the metal fitting caulked with polyurethane sealant.

EXHAUST SYSTEM

With exhaust systems, it's against standard practices to combine engines into a single through-hull fitting. ABYC practices require that each engine be provided with a separate exhaust system.

Traditional practice on powerboats is to send the exhaust out through the transom at the waterline. Sailboat exhausts are usually located well above the waterline. No matter which type of boat, the following recommendations apply:

➤ All systems must be gas-tight to the interior of the hull to prevent deadly carbon monoxide from leaking into the living spaces.

➤ Only approved, wire-reinforced rubber hose should be used in flexible portions of exhaust systems.

➤ The exhaust system should run as straight as possible from the engine to the outlet. There should be a minimum number of bends, which are never sharper than 45 degrees.

➤ Exhaust pipes and other parts of the system must be supported to minimize failure from vibration, shock, or expansion and contraction.

➤ Exhaust outlets in flat, broad, vertical transoms should be as far outboard as possible to minimize backflow of exhaust gases into the cockpit or boat interior.

Most powerboats are equipped with wet exhaust systems that use water from the engine to cool hot exhaust gases as they exit engine manifolds. Dry systems are found mostly on workboats and larger vessels. This type of system requires insulating material to withstand the high temperatures involved.

POWERBOAT SYSTEMS

Conventional practice is to provide each exhaust manifold of an engine with a separate exhaust line. V-8 engines normally have two exhaust systems, one for each bank of cylinders. Each exhaust line runs as straight as possible from the engine exhaust manifold to the transom. This routing avoids backpressure and drainage problems that might result from joining the two lines with a "Y" connector.

Until recently, few powerboats have been equipped with a muffler or an exhaust silencer. Wire-reinforced rubber exhaust hose has gone straight from the engine manifold to the transom fitting. This arrangement reduces backpressure to the bare minimum, but is increasingly becoming illegal as more jurisdictions pass anti-noise laws. The common practice now is to install an approved muffler or silencing device in each exhaust line.

Powerboat engines are commonly located at or above the waterline. This means their exhaust systems slope *downward* toward the stern discharge ports. It is unlikely that seawater will back up into the exhaust system and enter the cylinders, even in a following sea. Engines of some displacement power cruisers ("trawlers") may be located below the waterline. This type of installation should be constructed according to sailboat practices.

SAILBOAT SYSTEMS

"Waterlift" systems are used on most sailboats, especially those equipped with diesel engines. The key part of these systems is a waterlift chamber, which acts as muffler. Exhaust gases and cooling water are discharged into the chamber by the engine. Pressure builds up until it is sufficient to push the collecting water out of the chamber and down the exhaust pipe.

Sailboat engines typically sit below the boat's waterline. This location raises the possibility that seawater might siphon back through the exhaust system into the cylinders when the engine is not running. The discharge line from the waterlift chamber should loop as high in the boat as possible and the discharge outlet should be well above the waterline.

ABYC practices recommend equipping the loop with a siphon-breaking device to prevent water from siphoning back into the engine. These devices are not well liked by sailors, however, because they are subject to problems from corrosion and salt encrustation.

Placing the exhaust outlet on the centerline prevents seawater from entering the system on one tack, but not the other. Double-ended hulls often leave no option but a side-mounted discharge, forcing the use of a high loop and an antisiphon device. Many offshore sailors equip the exhaust outlet with a seacock, which can be closed on long passages when the engine will not be operated for extended periods of time. The obvious danger, however, is that opening the seacock will be forgotten in the excitement of making a landfall.

GENERAL USE RAW-WATER SYSTEM

(ABYC Practice H-27)
Modern vessels can make considerable use of raw seawater for everything from washing down the decks to flushing the toilet. Unlike

the engines, a single sea chest raw-water intake is acceptable for these needs. A sea chest reduces the number of through-hull fittings and, consequently, the opportunities for water to enter the core of the laminate.

A sea chest does not resemble a box. More likely, it is a "Christmas tree" of T-fittings and valves coming off a single pipe from a single seacock. Each T-fitting feeds a different use of raw water:

> ➤ Flush water for the marine toilet.
> ➤ Raw-water washdown pump for cleaning the cockpit and decks.
> ➤ Non-potable "hand washing" water for the galley and head sinks.
> ➤ Cooling water for reverse cycle air conditioning/heating systems.

The intake fitting for a sea chest must be large enough to allow passage of the maximum required amount of water. A fitting of 1½ inches (40mm) may not be oversized. It should be fitted with a seacock *before* the manifold pipe with its T-fittings is installed. Each T-fitting should be supplied with an individual shutoff valve to allow servicing one system without shutting down all systems on the sea chest. The entire sea chest assembly should be located where it will be below the waterline at normal angles of heel.

GLAZING MATERIALS

(ABYC Practice H-13)
Standard window glass has no place aboard a boat. When ordinary glass breaks, it forms sharp "daggers," which can injure or kill anyone in their way. All glazing materials used on your boat must be of approved safety materials:

> ➤ Laminated Glass—Two or more pieces of glass bonded together by an intervening layer or layers of plastic material.
> ➤ Tempered Glass—A single piece of specially treated glass possessing substantial mechanical strength.
> ➤ Wired Glass—A single piece of glass with a layer of mesh wire completely embedded in the glass.
> ➤ Safety Glazing Plastic—Materials predominantly organic in character, meeting the appropriate safety standards.

Of these materials, the easiest for the amateur builder to obtain are safety glazing plastic and tempered glass. Both are available from glass supply houses in larger cities. The plastic materials are normal stock items that can quickly be cut to shape. Tempered glass takes several days to obtain because it must be cut to shape and then sent to a tempering facility. Very large glass suppliers may have the ability to cut laminated glass to custom specifications.

No matter what type of glazing is used, the procedure for buying it remains the same. Make an exact pattern of the desired piece from stiff cardboard or ¼-inch (6mm) plywood. Take this pattern to the glass supply house along with an exact description of where and how it will be used. Let the glass supplier choose the appropriate glazing material.

Glazing in the helmsman's horizontal field of view must transmit not less than 70 percent of the available light. In addition, it should not distort the image of objects. The prohibition against ordinary window glass on boats applies to decorative uses as well as windows and ports. Table tops and picture glass should also be safety glazing.

12-VOLT ELECTRICAL WIRING

(ABYC Practices E-3 and E-9)
Neat wiring routed in wrapped bundles well out of the bilge is the hallmark of a careful builder. Proper wiring is not only less of a fire hazard, it's also a lot easier to repair or to alter when new equipment is added. Following the industry standard color code helps the job go even faster. The code eliminates hooking the wrong wire to the wrong switch. You don't have to spend hours trying to figure out which wire is which.

WIRING COLOR CODE

ABYC recommends the color code shown in the accompanying table. It is the standard for U.S. production boatbuilders. A full dozen different colors are needed to follow the code, although it may not be necessary to purchase all of them. For instance, the *yellow with red stripe* wire specified for the starter circuit is normally supplied in the engine wiring harness. *White* and *black* can both be used as negative (–) return mains to the battery, but only one of these colors is needed.

Wires can be identified by small pieces of colored tape at either end as well as the color insulation. This can introduce an element of mystery if the colored tapes come off. Large electrical supply houses offer self-stick numbers, which can also be used to identify circuits. These numbers are wrapped around the wire at both ends. If numbers are used, a complete log must be kept and this information permanently installed in the boat.

APPROVED WIRING

Marine electrical conductors must be made of insulated, stranded copper wire. Solid wire is not approved. Although slightly more expensive, the best wire to use on boats is that in which each individual strand of copper has been tinned. Tinning makes the wire less subject to corrosion. Insulation should be made of plastic or vinyl that does not absorb water.

Wiring sizes in the United States are specified by the American Wire Gauge (AWG) system. Under this system, large conductors have low numbers and small conductors have large numbers. A battery cable, for instance, could be a #0 or #1 cable; a nightlight might be served by a #16 or #18 wire.

Each conductor in a multi-conductor sheath must be at least a #18, while wires installed outside of a harness must be at least #16 AWG. This specification ensures that individual wires have enough strength to support themselves during years of vibration and impact loading.

All wiring experiences a loss of power, known as "voltage drop." The amount of voltage drop varies depending upon the length of the wire and its AWG size. A big, thick cable (#0 or #1) has very little loss compared to a tiny #18 wire. This loss must be considered when choosing the proper wire gauge for each circuit. Some electronic equipment, such as a VHF-radiotelephone, is quite sensitive to voltage drop. Low voltage will also cause navigation lights to be dimmer than required by law. Other circuits, such as bunk lights, are less critical and can accept a larger voltage drop. Wires should always have crimp-on terminals at both ends. It is not acceptable to wrap the copper conductors around the screw stud of a terminal block.

OVERCURRENT PROTECTION

All positive (+) conductors require overcurrent protection from either a fuse or a circuit breaker. (This assumes the normal negative ground situation.) The master fuse or breaker should be located as close to the battery as possible. If the boat is equipped with a battery switch, the master fuse should be on the output of the switch. Fuses or breakers for individual circuits can be located on a master switch panel, which is often placed near the helmsman.

BATTERY SWITCH

A battery switch must be included in the circuit feeding the starter motor of all inboard engines. This switch should have an intermittent amperage rating not less than the maximum cranking current of the largest engine starter it serves. The continuous rating of the battery switch should be greater than the total amperage of the main overcurrent protection device connected to it. Locate the battery switch in a readily accessible place, as close as practical to the battery.

Large boats are equipped with two batteries. In this case, the battery switch allows choosing which battery will be used to crank the engines or power the auxiliary circuits. It also allows connecting both batteries to the circuit or disconnecting all battery power.

BATTERY INSTALLATION

Boat batteries should be located as close to the engines as possible to keep starter cables short. On twin-screw powerboats they are often placed between the engines. Sailboat batteries should be as low in the boat as possible, but not in a place where they can get wet with bilge water. On all boats, batteries must be held in position against both horizontal and vertical movement in all directions. By Coast Guard regulation, batteries cannot be located directly above or below a fuel tank, fuel filter, or fitting in a fuel line.

Regulations also require that the positive (+) terminals of negative ground electrical systems be protected against coming in contact with metallic objects. Special rubber "boots" are available to protect the terminals. These boots are unnecessary on boats where the batteries are stored in plastic boxes with protective lids.

GLOSSARY

The following words are defined in the context of this book. They may have additional definitions outside of strip composite boat construction.

Batten—1. A long strip of wood used as an aid when drawing curved lines when lofting. 2. Several strips of DuraKore glued together for the purpose of planking a hull.

Cure—The chemical process by which the molecules in epoxy cross resin link and form a new solid.

DuraKore—Trade name for strips or planks of end-grain balsa laminated between hardwood veneers.

Epoxy—Generic term for a class of chemicals consisting of resins and hardeners, which when mixed in the proper proportions form an excellent marine glue or coating.

Fair—1. *(v)* The process of making all views on a lines drawing coincide. 2. *(v)* The process of removing large-scale imperfections from the shape of a hull. 3. *(adj)* The quality of having a pleasant appearance, "eye sweet."

Furniture—Permanent portions of the interior living accommodations such as settees, V-berths, galley units, and navigation tables. Does not apply to bulkheads, cabin soles, or floor timbers.

Girth—Specifically the distance from the keel line to the sheerline. Occasionally the distance from sheerline to sheerline across the keel.

Laminate—1. *(v)* The process of applying reinforcement material and epoxy to the DuraKore planking. 2. *(n)* The inner or outer skin of a strip composite hull, consisting of reinforcement material and cured epoxy.

Lines Drawing—The most important drawing in a set of boat plans, it shows the plan, profile, and section views superimposed. A lines drawing is used in lofting the boat.

Loft, Lofting—1. *(v)* The process of enlarging the lines drawing to full size. 2. *(n)* The full-size drawing showing all three views of the hull.

Mold—A piece of wood or particle board that gives shape to the hull but is not part of the finished boat. (Also station mold or section mold.)

Mylar—A thin but strong plastic material used in drafting because it does not change size with changes in humidity or temperature.

Outgassing—1. *(n)* Bubbles or pockmarks in the first coat of epoxy applied to raw wood, caused by expanding air in the fibers of the wood. 2. *(v)* The process of air expanding out of the fibers of wood and creating bubbles in an overlying coat of epoxy.

Plank—1. A piece of uncut DuraKore at least 12 inches wide and 8 feet long. 2. A strip of DuraKore after it has been installed on the building mold through the process of "planking."

Polyester—Generic term for a class of chemicals, which when catalyzed are used in fiberglass boat construction. Polyesters are not recommended for DuraKore strip composite construction.

Post-cure—Describes epoxy resins that gain additional strength after curing by being heated to a specific temperature for a period of time.

Primary Bond—The chemical linking of molecules in two layers of epoxy material. In a primary bond the two layers lose their identities into a single solid. The strongest bond possible with epoxies.

Secondary Bond—A weaker bond formed when uncured epoxy is applied to cured solid epoxy. Not as strong as a primary bond.

Spiling—The process of recording the shape on a pattern through the use of a tick stick or drafting compass.

Strip—A factory-cut, narrow piece of DuraKore with finger joints at both ends.

Timber—Generic term for solid wood (mahogany, teak, etc.) or for plywood. Specifically not DuraKore strips or balsa-core materials.

Vellum—A high-quality paper used in drafting and the preparation of blueprints.

INDEX